y you.
support
for the School. I hope
you will enjoy really something

STUDIES IN MODERNITY AND NATIONAL IDENTITY *on the*

Sibel Bozdoğan and Reşat Kasaba, Series Editors *Ottoman Empire.*

Reşat Kasaba
April 6, 2011

Studies in Modernity and National Identity examine the relationships among modernity, the nation-state, and nationalism as these have evolved in the nineteenth and twentieth centuries. Titles in this interdisciplinary and transregional series also illuminate how the nation-state is being undermined by the forces of globalization, international migration, and electronic information flows, as well as resurgent ethnic and religious affiliations. These books highlight historical parallels and continuities while documenting the social, cultural, and spatial expressions through which modern national identities have been constructed, contested, and reinvented.

A MOVEABLE EMPIRE

OTTOMAN NOMADS, MIGRANTS, AND REFUGEES

Reşat Kasaba

UNIVERSITY OF WASHINGTON PRESS · SEATTLE AND LONDON

*Publication of this book was made possible in part by the Jackson
School Publications Fund, established through the generous support
of the Henry M. Jackson Foundation and other donors, in cooperation
with the Henry M. Jackson School of International Studies and the
University of Washington Press.*

University of Washington Press
P.O. Box 50096, Seattle, WA 98145 U.S.A.
www.washington.edu/uwpress

Library of Congress Cataloging-in-Publication Data
Kasaba, Reşat, 1954–
A moveable empire : Ottoman nomads, migrants, and refugees /
Reşat Kasaba.
p. cm.
Includes bibliographical references and index.
ISBN 978-0-295-98947-1 (hardback : alk. paper)
ISBN 978-0-295-98948-8 (pbk. : alk. paper)
1. Nomads—Turkey—History. 2. Turkey—History—Ottoman
Empire, 1288-1918. 3. Turkey—Social conditions—1288-1918.
4. Internal migrants—Turkey—History. 5. Migration, Internal—
Turkey—History. I. Title.
DR434.K37 2009   305.9′069109561—dc22   2009027544

For Melis

The new men of Empire are the ones who believe in fresh starts, new chapters, clean pages; I struggle on with the old study hoping that before it is finished it will reveal to me why it was that I thought it worth the trouble. — J. M. COETZEE

Contents

Acknowledgments

It is impossible to properly acknowledge the support I received from many people and institutions as I worked on this book, but I must try. The origins of the book go back to leisurely conversations I regularly had with a handful of people, all of whom I first met many years ago when I was a student in Turkey. In particular, I would like to mention Çağlar Keyder, Şevket Pamuk, and Faruk Tabak, who have been crucial in sharpening my ideas over the many years I have known them. Sadly, Faruk Tabak did not live to see the end of this project. In the time I was writing this book, I cooperated with Sibel Bozdoğan on several other projects, through which she helped me see many things differently. Most important, she taught me how to appreciate modernity. I am fortunate to have her as a friend.

In Seattle, having Joel Migdal and Daniel Chirot as good friends and colleagues has broadened my vision and made me a much better scholar and teacher. I am also grateful to Selim Kuru for his feedback on earlier drafts and for his help in deciphering some of the archival documents. In the last two decades I have had the good fortune of having a stellar group of graduate students, most of whom are members of our Turkish Circle at the University of Washington. I hope that one day they, too, will have the opportunity to discover how inspiring it can be to be close to such a hard-working and enthusiastic group of young scholars.

The Social Science Research Council, the University of Washington's Graduate School, and the Simpson Center for Humanities at the University of Washington provided funding at crucial points in this project. I am happy to acknowledge their support, without which most of what is included here would have been impossible.

Over the years, writing this book became such an intense activity that it was almost like a part of our family. In a way Kathie and I brought the project up together. I cannot list all the ways in which she made this a much better book, but I want to express my heartfelt gratitude. Finally, when I became a father I was concerned that I would not have the time to finish the book. Melis turned out to be such a source of joy that her presence actually helped speed things up. To her I dedicate this book.

A MOVEABLE EMPIRE

1 Empire, State, and People

Several years before I began writing this book, I noticed that the sources I was reading for another project repeatedly mentioned large numbers of nomadic tribes and other unsettled peoples who roamed the vast territories of the Ottoman Empire. According to these sources and the accounts of contemporary travelers and other observers, such groups were not confined to frontier areas or peripheral provinces but lived across the entire empire, even in urban areas. Furthermore, rather than figuring solely as carriers of dissent, in many instances migratory and nomadic groups actually mediated and imposed the will of the imperial center. It was particularly intriguing that the economic, political, and social changes the empire underwent in its long history—from roughly 1300 to 1922—and the Ottoman state's repeated attempts to settle the tribes seemed not to have affected the position and prominence of tribal and other migratory groups. Tens of thousands of tribes, some encompassing thousands of people and animals, moved across great distances, crosscutting the Ottoman Empire, which at one point extended from Algeria in the west to the Iranian border in the east and from Crimea in the north to the Indian Ocean in the south. Together with the continuous migration of agricultural and urban workers within and across the many regions, this movement created a situation in which at any time a significant part of the people living within the borders of the Ottoman Empire was on the move. Far from being leftovers from a previous era, these mobile groups and individuals had become integral parts of the Ottoman Empire.

On one level, there is nothing surprising about the presence of large numbers of nomadic tribes and migrant workers in the Ottoman Empire. The lands the empire controlled for 600 years, from the Balkans to the Persian Gulf, cut across one of the five major areas of nomadic pastoralism in the world.[1] Central Asian tribes that played key roles in the creation of the Ottoman and other polities in the Near East migrated through these zones and arrived in Anatolia in the medieval era as nomads themselves.[2] At the same time, the mountainous terrain and the overall sparseness of population limited the development of large-scale sedentary farming in these lands. Instead, small to medium-size peasant farming became typical in large parts of the Ottoman Empire, and the farmers always depended on the availability of migrant labor.[3]

Hence, there are some answers to the question of why such a high degree of mobility exists in this part of the world. But if one asks how the nomadic tribes and itinerant workers managed to survive in an empire that was as bureaucratic and powerful as the Ottoman Empire, then the answer becomes less clear. Historians who tackled this issue in the 1930s and 1940s were more interested in exploring the role of nomadic tribes in the rise of the Ottoman Empire in the thirteenth and fourteenth centuries than in the long-term coexistence of settled and migratory communities.[4] Some of their studies were deeply ideological, seeking to "prove" the Turkishness of early tribes and show how that essence was maintained and carried over into the modern era.[5] A third area of interest for these scholars was what role, if any, Islam played in this history, and if it did, what kind of Islam it was.[6] In these studies the emphasis was especially on the Sufi orders that were organized in the frontier regions and on how such orders became the carriers of a uniquely "Turkish" version of Islam. Although these writers reflected a trend toward idealizing tribal forms, they shared an evolutionary understanding of history and considered tribal prominence as belonging to a more primitive stage that preceded the establishment of the central institutions of the Ottoman Empire.[7]

The question I pursue here is not the origins of the Ottoman Empire, the nature of its "Turkishness," or the role played by Islam in the empire's early expansion. I am interested in explaining how, despite the concerted efforts of the Ottoman and subsequently the Turkish state, tribes and other migrant groups survived over such a long period of history. A significant body of literature is focused on this question, but primarily from the perspective of the resistance of ethnically or religiously distinct communities, such as the Kurdish and Kızılbaş groups, that were organized in tribes. The writers of such studies tend to be more interested in the ethnic or religious aspects of these conflicts and treat tribal organization as secondary in importance.[8]

In order to gain a better understanding of the relationship between tribes and empires, one needs to move beyond the Ottoman context and consider the influential writings of the North African philosopher and statesman Ibn Khaldun, who lived in the fourteenth century. Ibn Khaldun described tribes as entities bonded by strong feelings of solidarity based on lineage.[9] According to him, the closeness of the ties that gave the tribes their unity also made them cohesive and powerful. As such, tribes were more effective than sedentary empires in fighting and in spreading their influence. Historically, however, tribes almost always lose their unity and succumb to the cosmopolitan ways of settled urban cultures after they defeat and displace urban civilizations. In Ibn Khaldun's scheme, it took four generations for this circle to close—that is, for tribes to become urbanized, grow weaker, and end up as targets of other tribes, ushering in another cycle of conquest and displacement.

Ibn Khaldun was translated into Turkish in the eighteenth century and read by Ottoman historians who were trying to figure out the reasons behind the difficulties the empire was facing. Ottomans found Ibn Khaldun's explanation for the decline of dynastic centers—that it could be attributed to their loss of familial solidarity and ideological purity—appealing. They used a Khaldunian framework, versions of which some Ottoman historians had developed on their own, to explain the decline of their empire and also to make recommendations to the sovereign about the best way of restoring good government and imperial power.[10]

Whereas an idealized, almost nostalgic vision of tribal culture permeates Khaldun's writings, scholars with a modern vantage point have grown suspicious of this form of existence. Modern writers have privileged settled forms of living and governance over those that are footloose and indeterminate. Just as empires such as the Roman and the Chinese labeled their nomadic and tribal adversaries "barbarians," so did early modern states regard them as threats to social peace. According to Simon Schama, "to be of no fixed abode constituted deviant behavior" in the Dutch republic in the seventeenth century. Such people were "civically indigestible" and were punished severely for being vagrants and vagabonds.[11] "Heathen hunts" targeting that perennially vagabond community, the Gypsies, offered big rewards. Such hunts continued in Europe well into the nineteenth century.[12]

Even without such overt hostility, Enlightenment thinkers still saw tribes as primitive entities. They used this way of thinking about tribes to interpret the new information that was arriving from the Americas and the Pacific. They considered the exotic "savages" of these lands as belonging to one of the early stages of human history. This was a simpler and happier age, but people could not be left to live in such an innocent state. European civilization, representing the more mature, older age of humanity, had the responsibility to pull these communities out of their childlike stage.[13] Karl Marx's writings on India provide a good example of such a point of view: "Arabs, Turks, Tartans [sic], Moguls, who had successively overrun India, soon became Hindized [sic], the barbarian conquerors being, by an eternal law of history, conquered themselves by the superior civilization of their subjects." According to Marx, "the British were the first conquerors superior and therefore inaccessible to Hindi civilization."[14]

With or without a negative gloss, from the medieval to the modern industrial period most scholars who wrote about tribes and mobility saw these communities as belonging to a more primitive stage of human development. Scholars such as Emile Durkheim lamented the implications of the development of modern life but still saw stable institutions as key components of civilized society. Durkheim regarded tribes, which he called "hordes," as the most elementary type of social organization. According to him these units acted as "protoplasm" out of which all social forms developed. Hordes created clans by coming together and forming associations. The underlying principle that held these units together was that of "mechanical division of labor," which was characterized by sameness and repetition. The key to transition to a higher form of society was the development of moral individualism, which ushered in a division of labor based on functional differentiation. Durkheim described this as "organic division of labor." For Durkheim, this change in the mode of solidarity necessitated a change in the structure of society.[15] In more recent years, the study of tribes in the Middle East has been influenced by the writings of Ernest Gellner, who is credited with helping Western scholars discover the writings of Ibn Khaldun and use them as a framework for analyzing not only the history but also the modern dynamics of "Muslim societies."[16]

Although they represented vastly different schools of thought, most authors who wrote about tribes until recently used an evolutionary perspective. By and large, they concurred that the persistence of nomadic and migratory communities and the formation of strong polities represented different stages of human development and as such were inherently incompatible with each other. Ibn Khaldun's cyclical framework might look like an exception, but on close examination one sees that he, too, found relations between tribal solidarities and urban civilizations to be fundamentally conflictual. Uncritical acceptance of such dichotomies led scholars such as James Scott to ask "why states are the enemy of the people who move around" and "why civilizations can't climb hills."[17]

Under the influence of their European contemporaries, and constrained by the requirements of running a modern state, Ottoman and Turkish intellectuals and Ottoman statesmen grew increasingly wary and harshly critical of nomadic tribes and other migrants in the nineteenth and early twentieth centuries. One of Emile Durkheim's followers was Ziya Gökalp, who became a key intellectual during the Young Turk and early Kemalist periods. Gökalp likened tribalism to a "disease" that needed to be cured. In his study of Kurdish tribes in Turkey, he identified five stages in the evolution of these communities: fully nomadic tribes, semi-nomadic tribes, settled tribes, tribes dominated by landlords, and settled villages. According to Gökalp, the new Turkish state had to understand the factors that led to the development of tribalism and take the necessary steps to hasten the move from the first stage of evolution to the last.[18]

The evolutionary perspective on tribes has been challenged in recent years, especially by some anthropologists who see tribes not as representing an early, primitive stage in human history but as a constantly changing, integral part of the modern world. Furthermore, instead of seeing states and tribes as exclusive entities belonging to different stages of social evolution, researchers have shown that in places such as Iran and Turkey, states have preserved and even created new tribes in order to perpetuate their rule.[19] In this book I question the assumption of a sharp divide between stasis and mobility as markers of civilization and barbarism, respectively. By looking at Ottoman history, I show how tribal interests were incorporated first into Ottoman institutions, then into the reformed institutions, and ultimately into early republican structures. In this way, migratory habits became a constitutive element in the making of modern Turkey and continue to be significant even in the twenty-first century, when more than two-thirds of Turkey's population is classified not only as settled but as urban.[20]

In this outcome, the power of the tribes and their ability to negotiate with the centralizing and reforming Ottoman authorities played a key role. Accordingly, I argue that researchers need to see the institutionalization of the Ottoman-Turkish state as a process unfolding in continuous relationship with other groups and elements of society and with counterparts in surrounding areas. As a result, conceptually and in real terms, the internal boundaries that separated the Ottoman state from the tribal social structures were never clear. Nor were the external borders separating the Ottoman Empire from its neighbors as clearly identifiable as historical atlases presume.[21] There was always movement of people, goods, and ideas, not to mention armed groups, that cut across internal divides as well as the borders of the Ottoman Empire. Consequently, both the imperial center and the modern state that emerged from it were deeply embedded in local practices, making it impossible to talk about centralization as having clear starting and end points. Similarly, dividing the history of the Ottoman Empire into distinct periods such as Classical, Transition, Reform, and Collapse, or imagining a unilinear progress from tribe to empire to nation, imposes too compact a framework on a complex history. Rather than being strictly separated, the phases of this historical transformation overlap, crosscut, and build on one another in myriad ways. They are not distinct steps in the staircase of universal civilization.

In this book I examine the status of tribes in the Ottoman Empire and their relationship to political authority in five chapters. Chapter 2 is focused on the early part of Ottoman history, when maintaining a nomadic presence, especially in the frontier regions of the empire, was an important source of strength. The imperial center used these communities as tentacles of its reach into neighboring territories. Sometimes the communities moved on their own, occupying new territories, and the imperial administration followed with its institutions and practices. These frontier communities also helped expand the influence of the empire by proselytizing in the border regions and laying the groundwork for subsequent invasion by Ottoman forces.

Tribes that were engaged in pastoral nomadism were important for the internal organization of the empire as well. They were the main suppliers of animals for military and civilian purposes. Through their mobility and part-time farming they helped cultivate a larger part of the Ottoman lands than would have been possible otherwise. They facilitated the internal movement of goods for trade and taxation purposes, and by carrying messages and maintaining a transportation network, they provided the main lines of communication between the imperial center and its provinces. The organization, functioning, and expansion of the Ottoman Empire involved the participation of many communities that were accustomed to living independently. The prominence and importance of nomadic activities meant that the power of the imperial center was refracted through tribal leaders, which allowed these chiefs to perpetuate their authority while providing the center with an effective way of reaching distant parts of the empire.

Tribal cooperation with imperial and subsequently state authorities was an important factor in guaranteeing the survival of tribes not only as an organizational form but also as bearers of distinct cultures and identities within the Ottoman Empire. Such cultural characteristics were neither insular nor static. On the contrary, the very mobility that defined these communities created eclectic lives and practices that were highly fluid and dynamic. Islam, for example, which was practiced among most of the people of the Ottoman lands, incorporated aspects of other religions and a wide range of vernacular practices, some of which were influenced by pre-Islamic traditions. Other religions developed their own local traditions and schisms, making them, too, resistant to simple categorizations. With unorthodox beliefs permeating all the religions practiced in the Ottoman Empire, and with a high degree of mobility characterizing the lives of a significant portion of the Ottoman population, how could Ottoman culture have been anything but fluid?

The fluidity and indeterminacy of Ottoman society gave the empire an advantage in earlier parts of its history, when it was faced with the remnants of medieval feudalism in the Balkans and with severely compromised Arab dynasties and tribes in the south. In chapter 3 I examine the way these conditions, which favored the Ottomans, changed significantly starting in the seventeenth century and how the Ottomans responded to the changes. The first important development was the emergence of a new system of states built on powerful, centralized structures and on the principle of international sovereignty. The Habsburg and Russian Empires, the two main neighbors and adversaries of the Ottomans, became part of this system and began to pressure the Ottoman Empire. They moved to shore up their borders with the Ottoman Empire by creating new settlements along the frontiers, engineering the religious and ethnic composition of existing settlements, and reaching into Ottoman territories to agitate their ethnic and religious brethren there. At the same time, indigenous communities, tribal and otherwise, that had prospered under the Ottoman Empire began to see new possibilities for expanding their economic and political power by pursuing local, regional, and even global opportunities independent of the Ottoman center. In some cases this new situation created the nuclei of nationalist movements; in others it became the basis for tribal uprisings and rural depredations. The loose and flexible relationship between the Ottoman center and migrant communities became a liability under these changing conditions, and the Ottoman state took its first steps toward settling and sedentarizing tribes and controlling migrations. However, the central government had limited means of enforcing these plans unless some of the very communities who were the targets agreed to go along with them. As a result, the early policies of centralization ended up giving even further power to the larger tribal confederations, which could now claim to be expanding their influence on behalf of the central government.

In chapter 4, I show how the Ottoman policy of creating a sedentary society became increasingly ambitious in the course of the nineteenth and early twentieth centuries. This policy combined coercive and consent-based practices, including land grants, tax exemptions, and guarantees of access to water, as well as military campaigns whereby tribes were broken, their animals confiscated, and their people forcefully resettled across long distances. The institutional reforms of the nineteenth and early twentieth centuries were accompanied by increasingly detailed surveys that collected as much information as possible about the itinerant populations of the empire. Questions about tribal identities, the identities of the leaders, tribal histories, tax liabilities, and migratory routes lay at the heart of these surveys. By this time, main Ottoman officials had become convinced that tribalism and nomadism had no place in modern state structures. They began to describe many of the tribes as untamed, wild, and animal-like.

There were two main problems with the way the reforms of the nineteenth century were conceived and implemented. The first had to do with the fact that the Ottomans needed powerful institutions in order to settle the tribes and carry out the reforms. But it was precisely the creation of these institutions that the reforms were supposed to achieve. In the absence of effective institutions of enforcement, the central government ended up resorting to the older practice of choosing and relying on some of the tribes and empowering them in order to draw them to the side of the central government and to the cause of reform. This afforded some tribes in the Kurdish zones, Arabia, and North Africa a further means of protecting their identity. These tribes survived more or less intact into the era of the modern state. This time they were using the reformed and modern institutions of the new states to protect their priorities against rival tribes.

The second problem had to do with the fact that the Ottomans, throughout this period of reform and until the very end of the empire, held onto the vision of rescuing and preserving some notion of an imperial arrangement and using it to retain the communities that sought to quit the empire. Many of the new institutions were created in order to bolster the empire, and many of the reforms were supposed to make the empire function better. But in an environment in which competing national, ethnic, religious, and tribal identities were gaining traction, the reformed institutions would have no staying power unless they were substantiated with a generalized sense of belonging that appealed to a significant part of the people of the empire. Proposals were made and interventions attempted to cultivate "Ottomanism" and Islamism as bases for such a civic identity. As I show in chapter 5, Turkish nationalism, as an exclusive program, emerged slowly and haltingly, although even in its incomplete state this ideology played a decisive role in the formulation of certain policies, especially in the deportation and murder of Armenians and the mandatory exchange of populations with Greece in 1923–24. Ultimately, World War I and the subsequent intervention of European powers made it possible for the narrow ideologies of local nationalisms to become fully fledged. So sudden was the war and so radical its aftermath that these ideologies carried forward the unresolved contradictions of the nineteenth century. Most important, a significant number of people who became engulfed in these changes had been part of networks and relationships that were fluid and open. As such, they had little familiarity with the increasingly closed and insular ideologies of new nationalisms that created clashes and conflicts that continue to this day.

The Ottoman Empire began and ended with migration. But the two migrations that bracketed the empire were substantively different from each other. The migrations that were prevalent during the formative years of the empire were largely spontaneous. They helped build the empire and made mobility an integral part of it. The migrations of the nineteenth and twentieth centuries were, to a large extent, administered by states on the basis of their ideological priorities. For this reason the latter wave could only undermine the empire. The nation-states that emerged appeared to be more compact and stable, but the historically rooted, spontaneous movements never disappeared completely and quickly reemerged as prominent characteristics of these societies.

2 A Moveable Empire

The Ottoman Empire became one of the largest and most powerful political structures in the world between the closing years of the thirteenth century and the turn of the seventeenth. By the latter date, the Black Sea basin, the Anatolian plateau, the Fertile Crescent of the Middle East, and North Africa had all become parts of the empire, putting the Ottomans in full control of all the important routes that had linked Europe, Asia, and Africa for several millennia. The speed with which the Ottomans swept these lands and the effective control they established over them continues to fascinate historians.

The arrival of the Ottomans ushered in a reversal in the history of the Near East, which had been going through a lengthy period of conflicts and crises that had all but destroyed its major centers and impoverished its economy. The Crusaders devastated some of the wealthiest cities and trade routes around the Mediterranean between the eleventh and thirteenth centuries. Originating in central Asia, Mongols spread in waves, attacking, burning, and pillaging much of what they encountered during the thirteenth and fourteenth centuries. Millennial movements that challenged both Islamic orthodoxy and orthodox rulers undermined the social order in Anatolia, causing massive and continuous displacements. Several empires, such as the Byzantine, Seljuk, and Abbasid, succumbed to these internal and external pressures and either lost much of their grandeur or collapsed completely. It is true that the retreat of these empires in quick succession left a vast void into which the Ottomans moved. But how exactly the Ottomans managed to rein in these unraveling social structures and relationships and mold them to serve as the foundation of a powerful and prosperous empire remains shrouded in mystery.[1]

It is unlikely that scholars will ever demystify this history entirely, because doing so would require the use not only of conventional historical records but also of written and oral literary sources along with exegesis and related discussions by Islamic scholars, Sufi sheikhs, and their disciples. Even if all these sources were available and accessible, it might well be beyond the capacity of any one scholar to use all of them to address fundamental questions about the early years of the Ottoman Empire.[2] One historian says that for most of this period, "and especially for the fourteenth century, the materials are usually non-existent. Where they exist they are fragmentary, problematic, and usually contradictory. For this period, to establish an event and, even more, to fix a secure date to an event is already an achievement. In these circumstances where almost any statement of fact needs a qualifying 'perhaps' or 'on balance, therefore,' no attempt to establish an explanatory framework can be more than an educated guess."[3]

In this chapter I focus on one aspect of the early history of the Ottoman Empire that, although well known, has not received the attention it deserves. This is the central role played by nomadic and other mobile groups in not only the expansion but also the organization and administration of the Ottoman Empire. In the first part of the chapter I describe the symbiosis that developed between nomadic tribes and other mobile groups, on the one hand, and the burgeoning Ottoman imperial institutions, on the other. The second part is an examination of how the integration of a large number of mobile groups into the empire influenced its borders and identities.

ENCOUNTERING MOBILITY

The territories of the Ottoman Empire intersected with what geographers refer to as the "sub-Arctic nomadic zone," which extended from the Mediterranean littoral through the Anatolian peninsula and the Iranian plateau into the mountains of central Asia.[4] Tens of thousands of tribes moved constantly across this belt of high mountains and dry steppes and deserts for millennia. Starting in the eleventh century, in addition to ongoing seasonal migrations within this zone, nomadic tribes steadily moved westward from Asia. Turkic and Mongolian tribes arrived in the eastern Mediterranean and Anatolia as parts of this movement, altering the social and political makeup and the history of these regions forever. As they passed through this geography, the tribes interacted with local communities. Some melded into local relations and networks and abandoned their journey; others continued to move. Some of the indigenous communities themselves were nomadic, moving over shorter distances with their own complex interactions and relations with sedentary communities and political authorities. The superimposition of the long-distance migrations onto these local movements created a highly fluid social environment throughout the territory, especially in Anatolia, where it became difficult to distinguish between the arriving, staying, and departing tribes between the eleventh and fourteenth centuries. Mobility thoroughly permeated Ottoman society and the nascent institutions of the empire. Consequently, the social makeup and even the geography of the region changed continuously, making it impossible to describe the late medieval history of these lands in terms of firm boundaries or fixed categories.

The Ottomans grew out of this complex environment. Although they subsequently adopted and propagated the fiction that they were the direct descendants of distinct central Asian tribes, in reality this was but one of several layers of identity that shaped early Ottoman culture and society.[5] Goat- and sheep-herding Türkmen communities of the Anatolian peninsula and camel-raising Bedouin and Arab tribes of North Africa and the Middle East, which had preserved their nomadic ways under the Seljuk Empire and the *beyliks*, or principalities, that preceded the Ottoman era, continued their highly autonomous lives even after they were integrated into the Ottoman Empire. Here is the way Ibn Batuta, who traveled in North Africa, Anatolia, and the Middle East in the fourteenth century, described the Ottoman ruler Sultan Orhan (r. 1326–62), who succeeded the dynastic founder, Osman I: "Of fortresses he possesses nearly a hundred, and for most of his time he is continually engaged in making the round of them, staying in each fortress for some days to put it into good order and examine its condition. It is said that he had never stayed for a whole month in any one town."[6]

Johannes Schlitberger spent more than thirty years, between 1394 and

HUNGARY

PODOLIA

TRANSYLVANIA

MOLDAVIA

SERBIA

WALACHIA

DALMATIA

DANUBIAN
PRINCIPALITIES

BLACK

ADRIATIC SEA

BULGARIA

Dubrovnik
İşkodra

MACEDONIA

THRACE
Edirne

Bosphorus

Istanbul

Adapazarı

RUMELIA
ALBANIA

Thessaloniki

*Sea of
Marmara*

Bursa

Eskişehir

THESSALY

Dardanelles

Ankar

GREECE

*Aegean
Sea*

Karasi

ANATOLIA

Manisa

Izmir

Gavur Daġ

Menderes River

Akşehi

MOREA

Denizli

Konya

Antalya

TAUR

CRETE

CYPRU

MEDITERRANEAN

SEA

Benghazi

EGYPT

LIBYA

Nile River

N
W — E
S

0   250 miles

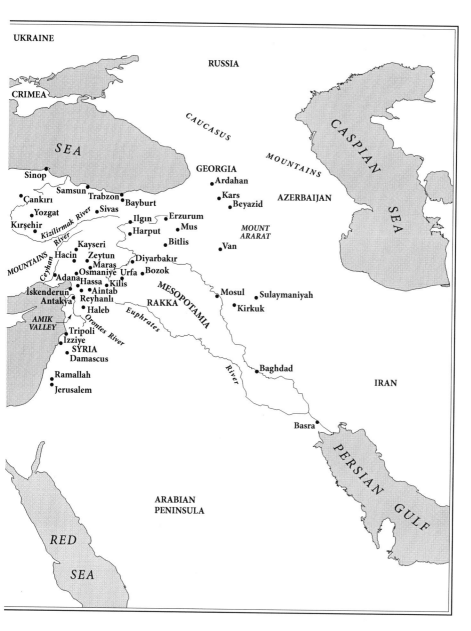

MAP 1 *Balkans, Anatolia, and the Middle East*

1427, in captivity, first with the Ottomans and then in the court of Tamerlane and his sons in Asia. "In Muslim lands," he observed, "it is customary for rulers to be constantly on the move with their herds. When they come across good grazing lands, they purchase the right to use these areas from local rulers."[7] One historian estimates that as much as 27 percent of the population of Anatolia was fully or semi-nomadic as late as the 1520s. Nomads were particularly concentrated in the old frontier zone between the Ottoman and Byzantine Empires in western Anatolia. According to one estimate, two-thirds of the nomadic population of Anatolia was there.[8] Moving farther from the so-called core provinces of the Ottoman Empire and examining eastern Anatolia, the Arab provinces, and beyond, one finds the proportion of the nomadic population to be as great as 60 percent.[9] So pervasive was the nomadic presence that Halil İnalcık described these tribes as "the backbone of the entire imperial organization," referring not only to their numerical strength but also to their important role in local networks of production, trade, and administration across the Ottoman lands.[10] It is difficult to imagine how such a large degree of mobility could have been maintained in the Ottoman Empire had the Ottomans not been accommodating to the nomadic tribes and other itinerant groups they met in Anatolia. This openness to different communities made the Ottoman Empire considerably more diverse, dynamic, and extraverted than its contemporaries.

In addition to leaving existing patterns of migration intact, Ottomans helped instigate mobility where there had been none. The practice of *sürgün*, whereby sedentary as well as nomadic communities were required to move across long distances, was central to the Ottomans' settlement of new territories.[11] Although this was primarily a way of punishing unruly tribes, it was also used to settle newly annexed territories and frontier areas, to which the tribes were given incentives to move. Many sedentary households were turned into migrants by an Ottoman law that required every ten peasant households in a given region to identify up to two households of deportees who would be required to move to a newly conquered area. Such households were exempted from all taxes for two years.[12] The forceful relocation of nomadic tribes, however, did not automatically entitle them to land, because they were not necessarily encouraged or expected to adopt sedentary farming in their new places.[13] Instead, in line with established practices in their places of origin, these communities were allocated grazing land and were fully expected to continue their pastoral nomadism in the new regions. When tribes were ordered to move, in part or in whole, their officials were required to move with them and take along the communities' official record books, or *defters*.[14] The widespread use of such measures suggests that during the early part of their history, the Ottomans expanded the scope of migrations rather than bringing about a general sedentarization of populations in the areas they ruled.

A well-established body of writing in Ottoman historiography insists that Ottomans were anti-nomadic from the very beginning.[15] Its authors point out indications such as endowment charters and court ceremonies to argue that from as early as the time of Sultan Orhan, visible symbols of statehood existed in the institutions and practices of the Ottoman Empire. Furthermore, the Ottomans were not starting from scratch; they could and did take over the institutions of the principalities that preceded them in Anatolia.[16] Ottoman princes, including the future sultans, were posted in the cities that had been the centers of these principalities, where they set up courts of their own with all the trappings of full-fledged rulers. These centers usually served as venues for preparing for the day when one of the princes would ascend to the throne, but they also became centers of dissent and even rebellion when succession was contested and the local prince lost out. In assessing the simultaneous existence of sedentary and nomadic communities, one should keep in mind that rather than existing in pure form, the two types constituted parts of a continuum, and in many instances they overlapped with and complemented each other. In the large territories that the empire encompassed during its long history, certain regions, periods, and reigns appear to have been more or less hospitable to nomadism. Even during the times of sultans such as Bayezid I (r. 1389–1403), when the state pursued a vigorous policy of settling and punishing tribes, the Ottomans continued to rely on the mobility of people in the expansion and organization of the empire. This is one of the ways in which to account for the persistence of mobility despite fluctuations in the numbers of nomads and other migrants.

The Ottoman Empire was not unique among empires for relying on the mobility of its subjects for its organization. People willing to move over long distances and to work, trade, explore, and settle in unfamiliar territories have been central features of all empires in history. It was such persons who embarked on the conquest of the New World on behalf of the Iberian empires. China's sphere of influence in south and southeast Asia was forged by Chinese merchants and other groups who lived and worked in those parts. Islamic empires expanded their influence in Asia and Africa not through armies but through the activities of itinerant merchants and scholars who traveled thousands of miles in the medieval world. As was the case in all these empires, the Ottomans relied on such figures in both the expansion and the integration of their empire.[17] *Akıncı* organizations, mobile units that were located in the frontier zones of the empire and served as the shock troops of imperial expansion, were similar to the frontier organizations known as the *akritai,* which the Byzantine Empire had maintained on its frontiers and used for the same purpose. Indeed, part of the early "lightning" success of the Ottomans may have been due to the complementarity (or symbiosis) that existed between these overlapping frontier societies.[18]

The groups whose mobility was crucial to the organization of the Ottoman Empire also had the power to escape, avoid, and, most important, negotiate the terms of their relations with other groups, including the rulers. The social order created by these interactions was much more fluid than the monolithic images one reads about in contemporaneous accounts, such as the following from Machiavelli: "The entire Turkish Empire is ruled by one master, and all other men are his servants, he divides his kingdom into sandjaks and dispatches various administrators to govern them, whom he transfers and changes at his pleasure. . . . they are all his slaves, bounden to him."[19] The fluidity of the Ottoman Empire's basic relations served the interests of the expanding empire well, especially because the areas into which it was expanding had weak political structures and dispersed communities. This situation would change in the second half of the seventeenth century, when territorially sovereign states with clearly demarcated boundaries became the norm in Europe. With this, the uncertainties of empire began to become liabilities for the Ottomans. And it was at the very end of the seventeenth century that the Ottomans first attempted to sedentarize the tribes.

ADMINISTERING MOBILITY

As their empire grew quickly in western Anatolia and the Balkans, the Ottomans tried to balance their interest in strengthening the empire's peasant base with the obvious need to define a clear place for nomads in Ottoman rural society. They developed special laws to monitor the activities of tribes, and they recorded tribal affairs separately in special documents.[20] Maintaining control over nomadic and tribal communities and administering them was no easy task. For one thing, the areas across which they moved could be large. A particular clan might spend summers at the source of the Euphrates in eastern Anatolia and then move south to the Syrian desert for the winter, a distance of more than 600 miles.[21] Some of the tribes were huge, with as many as 30,000 to 40,000 persons and sometimes several hundred thousand sheep and camels—even though Ottoman law recognized 300 sheep as constituting a herd, and the state used this as the unit of accounting in assessing the liabilities of tribes.[22]

At least initially, the Ottomans had neither the means nor the intention to permanently settle or discipline the tribes. They opted for classifying them in their existing situations. On the most general level they referred to a tribe as an *aşiret*. In order to facilitate administrative and especially taxation matters, they grouped tribes in eastern Anatolia, Iraq, Syria, and farther east in the Arab provinces as Türkmens, Kurds, Arabs, and Bedouins. Those who had moved west of the Kızılırmak River in Anatolia and on to the Balkans had become semi-nomads (*yarı-göçebe* or *konar-göçer*) and were called Yürüks.[23] The Kurds and Türkmens were closer to being absolute nomads; typically an entire tribe moved together between higher and lower terrain, taking all their animals and belongings with them. The largest administrative units the Ottomans recognized among the Kurds and Türkmens were the *il* and the *ulus*.[24] The two largest of these were the Boz Ulus, consisting largely but not exclusively of Türkmens, and the Kara Ulus, consisting largely but not exclusively of Kurds.[25] *Ulus* confederations were divided into smaller groups—in descending order, *boy* (sometimes *taife*), *cemaat*, and *kabile*. Yürüks, on the other hand, were spun off from Türkmen *kabile*s and were not organized in the larger units of *boy*, *il*, and *ulus*. Instead, they were classified and registered as *kabile*s and *cemaat*s, mostly on the basis of their tax and other obligations or the places where they circulated.[26]

For the most part, Yürük and Türkmen formations such as *ulus, il, boy, cemaat,* and *kabile* had evolved endogenously, without input from outside, and were later recognized by the Ottoman administration. In some cases the Ottoman government did intervene directly to alter existing organizations or create new ones in order to make the communities better serve its own interests. But these groupings were still built on existing practices of the tribes without introducing radical reorganization into their lives

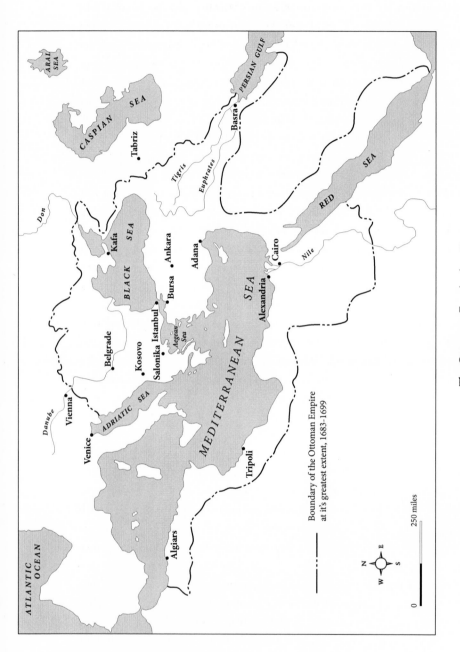

MAP 2 *The Ottoman Empire in 1683*

Boundary of the Ottoman Empire
at it's greatest extent, 1683-1699

250 miles

0

or the patterns of their migrations. Some of the new groupings created by the government were named after the pastures assigned to them (hence, Haleb [Aleppo] Türkmeni, Şam Türkmeni, and so forth) or after the place of residence of the tax-collecting unit to which the tribe was assigned (hence, Üsküdar Türkmeni, formerly Yeni İl).[27] Such designations, however, tended to be ad hoc and inconsistent. It would be impossible to trace the place where a particular tribe lived or moved in and out of on the basis of such a designation. In the Aleppo district alone the nomadic population was very large and diverse. In 1596, 241 tribes were registered there, with an estimated total population of more than 50,000. The tribes owned more than 2 million sheep and paid an annual sheep tax of more than 1 million *akçes*.[28] Being nonsedentary, they soon left Aleppo, but they carried their names with them. As early as the sixteenth century a large group of "Haleb Türkmeni" was living around İzmir in western Anatolia. Some of them had been relocated there by the central government and given land from the sultan's possessions. Others had come on their own as camel herders, some were complete nomads, and others combined nomadism with seasonal farming. It is clear that regardless of particular circumstances, they had at best a tenuous relationship with Aleppo.[29] Alternatively, in the case of the Üsküdar Türkmeni, the tribal groups had no direct relationship with Üsküdar except for their taxes being farmed to households there. As might be expected, these classifications overlapped to a certain degree. It was normal for a person to find himself covered under several labels and expected to fulfill the obligations that came with each.

The Ottomans devised measures to incorporate and administer the indigenous nomads in the Balkans as well. Among the indigenous communities there were the Vlachs, who had escaped from the earlier Slavic invasions. Vlachs practiced transhumance and cooperated with other nomadic groups such as the Cumans, Pechenegs, Tatars, and Albanians, all of whom were Muslims and played important roles in the local economy, organization of the military, and provincial administration.[30] The arrival of Ottoman forces and administration in the Balkans brought yet another wave of migrants that included Yürüks and Türkmens, who interacted with local residents, assimilating and being assimilated by them.

In addition to recognizing existing groups and sometimes regrouping them under new labels, the Ottoman government appointed high-ranking officers to administer the affairs of the nomadic communities and to assess and collect their taxes. Being mobile, these tribes were not subject to the authority of any subprovince governor (*sanjak beyi*). Instead, *ulus* units were governed by *voyvodas*, and *cemaats* by *kethüdas*. Nomads registered into the army were supervised by *seraskers*. Like other administrative units in the empire, each confederation of tribes was also assigned a *kadı*, who served as the direct representative of the central government and adjudicated in intra- and intertribal matters. As a further indication of the government's willingness to accommodate these communities, the *kadıs* accompanied the tribes through their seasonal cycles of migration.[31]

Although the titles of the officials in charge of tribes and of those responsible for peasant households and villages were identical, there were important differences in the way the two sets of administrators were appointed and in the units they administered. The tribal units that the Ottomans recognized for purposes of administering them were conceived of not on the basis of bounded areas but as confederations of tribes and clans themselves. Typically these units were very large yet territorially loose. In the sixteenth century more than 100 separate tribes of various sizes were registered as part of the Boz Ulus confederacy, whose population at the time is estimated to have been more than 60,000, with 2 million sheep. Its seasonal migrations covered an area extending from Mardin in southeastern Anatolia all the way to Persia and Georgia.[32] In the seventeenth century some groups broke off from this confederacy and went as far away as western Anatolia and the Balkans, signaling the end of Boz Ulus as a meaningful unit in eastern Anatolia.[33] Even the tribal units contained multiple communities with distinct names and lineages. For example, the Rişvanlı tribe, which occupied a prominent place in central Anatolia between the sixteenth and nineteenth centuries, contained forty-five such subunits.[34]

More often than not the Ottoman administration relied on the tribes themselves to identify their leaders, whom the central government then recognized and appointed with appropriate titles.[35] In a decree issued in 1574, Sultan Selim II ordered the Gypsies to identify a *cemaat başı* for each group of 50 and accepted these leaders as the main intermediaries between the central government and the Gypsy communities.[36] In some instances these positions became hereditary, creating a privileged "tribal aristocracy" with leaders who wielded enormous power in their regions. This was especially the case among Kurdish tribes in eastern Anatolia and in Mesopotamia.[37] In 1655 the Ottoman traveler Evliya Çelebi counted thirteen hereditary *sanjaks* in Diyarbakır, which constituted more than half such administrative units in that province. Large tracts of imperial land were granted to them, and they were free to use the income from these domains in any way they wished.[38] The hereditary nature of local rule and the organic ties that existed between the communities and their leaders reinforced local customs and cultural specificities and contributed to their survival over generations.[39]

Of the indigenous tribes that the Ottomans came to dominate, the Kurdish communities constitute a special category. The Kurds were one of the largest ethnically distinct and predominantly Muslim groups, and their presence in this part of the world long predated the Ottomans. Ottomans were aware of the local power of this community, and their policies contributed to the long-term survival of the Kurds as a distinct people. They used a policy of accommodation, sometimes referred to as *istimalet,* which consisted of making generous concessions to win over people while helping consolidate the power of local chiefs.[40] They used the same policy toward the Christian communities in western Anatolia and the Balkans in the fourteenth and fifteenth centuries.[41] By working especially with the Sunni Kurds through such methods, the Ottomans tried to separate them from the Alevi Kurds, who practiced Shi'i Islam, and cultivate them as a buffer against Iran and as allies in their lengthy battles with local Shi'i communities (Kurdish and otherwise), some of whom supported the Persian rulers. According to Evliya Çelebi, some of the Kurdish areas in this frontier zone "were allowed their own governorship. . . . They have the status of *sanjak* but are governed as ancestral properties. . . . When one dies, his place is given to his son, or else to a worthy elder kinsman."[42]

Kurdish chiefs took advantage of these conditions and used their ties with the Ottoman government to amass fortunes and power in eastern Anatolia. So powerful were some of the chieftains that they were able to influence Ottoman policies and affect the shapes of military campaigns in their areas.[43] Sultan Murad IV issued a series of imperial orders in 1632 and 1633 reinforcing the hereditary nature of Kurdish tribal chiefdom and prohibiting local military commanders and governors from harassing and abusing the Kurdish tribes. In one of them he said, "God made Kurdistan act in the protection of my imperial kingdom like a strong barrier and an iron fortress against the sedition of the demon Gog of Persia."[44] In another he stated, "The Kurdish commanders are loyal and faithful well-wishers of the Ottoman state and have from the noble time of our great ancestors until the present time performed a variety of praiseworthy services on behalf of the crown and expended incalculable laudable efforts thus making it incumbent on the imperial zeal that they be treated with respect and care."[45] The Kurdish chief Abdel Khan, who ruled Bitlis for thirty years, was described by Evliya Çelebi as someone "whose generosity to the people of Kurdistan has made all the free and noble tribesmen his servants" and who "at battle time is able to muster fifty thousand troops."[46] According to Evliya, Abdel Khan was a "master physician, and surgeon, a falconer, an oculist, a poet in Arabic, Persian, and Turkish, a goldsmith, and watchmaker, a singer and musician, etc."[47] The Bedouin were another group whose presence and local power the Ottomans used to advance their imperial interests in the Arab provinces in the sixteenth and seventeenth centuries. Some members of the Bedouin Bani Haritha tribe were even appointed as district governors of Jerusalem in the early seventeenth century.[48]

These special arrangements show that in incorporating nomadic tribes into their administrative structures, the Ottomans acted with full appreciation of their dependence on these units for extending their rule, especially in the eastern reaches of the empire. The arrangements served the interests of the tribes and especially the tribal leaders, who used their connections to the Ottoman government as added sources of legitimacy in wielding their power locally. The Ottoman government was also an important source of security, not only for the tribal leaders but also for the ordinary members of the tribes. Nomads who specialized in sheep and goat herding needed especially to stay always within easy access of water. This and the mountainous terrain put some restrictions on their mobility and made them dependent for their survival on the protection of supratribal confederations, which were strongest and most secure when linked to empires.[49]

In addition to tribal confederacies and their leaders, with whom the Ottomans dealt regularly, there were also single tribes and unattached individuals, all of whom provided the government with additional avenues for influencing local relations. Individual Muslim tribes were described in court records and government documents by reference to their skills, crafts, or occupations. Some examples are the Keçili (with goat), Koyuncu (sheep seller), Saraç (tanner), Kaşıkçı (spoon maker), Yarı-Çoban (half-shepherd), Kürkçü (fur maker), Yağcı (oil maker), Yaycı (bow maker), Çeng (musician), Atçeken (horse puller), and Koyuneri (sheep master) tribes. Sometimes the name of the tribe derived from a historical event or experience specific to that community, such as the Öksüzler (orphans), Sakallı (bearded), and Şehitler (martyrs).[50] For the most part these identifications were based on what the tribes did and who they were, rather than being categories imposed from above.

Although the Ottoman government regarded tribes as communities and approached them typically through their rulers, this did not preclude the possibility of Ottomans interacting directly with individual members of a tribe. Tribal members could be summoned for government service or sued as individuals. In such orders the names of the persons would be qualified with reference to the larger grouping, such as Yürük, Türkmen, Kıpti, Çingene, and Kürd. This has led to confusion among later researchers who assumed that *Yürük* referred not just to an administrative status but also to ethnic identity. Other itinerant individuals, too, appear in government documents: lawless vagabonds (*levend*),[51] unmarried tax payers (mücerred), unmarried and landless persons including migrant workers in Istanbul (*bekâr* or *caba*), and young boys who worked as footservants for military officers (*civelek*).[52]

Even though the basis of these classifications is far from clear and the results are anything but consistent or reliable, for the Ottomans the primary purpose of going through this exercise was to ensure the security of the countryside and to facilitate the assessment and collection of taxes from the rural communities. The most commonly imposed tax on pastoral nomads was the *adet-i ağnam,* or sheep tax, which was determined on the basis of the size and quality of the herds a particular tribe or confederation owned. Nomads were also required to pay fees for their grazing land and pastures, as well as special dues if they harmed or lost their own or other people's animals or slaves. Along with the rest of the peasants, nomads had to pay a marriage tax (*resm-i arus* or *gerdek akçesi*) as well. Most of these taxes were assessed and the obligations of nomads determined by taking into consideration whether the payer was well off and whether he was single, living with his parents, or living alone.[53] Nomads were exempted from many of the taxes and dues that were imposed on most peasant households. Even with the special taxes imposed on them, the tax burden on nomads ended up being lighter than the obligations of sedentary farmers. Naturally, nomads were aware of their special status and used it in raising complaints against officials who sought to impose unlawful dues on them. In such complaints they insisted that they were not tax-paying subjects (*reaya*) but had special status because of the services they performed for the sultan.[54] The special status and power of the tribal leaders became particularly important in this regard, playing an important role in the tribes' voicing of such concerns and affecting the outcomes of complaints.

The administrative categories I have described should not be taken as consistent, universally applied ways of naming tribal communities across the Ottoman Empire. It was normal for officials in different regions to use different titles or to group and describe the same tribes with different names. Furthermore, because of the very nature of tribal life and its relationship to an administration still being formed, the lines of division and categories of administration employed by the Ottomans did not remain constant over the long history of the Ottoman Empire. Nor was there any consistency in the exact meaning of these categories or in the tax obligations that corresponded to each across the provinces of the empire. As Rhoads Murphey cautioned, "instead of being made to conform to the patterns of organization imposed by the highly centralized bureaucratic institutions of the steppe empires, the Anatolian tribes developed individualized, localized, and idiosyncratic bureaucratic models of their own."[55] Nevertheless, these categories and the related terminology provide a fair reflection of the Ottoman approach to tribal administration, which combined the granting of considerable freedom to the tribes with increasingly complex interventions intended both to govern the empire and to protect the tribal communities.

The Ottoman practice of using fluid categories to describe its subjects affected the organization not only of the tribal areas but of the entire empire. This was because nomadic tribes and migrant workers constituted a large portion of the rural population of the Ottoman realm. They continually interacted with nontribal and non-nomadic populations. These conditions on the ground did not change even after the Ottomans strengthened their bureaucracy after the conquest of Istanbul in 1453. In empire-wide fiscal surveys, people were classified broadly on the basis of religion as Muslim, Christian, or Jewish, and their status was categorized as peasant, townsman, or nomad.[56] Of these categories, religion was the most generally used identifier in all other official documents, but the denominations were drawn broadly, with little attention paid to the subgroupings that developed within the religious communities as part of their historical development. Generally, Christians were referred to as *zimmi* or *nasrani,* and Jews as Yahud, Yehud, or *çıfıt,* but in some cases *zimmi* was applied to all non-Muslims, not just Christians. Some groupings within the Muslim community were differentiated as well. For example, the names of individual Gypsies were qualified with *kıpti,* and after the sixteenth century, those who belonged to the Twelver branch of Shi'i Islam, known as Alevi (or Alawite), were identified as Kızılbaş (redhead) in reference to their defection to and service under the Shah of Iran in specially designated troops wearing red caps. The Ottoman government was always careful to identify Kurds, Kızılbaş, and Yezidis, who were the followers of an indigenous syncretic religion. Among other things, the locations of these groups along the Iranian and Russian borders made them suspect and a potential threat to the authority of the central government.[57] It is worth noting that of all the religious and other groups who came under the control of the Ottoman Empire, Gypsies and Kurds were the only ones categorized on the basis of ethnicity and not religion. Even though both groups included Muslim and non-Muslim segments, such distinctions were subsumed under the general categories of Kurds and Gypsies.[58]

PROTECTING MOBILITY

Although the Ottoman land system was premised on the existence and preservation of peasant households (*çift hane*), it also preserved and incorporated the large number of nomadic tribes and regulated their interaction with sedentary farmers. In other words, far from being a residual category that was simply contained, transhumance was "institutionalized in the Ottoman Empire and was protected by the state with special safeguards, rules, and privileges."[59] Ottoman officials issued numerous laws and regulations to govern the migratory routes of nomads and guarantee their livelihood and safety.[60] The plethora of laws protecting the rights of peasants against the incursions of nomads and their animals did not leave the nomadic population without safeguards. In many regions, tribes were expected to herd their animals over specially designated paths, but peasants were also required to mark their land clearly and build fences around it if the land lay on the migratory route of a tribe.[61]

The Ottoman Empire did not undertake a comprehensive policy of sedentarization until the eighteenth century. Before that, the settlement activities the Ottoman government promoted and enforced were limited in focus and purpose. They were carried out in order to populate or repopulate newly conquered areas in the Balkans, to enhance the security of the frontier zones by settling nomads—but without necessarily requiring them to abandon nomadism—to punish unruly tribes, and to resettle *reaya* (tax-paying peasants) who had fled their land.[62] The only large-scale resettlement carried out before the eighteenth century targeted not nomads but peasants who had fled in the face of the Celali uprisings in the seventeenth century, who were encouraged to return to their villages.[63] Even in such campaigns, the nomadic tribes were protected.

Throughout its early centuries, the Ottoman government was careful to preserve nomadism as a legally constituted administrative category as well. It was as difficult to quit nomad status as to acquire it. Even though the empire allowed considerable mobility across social and political strata, formidable barriers made it difficult for sedentary peasants to gain recognition as nomads and vice versa. In 1574, when some peasants wanted to quit their land and work in mines or as falconers, the central government insisted that only members of families who had worked in those capacities for several generations were eligible for such employment. It was usually landless itinerant persons and members of nomadic tribes who were chosen for such positions.[64] On the other hand, even Yürüks who had settled by order of the government and been given land were still drafted for services typically performed by nomads.[65] A formerly nomadic household could apply to change its status only after living and farming in one place for many years. Its members could register as peasants and be exempt from the special service and military obligations that fell on nomads only after their application was approved by the central government.[66]

The practice of petitioning the state has received the attention of Ottoman historians in recent years. Suraiya Faroqhi, among others, has described many instances of peasants appealing to the government in the person of the sultan over perceived injustices or breach of contract.[67] It seems that as far as the Ottoman government was concerned, petitions filed on behalf of nomadic tribes carried the same weight as those written by peasants. This was especially so in areas of strategic importance to the empire. In one of many examples, a (Kurdish?) tribal confederation that was ordered to settle around Diyarbakır in the early 1560s found that the areas designated as its pastures had been claimed by local fief holders, and these presumed landlords demanded a special pasture fee from the tribes. Not having the resources to pay, the tribes quit their land altogether and decided to move to Iran. As they were preparing to leave, they were subjected to onerous duties and taxes by local officials, and they petitioned the court, seeking protection and reprieve. In a detailed response, the central government ordered two separate inspections and concluded that unless such infringements were not prevented and tribal privileges respected, it would be impossible to attract tribes to this area and restore peace and security there. The government ordered the local officials to determine and report the exact locations and the sizes of the pastures. They were also required to put an end to all private claims on these tracts of land. Government officials in the area were instructed to charge no extra tax, fee, or duty from the tribes. According to common practice, the government held the local officials responsible for ensuring that the members of the confederation prospered, free of any cruel treatment.[68] Although it was usual for peasants to complain about the actions of nomads, it was by no means a foregone conclusion that the central government would decide in favor of the peasants. When peasants in Bitola, Thrace, sought government help in preventing Gypsies from coming into their villages in 1634, the government sided with the Gypsies. The order stipulated that they could continue their migration as long as they agreed to pay compensation for any damage they or their animals caused.[69]

In these petitions and responses, what is noteworthy is the close attention the central government paid to the details of the cases. For example, when the government tried to draft some members of a Yürük tribe around Manisa for services to support the military, the tribal members objected, claiming that they were too poor, and their families would have no way of supporting themselves if those who were drafted actually left the area. When representatives of the government arrived from Istanbul to carry out this order in 1572–73, the local *kadı* sided with the tribes, trying to put an end to the demands. After insisting and requesting a special surtax for noncompliance, the central government eventually yielded and dropped its demands.[70]

MOBILITY AND THE INTEGRATION OF THE EMPIRE

The inclusion of tribal communities in the Ottoman system of administration provides only part of the explanation for the long-term presence and resilience of nomadism in the Ottoman Empire. The other significant factor was the tribes' integral position in the Ottoman economy, on both the micro and macro levels.

Land was relatively plentiful across the Ottoman Empire. This meant that in most regions, especially in western Anatolia, a shortage of labor existed, which became particularly pronounced at harvest time. Migrant laborers who belonged to nomadic tribes moved long distances to participate in harvests in the west. In and around Bursa and İzmir, one could find workers who came from northern and eastern Anatolia. They routinely took advantage of higher wages, which could rise as much as threefold during harvest season.[71] Their participation in a variety of economic activities meant that most of the time the tribes functioned as transhumant communities, in which only a part of each tribe moved between the lowlands and mountain pastures while the rest became involved in sedentary activities, including farming. Even those who moved were not necessarily cut off from farming completely, because they could incorporate it into their seasonal migration. In the course of their migration they cultivated the abandoned or unclaimed land they encountered (which could be plenty) or worked as sharecroppers or seasonal laborers on land cultivated by peasants. The existence of these relationships shows that the underlying system of settled agriculture was strong, and a division of labor existed between this sector and the migrating groups and individuals.[72]

The interchange between villages and migrants could take even more complex forms. For example, the collective ownership of land, called *mush'a,* that prevailed in some of the Arab provinces, particularly in western Syria, did not grant permanent ownership or possession to any single household that was part of the system. Instead, individual parcels were periodically redistributed among households, including those of seasonal migrants who might be residing in the village. In this way *mush'a* provided migrants another entry into local economic networks.[73] All this shows that despite appearances, neither migration in rural areas nor the interaction of nomads with local economies was random. The central government was aware of the systematic nature of these relations and taxed nomads separately for the settled farming in which they participated.

In addition to farming, nomads participated in manufacturing, including carpet weaving, rug making, and the production of other textiles.[74] Around Jerusalem, both settled peasants and nomads were engaged in producing soap in the seventeenth century, and the two groups competed with each other to obtain raw materials such as alkaline ash, a key ingredient.[75] Some important export items, such as natural dyes and timber, were gathered from the interior of Anatolia by nomads and sold to merchants on major trade routes.[76] Often, nomadic tribes were the sole purveyors of camels, donkeys, mules, and horses, which were the main means of transportation for civilian and military purposes. They also specialized in raising sheep, which made them the main suppliers of meat in the Ottoman Empire. Their control of the empire's large and small animal stock meant that nomads were indispensable for the operation of regional and imperial networks of trade. In this context it is important to point out the mutual dependence that characterized relations between nomads and settled villagers and townspeople. Just as much as the sedentary groups, the nomads depended on the commercial nexus that linked them to other groups along their paths. They had to have access to regional markets in order to obtain a wide variety of necessities, including food items, construction materials, horseshoes, and even some of their weapons. Such exchanges were regular parts of the economies of various parts of the Ottoman Empire.[77]

Nomads provided important services in the integration and organization of the Ottoman Empire on a macro level as well. For example, so-called Arab camel drivers could be found in most provinces of Anatolia, sometimes moving with their animals across a large swath of territory extending from the Dardanelles to Adana in the south.[78] Nomads facilitated the flow of goods and resources, made it possible for Ottoman troops to move quickly across great distances, and herded, gathered, grew, and manufactured valuable goods of consumption and trade. In times of famines and other natural or man-made disasters, the Ottoman government relied on the services of nomadic tribes to move large quantities of grains and other foodstuffs and necessities to areas of disaster.[79] Nomads were also employed in state-owned mines and in the construction of roads, bridges, forts, and castles, as well as in guarding and protecting such structures.[80]

Nomads made equally significant contributions to the military organization and success of the Ottoman Empire in the early part of its history. By relying on intrinsically mobile groups such as nomads and unattached single men, the Ottoman government could mobilize large numbers of troops without threatening the integrity and viability of the peasant economy. An Arab historian writing in about 1330 estimated that western Anatolia could easily mobilize more than a quarter million cavalrymen from among the nomadic tribes there.[81] Indeed, so central were the local tribes' military activities that between the fifteenth and sixteenth centuries the Ottoman government registered many Yürük communities as military companies (müsellem), ready to be called to the front in times of war or provide support services in war or peace.[82]

For the bands of fighters raised from among nomadic tribes in the frontier regions, it proved relatively easy to defeat and incorporate the land-bound troops of the weak feudal states of southeastern Europe and eventually to vanquish the other principalities in Anatolia.[83] In some instances the Ottomans did not even have to channel or harness the movements of local tribes but simply followed them. This was the case with the 10,000 nomads who spontaneously moved from northwestern Anatolia and settled in the Balkans, where they linked up with the semi-nomadic communities of Vlachs and Albanians in the fourteenth century. By working with each other, they prepared the ground for the subsequent victories of the Ottomans' conquering armies.[84] Tribal groups were assigned the task of guarding fortresses on the frontiers, bridges, and major highways, all of which were crucial in military campaigns as well as in peace. Nomadic tribes were also the sole suppliers of the more than 40,000 camels and as many mules that the Ottoman army required in its campaigns.[85] In the Arab provinces, the government paid the Bedouin to provide some of these services and particularly to keep pilgrimage routes open and safe.[86]

Not surprisingly, the importance and variety of the activities in which nomads were involved and the crucial role the chiefs played in mobilizing their followers made some of these leaders extremely wealthy, powerful, and autonomous. One historian estimates that "even the poorest herdsman could be placed in the same category as a peasant cultivating a full *çift* of 60–100 *dönüm*s or 15–25 acres of land."[87] In 1540 two confederacies in eastern Anatolia paid the central government 2 million *akçes* in taxes.[88] Tribal chiefs used their power and wealth to negotiate the amount and manner of their obligations to the state and made sure that their participation in imperial projects did not go unrewarded. When the two sides disagreed, it was not uncommon for the government to back down and give in to the demands of the tribes as put forth by their chiefs. In one case in 1577, a tribal chief complained that he could not acquire the number of camels he would need to transport from Diyarbakır to Van the 100,000 *kile* of wheat required of him as a service to the central government. Hearing this, the sultan agreed to reduce the amount this tribe had to transport to 2,000 *kile*. Two years later, in 1579, camel drivers refused to transport wheat from Ramallah to Jerusalem for 10 *para* per load, which had been the going rate, and demanded a higher fee, which they received.[89]

In sum, nomads facilitated the flow of goods and resources, made it possible for Ottoman troops to move quickly over long distances, and herded, gathered, planted, and manufactured valuable goods of consumption and trade. Indeed, they were key to the creation of an impressive organization that attracted the envy and admiration of contemporary observers. Ironically, recognizing the nomadic contribution to so many parts of the imperial administration and economy leads us to think of the Ottoman Empire not as a tightly organized and highly centralized entity, as the older models of oriental despotism suggested, but more as a body in flux that displayed considerable capacity to adjust to changes in external conditions and to its own changing needs.

RESISTING THE STATE

To be sure, if they felt their status was threatened or their privileges were undermined, tribes could and did use their distinctive social organization as a weapon. They resisted in different manners, including the organizing of widespread rebellions that lasted for years or even decades. Especially in the Anatolian countryside, the mixture of Sufi teachings, deviant dervish groups, and nomadic and tribal social organization tended to be explosive. Anatolian history is full of examples of rural uprisings in which these elements effectively and sometimes violently resisted when the pre-Ottoman and Ottoman states took steps to enhance their power at the expense of tribes. Some of the better known examples of such rural uprisings are the Karamiyya movement, which extended from Afghanistan into Iran and Anatolia in the ninth through eleventh centuries; the Baba Ishak uprising against the Seljuks in 1240; the Şeyh Bedreddin, which, according to Heath Lowry, was an interfaith popular uprising against the Ottomans, in 1416;[90] and the revolt of Kalender Çelebi, who belonged to the predominantly Shi'i Bektaşi order, and his followers against the Ottomans in 1527.[91]

When these movements spilled over the porous borders and joined forces with their equivalents in neighboring regions, they became particularly serious liabilities for the Ottomans. The Alevi Türkmens, who belonged to the Twelver branch of Shi'i Islam and were divided into several orders (*tarikats*), repeatedly found themselves in such a position in the border zone between the Ottoman and Persian Empires. Starting in the late fifteenth century, when the Ottoman administration adopted elements of orthodox Islam as its principal means of legitimacy to empower its central institutions, some of the tribes among the Alevi Türkmens joined forces with the Safavid ruler Shah Ismail and fought in his army in companies named after their places of origin in Anatolia, such as the Rum-lü, Kara-man-lü, and Tekke-lü.[92] These were the Alevi Türkmens who came to be called Kızılbaş in the Ottoman Empire because of the red caps they wore during their campaigns. Eventually, Kızılbaş became a generic name used to refer to all Alevis in the Ottoman Empire, which reflected a deep suspicion among the ruling elite, who had come to equate being an Alevi with being a rebel and a collaborator with the enemy. After this, Ottoman policies became increasingly discriminatory and violently oppressive toward this community. The wars and the spreading Kızılbaş rebellions ushered in a long and bloody period of suppression by the Ottoman government between the late fifteenth and early seventeenth centuries. The government set up a vast network of spies to monitor the activities and movements of Alevis. Many Alevi orders were banned. Tens of thousands of the followers of these orders, including men, women, and children, were killed, and many were deported to the Balkans, as far away as Hungary.[93]

Ottoman distrust of the Kızılbaş extended to the Bektaşis, just because most members of this Shi'i order were followers of Imam Ali, even though they were predominantly urban, were organized around lodges, and had historical ties to the governing elites and the Ottoman professional army. One of the founders of the Bektaşi order, Abdal Musa, had even been among the comrades of Osman Bey, the founder of the Ottoman dynasty.[94] Despite this pedigree, in 1501 Sultan Bayezid II went so far as to set a loyal lodge in central Anatolia, away from the Bektaşi center in the east. He appointed one of his trusted advisers as its head and imposed the requirement that all resident dervishes take a vow of celibacy, a way of limiting the growth of the order.[95]

Like all other itinerant groups in history, nomadic tribes in the Ottoman Empire had the option of using their mobility as a weapon. When they lacked the means to organize a rebellion, they simply abandoned their designated pastures and paths of circulation, left the towns in which they were settled, and hid in the mountains or the countryside to avoid the authorities.[96] In times of famine, war, or political crisis they joined other unemployed youths or soldiers who had deserted or been discharged from the army, and together they roamed the countryside, raiding and robbing villagers and merchant caravans. The end of the sixteenth century was one such period of upheaval in the Ottoman Empire, and it overlapped with a Mediterranean-wide increase in banditry that Fernand Braudel described as "an explosion of liberation from the Mediterranean mountains."[97]

The Ottoman response to such actions was typically punitive and involved the forced displacement of individuals and tribes who were involved in them. But even such confrontations did not necessarily imply a categorical opposition to nomadism on the part of the central government; instead, they were more focused responses to ideological, political, or foreign pressures. In any event, tribes that had been forced to relocate as punishment did not necessarily stay in the places they were sent to but moved back and forth between their places of origin and their new areas of settlement. For example, Saruhan, in western Anatolia, an important source of emigration to the Balkans from early on, was never completely emptied of nomads but became an end point in the back and forth movement of migrants and nomads.[98] Hence, in most instances in the early part of the empire's history, pressuring nomads had the effect of spreading nomadism over an even larger part of the empire, a process one writer characterized as the "reseeding of nomadism" across the Ottoman territories.[99]

RESULTS

As a result of the Ottoman government's policies and the responses they provoked, parts of the empire witnessed not decreases but increases in numbers of nomadic and semi-nomadic communities during the first half of Ottoman rule. In the main Anatolian provinces, the increase in the number of nomads is estimated to have been about 37 percent between 1520–30 and 1570–80, from 160,564 to 220,217.[100] In Manisa, for example, the number of nomadic households increased by 27 percent between 1531 and 1575, and that of single nomads, by 433 percent.[101]

Awareness of the large number of tribes and unattached individuals who were constantly moving into, out of, across, and around the empire alters our understanding of the way the Ottoman Empire was organized and functioned. This was a political entity with imprecise and constantly changing borders, in which not only spatial but also social mobility blurred the lines of division within the society. It is impossible to discuss questions of ethnic and even religious identity in the early Ottoman Empire in terms of well-defined categories, whether in reference to frontier areas or the very center of Ottoman administration. Far from seeing this flexibility as a source of weakness, the Ottomans regarded it as highly beneficial for their purposes.[102] It was only in the eighteenth century, when changing conditions in Europe put a premium on territorial boundaries and sovereignty, that the Ottoman government began to follow a consistent policy of stopping some of these flows. In the rest of this chapter I look at the consequences of large numbers of unsettled and mobile people for defining and maintaining the empire's borders and the implications these conditions hold for questions of identity in the Ottoman Empire.

Borders

The borders that are so carefully drawn in modern maps indicate primarily the spatial extent over which states can legitimately exercise their authority and, in particular, contain and govern their citizens and subjects and regulate their movements. But the boundaries that separate states acquired this sense of impermeability only in the last 200 years. Outside of well-fortified cities, the idea that people who happened to live in a certain region belonged there, formed a distinct community on the basis of that belonging, and could not legally move outside that region had no bearing on the realities of life before the second half of the eighteenth century. Only in the last two centuries did borders acquire a substantive reality not just for delineating the claims of contiguous states and empires but also, and more important, as universally recognized indicators of the sovereign power of states.

Even without the presence of nomads and other itinerant groups who crisscrossed the frontier regions of the Ottoman Empire, it would have been difficult to determine the exact boundaries of the empire to serve either or both of these purposes during the fourteenth and fifteenth centuries. For one thing, the Ottomans never built walls to protect themselves from the outside world, because, unlike the Chinese, they never regarded themselves or their empire as a distinct and insular entity. Natural boundaries such as rivers, mountains, and coastlines provided some guidance in dividing vast expanses, but only in the nineteenth century did reliable methods of harnessing major rivers and conducting reliable surveys of mountains and seas become widely available. Before then, rivers frequently changed size, direction, and volume, which made them unreliable as signposts in marking off international boundaries.[103] The Arabian and North African deserts, which encircled most of the southern borders of the Ottoman Empire, contained few landmarks of any kind. The concentration of nomads in these regions increased steadily under Ottoman rule. Some tribes fled there to avoid Ottoman demands, but the government itself settled some of them so that they could be mobilized as fighting forces and their normal patterns of migration used as a means of making inroads into new territories. This practice blurred even further the already uncertain borders between the empire and its external arena, making it that much more difficult to ascertain where the empire began and where it ended. The position of the Mediterranean Sea, another seemingly clear and natural barrier, was not that different. As Braudel demonstrated more than half a century ago, the Mediterranean was a "complex of seas," marked with "mountainous peninsulas that were interrupted by vital plains."[104] Thousands of sailors, merchants, commercial ships, and corsairs formed multiple links in and around most of these waters. The Balkans, Anatolia, and North Africa, which became parts of the Ottoman Empire, were and remained integral parts of this economic and cultural medium identified with the Mediterranean world.[105]

Consequently, until the eighteenth century the geographical and political boundaries of the Ottoman Empire functioned more like zones that mediated and even facilitated the interaction of peoples of different backgrounds and origins. Some of the Ottoman government's administrative practices were deliberately designed to maintain a certain degree of flexibility. This was particularly pronounced in monetary policies, in which gold and multiple silver standards were used in different kinds of transactions.[106] This is the opposite of what modern borders are supposed to do in terms of controlling and stopping such flows. Furthermore, the presence of nomads and other migratory people made the frontier areas distinct, with unique institutions and their own ethos, culture, and special practices.[107] Whether following rivers, deserts, seas, or mountains, any line that attempted to divide the premodern world into distinct imperial or civilizational zones would have had little relationship to reality on the ground and would have ended up disrupting existing networks in an arbitrary and destructive way. Many of the well-known pronouncements of the Ottoman sultans concerning their possessions and power reflect the underlying difficulties of delineating precisely the ends of the empire. Here is the way Süleyman I described who he was and what the Ottoman Empire consisted of: "I, emperor of emperors, crowned king of men over the whole face of earth, shadow of god on the two continents, emperor of the White Sea and the Black Sea, of Romania and Anatolia, of the countries of Greece and of Caramania, of Dulkadir, Diyarbekir, Dirinâzim, Damascus, Aleppo,

Cairo, Holy Jerusalem, and sublime Mecca and revered Medina, of Zide, of Yemen, and of many other countries."[108]

The places that Sultan Süleyman mentioned are either stretches with no clear "ends," such as the White Sea (the Mediterranean), Anatolia, Caramania, and Yemen, or cities that were circumscribed by walls and other physical barriers. It is also noteworthy that more than 100 years after they were incorporated into the Ottoman Empire, some of the principalities that preceded the Ottomans were still being described as the "countries" of Caramina, Dulkadir, and so on. This is in part a reflection of the Ottoman practice, upon conquering such lands, of taking over their administrative practices and records rather than centrally restructuring their existing institutions.[109] It is doubtful that the sultan or any of his officials or clerks knew in any detail what existed in these lands, to whom the zones across the western Balkans that separated the Habsburgs from the Ottomans belonged, or how far beyond the city walls of Baghdad Ottoman territory extended.

One of the ways in which the Ottoman court kept an inventory of its possessions and acquisitions was to make use of the region's rich tradition of cartography and pictorial texts, which included detailed descriptions of cities and battles.[110] But along with the desire to know and depict the extent of the empire, these sources were shaped by the temptation to exaggerate the glories of the Ottomans for the enjoyment and satisfaction of the court, which, after all, was the only constituency that had a chance to see such works. The maps typically lack scales and consistent directional viewpoints or orientations, so they are of little use in measuring actual distances between places or the true extent or size of the empire.[111] One well-known source is the *Kitab-ı Bahriye,* written in the sixteenth century by the Ottoman admiral Piri Reis. In addition to including maps of the various parts of the empire, it presents diagrams and pictures of sea castles and coastal towns that were not part of the Ottoman Empire, such as in southern France and around the Atlantic Ocean, including the coastline of the New World.[112] It is obvious that the purpose of such texts and drawings was to inform the sultan about the wider world and even to entice him to set sail to these places and perhaps conquer them for the empire. It was with such concerns that a book written for Sultan Murad III in 1587 stated that "within twenty years the Spanish people conquered all the islands and captured forty thousand people and killed thousands of them. Let us hope to God that some time these valuable lands will be conquered by the family of Islam and will be inhabited by Moslems and become part of the Ottoman lands."[113]

The inadequacy of cartographic representation was not specific to the Ottoman Empire or to Islamic civilization. For Europeans, too, before the nineteenth century the "idea that a map must ipso facto be a guide, or that an atlas must be a handbook, was far from being universally accepted."[114] Concerns other than creating a true picture of the world played a prominent role in the creation of European maps in the early modern era. A 1566 Venetian map of the area between the Ottoman and Habsburg Empires ignored the Ottoman presence altogether and used the pre-Ottoman names and allegiances of cities and places. In addition to political concerns, which sometime resulted in the distortion of reality, there was also the fact that for many Europeans, including the Venetians and the Habsburgs, the extremes of eastern Europe and the Balkans remained as much terra incognito as they were for the Ottomans for many years. Even the exact size, direction, and tributaries of the river Danube remained uncertain until the late eighteenth century.[115] Before then, the exact significance of this river as a marker changed as Belgrade changed hands between the Ottomans and the Hapsburgs.

Today, to figure out the borders of the Ottoman Empire, historians consult the texts of peace treaties and other agreements the Ottomans signed with their neighbors and other foreign powers. Before the sixteenth century, however, Ottomans considered most such treaties to be "tributary-protection compacts" involving a temporary halt to hostilities and the exchange of protection for tribute. As such, they cannot be used as guides in determining boundaries. Typically these documents were limited to mentioning castles, cities, and other visible landmarks and whether these could be fortified and repaired or should be destroyed, leaving the exact shape of the boundaries to the contention of the people involved. Here is the way the border with Poland was drawn in 1699: "After following the [valet of the Jahorlyk] for an hour we crossed the 'Nomad track' at the source of the river Kujal'nyk . . . where 'Lamb Hill' is situated; as there is no hill similar to this one in this neighborhood, it has been reckoned as the boundary marker."[116]

Only in the eighteenth century were such agreements more properly drafted as "truce agreements" spelling out the responsibilities of the parties with clauses dealing with foreign policy, boundaries, envoys, captives, trade, and so forth.[117] The agreements also began to describe in increasing detail the exact status of the newly conquered regions and the people who lived in them, including the mode of taxation and other agricultural and commercial arrangements that would be applied.

The situation on the southern borders of the Ottoman Empire was always particularly complex, because even a hypothetical line separating what Ottoman officials described as the "abode of Islam" (*darülislam*) from the non-tribute-paying lands belonging to non-Muslims, described as the "abode of war" (*darülharb*), was impossible to contemplate. Consequently, the causes for conflict between the Ottoman Empire and its Muslim neighbors varied and changed over time, and the borders themselves remained undefined. The landmarks delineating Ottoman territories were left to the protection of tribal chiefs, who were Bedouin, Kurdish, or Yezidi.[118] Some of these sites remained under the control of the same lineage for several generations, as in the case of some Kurdish tribes on the Iranian border. But having the appropriate title and being entrusted with the administration of a border post or a castle did not mean a tribal chief always remained loyal to the Ottoman sultan. On the contrary, such titles made the chiefs that much more powerful and autonomous. They had their own interests, and they used their strategic positions not only to broaden their spheres of influence but also to enter into regional alliances with peasants, townsmen, or Ottoman officials to protect their positions.[119] So close was the relationship between the Bedouins and the government around Jerusalem that, according to Amy Singer, it was "difficult to state which of the various roles was the most typical of the Bedouin: raider, ally, brigand, or farmer" for any length of time.[120] Kurdish chiefs frequently switched sides, as happened in 1533 when the emir of Bitlis, Şerif Bey, changed his allegiance, became a subject of the Iranian court, and proceeded to attack the Ottoman governor of the district. The result was a series of battles against the Kurdish tribes and the Iranians that lasted almost twenty years.[121]

These border arrangements and early treaties created a chain of tributary states and princedoms encircling the outer reaches of the Ottoman Empire: Byzantium (1372–1453), Serbia (1372–1459), a series of Bulgarian principalities in the late fourteenth century, Bosnia (1389–1463), Albania (1385–1478), Transylvania (1541–1699), Crimea (1475–1783), the Morea (the Peloponnese peninsula) and several northern Aegean islands during the fifteenth century, Ragusa between the fifteenth and eighteenth centuries, and several southern Aegean islands as well as Walachia and Moldavia between the fifteenth and nineteenth centuries. Some of these tributary arrangements were preludes to the full incorporation of the territory into the Ottoman Empire, whereas other territories maintained their special ties to the Ottoman government on a long-term basis.[122] While providing the Ottomans with an added cushion of protection, these tributary states and princedoms introduced another layer of uncertainty in the frontier regions.[123]

Ottoman trade policies also played an important role in keeping the borders open and guaranteeing continuous interaction between the empire and its Christian and Muslim neighbors. Because commercial interactions were particularly intense in the borderlands of the empire, those areas were covered by intricate networks that involved the many-directional movement of goods, people, and money. Itinerant merchants of different religious backgrounds were, in addition to nomadic tribes, the most prominent trespassers of these frontier areas.

Identities

The Ottoman Empire's vague borders were far from serving as markers for an Ottoman identity or as lines of division between Islam and Christianity. Depending on their perception of their own local interests and priorities, Christian nobles in the frontier regions frequently joined Ottoman campaigns against other European states during the fourteenth and fifteenth centuries. Some of them became officials of the Ottoman state and governed the castles that marked the empire's constantly expanding boundaries in the Balkans. In a survey of the most important places in this frontier area in the 1460s, İnalcık found no more than ten professional soldiers of the army stationed in them.[124]

Christian mercenaries and soldiers from different parts of Europe fought alongside the Ottomans against other Christian armies, especially those of the Byzantine Empire. Heath Lowry cites a Byzantine chronicler who described how some Catalan fighters joined the Ottomans against the Byzantine Empire in 1305.[125] When the young Ottoman sultan Mehmed II laid siege to Constantinople in 1453, his army included Serbian, Greek, and Bulgarian troops and also received help from the Genoese, who had a trading colony in the Pera section of the city.[126] The powerful cannon that proved to be the decisive weapon of the battle was cast by a Hungarian engineer who sold his services to the Ottoman sultan after the Byzantine emperor turned him down.[127] Two, possibly three, nephews of the last Byzantine emperor, Constantine, ended up serving the Ottoman state, one as a governor general, another as an admiral, and possibly a third as grand vizier, several years after the capture of the city by the Ottomans.[128] Neither was it uncommon for Muslims to go to the other side and fight against the Ottoman empire. Among the defenders of Constantinople was Orhan Bey, a distant cousin of Sultan Mehmed II, who had been in exile in the city. After the fall of the city, his maintenance continued to be covered by the Ottoman court.[129]

Even at the heart of the Ottoman dynasty, lines of division and sources of identity were by no means unambiguous.[130] Like other Turkic and Islamic rulers of the time, Ottoman sultans and princes routinely married members of the Christian nobility. Some of these marriages were enacted deliberately, with full cognizance of the diplomatic and political advantages they bestowed upon the parties. In 1343 Sultan Orhan married the daughter of Kantakouzenos, an important member of the Byzantine royal family. This gave the Ottomans a valuable means of influencing dynastic feuds in the Byzantine Empire, which they did until the end of that empire in 1453.[131] The Christian women who entered the Ottoman court gained considerable power and influence both in the empire and in relations with their homelands, even after they converted to Islam. Mehmed II's stepmother, Mara, was the daughter of the Serbian prince George Bankonić. When Mehmed's father, Sultan Murad, died in 1451, Mara returned to her father's court and gained considerable fame as a shrewd diplomat with influence among the Ottomans, especially over Murad's stepson, the young Mehmed II. Mara returned to the Ottoman Empire upon the death of her father and lived the rest of her days outside Salonica (twentieth-century Thessaloniki), where she died in 1487.[132] Ottomans used marriage alliances in their dealings with neighboring Muslim dynasties as well, but interestingly, such contacts were less common than those with Christians. The last marriage between an Ottoman sultan and a member of a neighboring Muslim royal family was the one between Selim I and Hafsa Sultan, the daughter of the Crimean ruler Mengli Giray Khan. Süleyman I (the Magnificent) was born to this couple.[133]

By far the most common relationship, which produced almost all the succession of Ottoman sultans, was that between a reigning sultan and a young, enslaved Christian woman. These relationships originated in a special type of forced migration, called *devşirme,* in which large numbers of

Christian children and young men and women were brought to the capital as slaves and forced to convert to Islam.[134] From among them, some males were chosen to be trained for army or high bureaucratic service. Some girls and young women were taken to the palace, where a few ended up being the sultan's favorites and occasionally even his legal wives. Sultan Mehmed II's interest in geography and his deep knowledge of Christianity and of Greek, Roman, and European history are credited to the influence of his mother, a convert to Islam.[135] Contrary to prevailing myths, the women seem to have maintained varying degrees of contact with their birthplaces and families, sometimes using this as a way of wielding power and influence both in the palace and in the empire's foreign relations.

Hürrem Sultan, wife of the long-reigning Süleyman and mother of his son, Sultan Selim II, is a good example of how even women who came to the court as slaves and concubines managed to use their relations with their places of birth to their own benefit as well as to that of the Ottoman state. Hürrem was originally from western Ukraine, which was then a part of Poland. She was presented to Süleyman as a gift on the occasion of his accession to the throne in 1520. For thirty-seven years, between the birth of her first son in 1521 and her death in 1558, when the empire was at the pinnacle of its power and influence in the world, Hürrem—known to Europeans as Roxelana—was one of the most powerful figures in the Ottoman court. In addition to playing a pivotal role in domestic and court politics, she figured prominently in the empire's foreign diplomacy. She corresponded with kings Sigismund I and Sigismund II of her native Poland and played a key role in maintaining peace between the two empires during Süleyman's reign.[136]

Nurbanu, the mother of Sultan Murat III (r. 1574–95), was Venetian by birth. She was taken prisoner and brought to Istanbul in 1537. Throughout her life she maintained a keen interest in Ottoman relations with Venice. So valuable were Nurbanu's interventions on behalf of Venice that in 1583 the Venetian Senate presented her with a gift of 2,000 sequins.[137] Similarly, many of the high-ranking bureaucrats who entered the Ottoman court as slaves kept alive their ties to their families and used their power and influence in the court to channel state resources to their places of birth.[138] The illustrious architect Sinan used his influence in the palace to gain exemption for his relatives in Kayseri, who were to be deported to Cyprus in the sixteenth century.[139]

In what was supposed to be the most secluded core of the empire's administration, then, the movement of individuals and groups helped maintain crucial ties to the outside world, making it difficult to draw clear lines of distinction and identification. Ottoman rulers saw their slave origins as a more important source of power and privilege than their affinity with their Muslim neighbors. Leading intellectuals of the empire argued that those who were not products of the *devşirme* system and not trained as scholars were "neither slaves nor scholars" and so should have "no right to enter the system." Moreover, those who were from outside the geographical region of "Rum"—central and western Anatolia—were not seen as true Ottomans and therefore were deemed unqualified to serve as rulers. Such skepticism and even outright hostility was directed particularly against Iranians and Alevis.[140]

Once they were fully in charge of the east-west passages, the Ottomans continued an active trade with India while maintaining good relations with at least one of the major commercial powers, including the Venetians, the Genoese, the Florentines, and later the Dutch, at any given time.[141] As a result of these policies, frontier regions and especially the major ports of the eastern Mediterranean grew as open and cosmopolitan cities under the control of the Ottoman Empire. The population of the port cities grew significantly in the second half of the sixteenth century, a time of commercial growth in Europe and the Ottoman Empire. Cities such as Dubrovnik, Constantinople, İzmir, and Aleppo housed expanding and overlapping communities of European, Arab, Persian, Armenian, Greek, Jewish, and Indian merchants who resided in these places and traveled east and west by following the ancient trade routes.[142] These cities also became points of attraction for migrant workers. People who might or might not be members of nomadic tribes arrived in these places in search of employment and filled the ranks of porters, water carriers, boatmen, bath attendants, hawkers, and day laborers.[143] The non-Muslim segment of the population in these cities, which had particularly vibrant commercial ties to the outside world, grew faster than the Muslim population. In İzmir between 1528 and 1575, the growth rates were 155 percent and 118 percent, respectively.[144]

The growing diversity at such points of contact did not mean that peopling various regions, especially the border areas, in a way that would enhance the security of the empire was not an important concern for the Ottomans in the fourteenth and fifteenth centuries. But making these areas secure did not necessarily entail the creation of ethnically or religiously homogeneous communities and containing them within well-defined and well-protected borders. The Ottomans made a point of maintaining largely open and mostly unmarked borders over which merchants, nomads, and other itinerant groups and individuals continued to move. There is little doubt that Ottoman rulers saw such openness and mobility as a source of strength. They supported social structures and policies that accommodated and strengthened the interaction of different communities across and beyond the empire.

Accordingly, the settlement policies of the new empire were not aimed at creating religiously homogeneous (that is, uniformly Muslim) or distinctly Ottoman populations along the empire's borders. On the contrary, the goal was to replicate the conditions of religious diversity that prevailed in most other parts of the empire. Although some settlement was carried out on the basis of centrally drawn rules and even ratios, in other instances the ongoing movements of tribes in the provinces were allowed to continue and even made easy by the central government and by the commanders of the frontier troops, who operated freely and autonomously in the borderlands.[145] In carrying out these policies of resettlement, the Ottomans sometimes took steps to alter the religious composition of the settled territory, but not in a way that created insular, homogeneous areas. In 1397, for example, 30,000 people from the Morea were resettled in parts of Anatolia while groups of Türkmens and Tatars were forced to move in the other direction and were settled in Thessaly and other parts of the eastern Balkans.[146]

The growing power and influence of the new Ottoman state extended even to neighboring states. The Ottoman sultan Bayezid I was able to pressure the Byzantine emperor Manuel II to establish a Muslim quarter in Constantinople in 1397, which had its own *kadı* and a church converted into a mosque. The populations of two Muslim villages, Taraklıyenice and Köyünk, were resettled in this district.[147] Undoubtedly the action was conceived as a step toward the eventual incorporation of the city into the Ottoman Empire. Tatar fighters who had originally belonged to Tamerlane's army but who had stayed behind in Anatolia were moved to Rumelia, where they established the town of Tatarpazarı (which still exists in Bulgaria as Pazardjik) in 1418.[148] In 1521 some 2,000 Serbs were relocated from Sirem, outside of Belgrade between the rivers Danube and Sava, to Gelibolu on the Dardanelles.[149] In Thrace and the eastern Balkans, local communities including Christian monks and priests complained that the land being given to the newly resettled groups belonged to them, and the orders granting these settlers access should be reversed.[150]

In managing the populations of their major cities, the Ottomans also monitored and managed the spontaneous migrations of groups and individuals. In most measures pertaining to the populations of major cities, maintaining a degree of religious diversity was important to the Ottoman government. This can be seen most clearly in measures enacted for repopulating Constantinople following its conquest in 1453, whereby thousands of Jewish, Christian, and Muslim families from different parts of the empire were forced to move to the new capital. As is well known, Mehmed II insisted that the Ottoman Empire be seen as the heir not only to classical Islam but also to the Byzantine Empire and especially to the Roman Empire. His successors took similar approaches, which included measures encouraging or providing the conditions for the mixing of populations on different levels. For example, Mehmed II's considerably more conservative son, Bayezid II, was particularly welcoming toward Jews who had been expelled from Spain in 1492. At least initially, Istanbul experienced a shortage of labor, and the Ottoman policies of encouraging immigration into the city were designed to fill the gap. Yet this relatively liberal policy of labor migration continued even after population increase became a source of concern for the central government. Only worries about the security of the city prompted the Ottomans to institute a degree of control and even reverse the flow of people into Istanbul and other large cities.[151] In a typical order issued in 1567, the sultan asked the military chief of Istanbul to register all those who had arrived in the city in the preceding five years. He wanted to know where these people had come from, where they were living, and whether or not they owned property. Those who did not own property and therefore did not belong to their neighborhoods, and those who were involved with local prostitutes, would be sent back to their places of origin.[152]

These crisscrossing and overlapping networks and relations notwithstanding, Christian Europeans, both Catholics and Protestants, eventually did identify the Ottoman Empire as the embodiment of Islam and therefore as representing everything that European Christendom was not. In the eyes of Europeans this made the Ottoman Empire a unified and monolithic source of danger. But such claims were more effective in helping Europe to define itself than in describing the true nature of the Ottoman Empire. The fourteenth, fifteenth, and sixteenth centuries, when the Ottoman Empire was expanding and interacting with Europeans, were particularly troublesome for Europe. Persistent warfare undermined both the legitimacy of the large empires and the authority of the pope in Europe, pushing some local vassals to declare their allegiance to the Ottoman sultan. Persecution of Jews in parts of Europe further exposed the latent tensions and rifts in the continent and opened another link with the Ottoman Empire as hundreds of thousands of Jews expelled from Spain migrated east and settled in Ottoman lands.

At the same time in central and western Europe, the Protestant movement gained strength, challenging in the strongest terms the power and credibility of the Catholic hierarchy. For a while it even looked as if the Protestants and the Ottomans might join forces and together deal a death blow to the Catholic monarchies of Europe. Although Luther eventually came to see Turks and Muslims as God's punishment on Christians for their sinful ways, he was initially opposed to the idea of fighting the Turks. He found the concept of holy war offensive and suspected that Pope Leo X was reviving the idea of the crusade as a way of imposing taxes on Christians and thereby reinforcing his own authority and wealth. Luther wrote in 1521, "How shamefully the pope has this long time baited us with the war against the Turks, gotten our money, destroyed so many Christians and made so much mischief!"[153] To Luther it was scandalous that Turks appeared to be more modest, enjoyed a simpler life, and acted more honorably than the pope.[154] Apparently Sultan Süleyman was aware of this schism. In 1531, upon learning from a German diplomat that Luther was forty-eight years old, he said, "I wish he were even younger; he would find in me a gracious protector."[155] As is well known, Luther eventually became adamant in his negative opinion of the Ottomans: "Antichrist is at the same time the pope and the Turk," he said. "The spirit of Antichrist is the pope, his flesh the Turk. . . . Both . . . are of one lord, the devil, since the pope is a liar and the Turk a murderer."[156] He continued to believe, however, that defense against the Ottoman armies would have to carried out not by crusading armies organized by the pope but by princes and states.[157]

Instead of "Turkifying" the Near East, migration in all its hues made this geography more diverse and heterogeneous. This diversity affected ethnic and religious identity not only in the frontier zones but also in the interior of the empire—especially in terms of the kind of Islam practiced there. Even though they were almost all Muslims, the nomadic tribes that populated late medieval Anatolia and became the building blocks of the rural and urban networks of the Ottoman Empire adhered not to Sunni orthodoxy but to one of the many Sufi *tarikats* or the Alawite or Shi'i branches of Islam. The initial spread of Sufi orders such as the Mevlevis, Bektaşi, Bayramis, Khalwatis, Rifais, and Kazerunis in the Near East dates back to the Mongol invasions. By that time these communities, which embodied locally specific interpretations of the Islamic faith, had each established its own hierarchical formal structure. In the middle of the thirteenth century the Mongols destroyed the urban centers where the leaders of these communities resided and from which they exercised control over their respective orders. In the chaotic years that followed, power gradually devolved away from these centers and toward the lodges located on the peripheries of the urban centers and farther away in the countryside. In the absence of a coherent central direction, in many places disciples took it upon themselves to protect the shrines of their holy figures and developed ideologies that increasingly privileged independent thinking, innovation, and decentralized administration.[158] Many of these ideologies were much more influenced by local beliefs than by any religious or scriptural orthodoxy originating in the center.

The nomadic Turkic tribes arrived and eventually incorporated themselves into these relatively anarchic structures between the eleventh and fourteenth centuries. The compatibilities between the traditions and practices of the Sufi orders and those of tribal organizations made it easy for Sufi missionaries to propagate their orders among the Turkic tribes in the late Middle Ages. Poetry and music, which were integral to tribal activities, were also central to the services and traditions of the Sufis and became important media for spreading the influence of these orders among the tribes. From the combination of tribal social structures and the malleable beliefs of the Sufi orders emerged the "colonizing dervishes" who played a leading role in the Ottomans' expansionary drive in the Balkans.[159] In time these dervishes and the Turkic communities in general would become some of the most devoted followers and defenders of both Islam in general and the specific beliefs and traditions of their orders.[160] As Ahmet Karamustafa has shown, the early centuries of Ottoman rule overlapped with the spread of many deviant orders that "elevated ascetic principles of mendicancy, itinerancy, celibacy, and self-mortification to unprecedented heights through a radical interpretation of the doctrine of poverty."[161]

The belief systems of Alevis and Sufis as well as those of deviant orders were conducive to the continuous movement of the groups that adhered to them. Sufis were generally organized around their own sheikhs, with whom personal contact and interaction were essential. Followers of particular sheikhs traveled with their leaders in order to stay close to them. The same was true for Alevis, especially those outside of the main hierarchies, such as the followers of Hacı Bektaş. Like Sufis, they had their own leaders, called *dedes*, to whom they tried to stay close. Alternatively, in several cases the *dedes* circulated and performed their duties in different places.[162] In their migrations these groups interacted with many Christian and Jewish communities, incorporating aspects of those religions, including some of their saints, into their own traditions. This was particularly the case in the relationship between the Sufis and the Armenian Paulicans in the east, Pontus Greeks in the northeast, and Jews in the southeast.[163] There were also loose ties between the Mevlevi orders and the mystical Jewish circles in Istanbul and the Balkans. In the music and poetry of some of these artists one sees the influence of Sufi traditions that originated in different places.[164] The result of this cross-fertilization was a series of hybrid social, economic, political, and cultural institutions and practices. It was in and through these diverse settings that the people of Anatolia and the Balkans came to practice Islam, creating a version of the religion that was strikingly different from the more orthodox versions that prevailed in the urban centers of the Arabian peninsula and the Fertile Crescent and intermittently in the imperial capital, Istanbul.

The influence of orders such as the Mevlevis, Bektaşis, Bayramis, Kadiris, Nakşibendis, and Halvetis spread among the major urban centers and Ottoman officialdom as well as the rural population at large. Some of the sultans were schooled and influenced by these orders. Osman, who gave his name to the Ottoman dynasty, had a father-in-law who belonged to the Akhi order and had close relations with Hacı Bektaş himself. One of the brothers of Orhan, who succeeded Osman to the throne, was an Akhi as well.[165] Mehmed II, who was known for his antagonism toward Sufism in general, was nevertheless a follower of Seyh Akşemseddin, the successor to Hacı Bayram.[166] Following the conquest of Istanbul, the growing influence of these orders within the Ottoman administration led Mehmed II to name some districts of the city after leaders of important Sufi *tarikat*s, such as Şeyh Ebu'l Vefa, Şeyh Akşemseddin, and Şeyh Sevinduk Halveti.[167] Mehmed II's son, Sultan Bayezid II, who was particularly close to some of the *tarikat*s, established the Halveti and Nakşibendi orders in Istanbul in the late fifteenth century. As they became established in urban centers, they served as magnets for migration from rural areas and became important parts of civic life in cities.[168] Other orders had more direct and long-lasting effects on specific organs of government. The most famous of these is the Bektaşi order, which came to be closely identified with the Janissary army. Indeed, many contemporary chroniclers and modern historians argue that the Janissaries' relationship with such Sufi orders became a venue for the soldiers to learn and practice various arts, crafts, and manufacturing activities, leading eventually to the weakening of the empire's military organization.

THE EMPIRE CHANGES

By the end of the seventeenth century, it had become clear to the Ottomans that in the newly emerging circumstances of early modern Europe, flexible borders and imprecise identities no longer served them well. They had spent most of the seventeenth century in war with several of their neighbors while trying to deal with internal unrest, rural rebellions, and military uprisings. They had little to show for the extraordinary effort and resources they had expended in ventures such as the disastrous second siege of Vienna in 1683. As early as 1606 they had signed a treaty with Austria in which they had to accept that they were no longer in a position to dictate the terms of such agreements but were dealing with other states on equal footing. That treaty and several that followed it included clauses requiring the regulation of borders. Specifically, the Ottomans were required to put an end to the cross-border raids of the frontier regiments.[169] The seventeenth century ended with the Treaty of Karlowitz in 1699, by which the Ottomans experienced their first major loss of territory in Europe and were forced to leave Hungary, Transylvania, Croatia, and other European territories.

The Ottoman Empire responded to the new world of expanding trade networks and territorial states by initiating measures aimed at improving its security. These measures can be interpreted as the first steps toward creating a functionally differentiated state structure that continually sought to improve its capacity to rule over an unruly society that was highly mobile. A key component of this shift in priorities was a growing interest on the part of Ottoman officials in counting, registering, and ultimately settling the nomadic and other itinerant groups within the borders of the empire. It was becoming clear that in the new modern world, the territorial and political uncertainty that came with nomads and migrants was no longer an asset. Indeed, such fluidity was fast becoming a liability.

3 Toward Settlement

In 1691 a group of villagers in western Anatolia filed a petition with six judges who had jurisdiction over their region. In it they complained that seven of twenty-two tribes that had been ordered by the central government to settle in parts of western Anatolia had set up their tents not on the properties reserved for them but on communally held pasture land. From these sites the tribal members were letting their animals loose, causing damage to planted fields in the surrounding area. Tribal members were also raiding villages, looting property and food, and robbing travelers on public roads. The villagers described how their properties were breaking up and how they were becoming destitute. They pleaded with the government to intervene to protect them.

The judges referred this complaint to Istanbul because it involved issues of primary concern to the central government. The government responded by reiterating the terms of the original decree, which had been written two years before, in 1689, ordering a large number of nomadic tribes to settle on land reserved for them. The response listed the names, brief histories, and leaders of the specific tribes, when and why they were ordered to settle, the precise locations and sizes of the areas they were supposed to settle in, and the terms of their settlement. The government urged the local authorities to see to it that the terms of the order were carried out fully and without delay.[1] Among other things, this exchange is valuable for the detail included in it and the close attention with which the government's response was obviously drafted. Far from being an isolated episode, this settlement order was part of a larger project. Indeed, the 1689 decree, which the central government reiterated in 1691, was one of a series of similar orders the Ottoman government issued around that time, all dealing with the sedentarization of tribes.

Impressive as the government's reiteration of its original order was, there is no way to discover whether it made any difference in getting the tribes to conform to the terms of their charge. Like most such cases, this one stops at this point, making further inquiry impossible. What is beyond dispute is that by the end of the seventeenth century, bringing about a more sedentary rural life had become a concern for the Ottoman government. Numerous orders were issued, their implementation was closely monitored, and government officials and tribal chiefs who did not comply were severely punished. This represents a significant departure from earlier methods of imperial rule, which relied on the continuing mobility of large numbers of imperial subjects to extend and exercise the authority of the Ottoman center. Interest was now growing on the part of the Ottoman rulers in creating a political unit with plainly demarcated borders that would contain people who were clearly identified, registered, and counted. To be sure, the completion of this shift took much longer than the brief span at the close of the seventeenth and the beginning of the eighteenth century. It can be argued that the process was still incomplete even when the empire collapsed and disappeared at the end of World War I. Nevertheless, the first significant push in this direction can be seen in the Ottoman Empire in the last two decades of the seventeenth century.

In the rest of this chapter, I first identify the external and internal factors that prompted the Ottoman government to begin regarding mobility not as an asset to be manipulated and taken advantage of but as a potential source of weakness to be contained. I continue with an assessment of three policies the Ottomans instituted in order to control the nomadic and migrant population. The first was the issuing of increasingly detailed directives that identified specific tribes for removal and resettlement. The second was the expansion of the empire's network of guards and couriers and the enrollment of tribal members in it, a practice conceived as another way of bringing the tribes under closer government supervision. The third was the registration of nomadic tribes and other migratory groups into the military and their integration in specially constituted military units. The results of these policies, however, were not always what the central government intended. The main problem lay in implementation. Because the Ottoman bureaucracy was still relatively small, it was difficult to transmit the will of the authorities in Istanbul to the far corners of the empire. Therefore, instead of realizing a comprehensive program of sedentarization in the seventeenth century, the central government ended up giving even more power and autonomy to some nomadic and migrant groups, because this was the only way it could reach into the countryside and control some such groups. As a result, the eighteenth century became a transitional one, with some important elements of the Ottoman state under reform but with many of its older institutions stronger than ever.

EXTERNAL PRESSURES

The first factor that pushed Ottoman officials to reassess the status of nomadic tribes was their reversal of fortune in Europe. The turning point came in the second half the sixteenth century. In looking at the Ottoman Empire's relations with its neighbors and other European powers, it is hard not to be struck by the sharp turn separating the second half of the sixteenth century from the first. The last major territorial conquest by the Ottomans in Europe came in 1541–43, when they took Hungary from the Habsburgs. This marked the culmination of more than 200 years of more or less continuous growth. Ottoman borders did expand farther, in both the west and the east, through the latter half of the seventeenth century, but these conquests were more in the nature of minor adjustments and amounted to little more than marginal gains in southern Ukraine, North Africa, and the Caucasus. Furthermore, some of the territories changed hands several times among the Ottoman, Russian, and Habsburg Empires without ever being firmly integrated into any of them.

The slowdown and ultimately the complete cessation of territorial gains pushed Ottoman officials to reassess a number of aspects of their imperial administration. They focused on their border areas, trying to find out who lived there, how the borders were defined, and what were the best ways of defending them. They also sought information more systematically about Europe and European affairs. Permanent legations were dispatched to

Europe, and their reports began to be included in the official histories of the Ottoman Empire for the first time in the second half of the seventeenth century.[2] Kâtip Çelebi (1609–1657), an extraordinarily well-informed scholar, combined these two trends and took the lead in making geography a key concern for the empire's elite. In the introduction to his book on naval warfare, *The Gift of the Noble, on Naval Campaigns,* he wrote:

> For a man who is in charge of the affairs of the state, the science of geography is one of the matters of which knowledge is necessary. . . . He should at least know the map of the Ottoman domains and that of the states adjoining so that when there is a campaign and military forces have to be sent, he can proceed on the basis of knowledge and so that the invasion of the enemy's and also the protection and defence of the Ottoman frontiers become an easier task. . . . Unbelievers, by their application to and their esteem for those branches of learning, have discovered the new world and have overrun the ports in India and East Indies. . . . Even such a miserable lot as the Venetians, a people whose ruler has only the rank of duke among unbeliever kings, and whom those kings call "the fisherman," has actually advanced to the Dardanelles in the Ottoman domains and has set itself to oppose the all-glorious state which rules over east and west.[3]

The growing diplomatic and intellectual engagement with Europe bore fruit. In various treaty negotiations the Ottomans appeared well informed about European affairs, and they used this knowledge effectively in the seventeenth century.[4] This intelligence came both from European diplomats and others who passed through or resided in the Ottoman Empire and from Ottomans who traveled abroad for business and, starting in the second half of the century, in official capacities.

While the Ottomans were trying to adjust to the new conditions confronting them, they were also fighting wars in order to halt and even reverse their losses. The intensity of these conflicts and the territorial, human, and material losses the empire suffered increased significantly in the seventeenth century. For the Ottomans, the fifty-four years between 1683 and 1737 were consumed by almost constant warfare, punctuated only by brief intervals of peace. It was almost as if war had become the normal state of things in relations with other powers. Despite the mobilization of large numbers of troops for lengthy periods and the tremendous expenditures the government had to undertake to finance them, the Ottomans had little to show for their seemingly interminable entanglements with their neighbors or for staging spectacular ventures such as the second siege of Vienna in 1683. Most of these confrontations ended in defeat and loss of territory for the empire.

It is fitting that the end of the seventeenth century was marked by the Treaty of Karlowitz, which the Ottomans signed with Holy League powers—the Habsburg monarchy, Poland, and Russia—in 1699, whereby they agreed to retreat from Hungary, Transylvania, Croatia, Slovenia, Dalmatia, the Morea, some Aegean islands, Podolia, and southern Ukraine. This was the first time the Ottomans had to evacuate, at once, such a large swath of territory in the Balkans and eastern Europe, after dominating those lands for three centuries. It was also the first time the imperial administration was confronted with waves of Muslim refugees who were abandoning land lost to the Austrian Empire and seeking protection in the Ottoman realm. The Muslim exodus, which would grow to more than a hundred thousand people in the early years of the eighteenth century, was engineered in part by the Habsburg monarchy.[5] In addition to refugee flows, these population movements included the migrations of tribes who were adjusting their migratory routes to the interruptions caused by newly erected citadels along the borders. Not surprisingly, the Ottoman bureaucracy was unprepared to absorb and settle these people in an orderly fashion. The problem would become only more serious in the eighteenth and nineteenth centuries.

The century between 1550 and 1650, when Ottoman expansion reached a plateau, coincided with far-reaching transformations that affected Europe and the rest of the world. The Mediterranean, where Ottoman efforts had always been concentrated, began to lose its central position in international trade in favor of the Atlantic, where the Dutch, French, and British quickly became the main players. In other words, the territories in which the Ottoman, Austrian, and Russian Empires intersected and where they were fighting their interminable wars were losing the pivotal role they had played in cross-continental networks in previous centuries. Paralleling this shift of center in the global economy was the development of a new understanding of sovereignty, which was formally agreed upon for the first time in the Treaty of Westphalia, ending the Thirty Years' War in Europe in 1648. Westphalia recognized the sovereign rights of each ruler to decide all matters of state within the internationally recognized borders of his or her realm. It delegitimated the notion that it was acceptable to fight to establish either a universal religion in Europe or a Europe-wide empire.[6] Europe was, in short, becoming a new place whose center of gravity was shifting toward the Atlantic coast and whose international borders were acquiring new significance as inviolable markers of state sovereignty.

The Ottoman Empire was not a party to the Thirty Years' War or the Treaty of Westphalia, but it was directly affected by the outcome of the treaty. Along with all the major European powers, the Ottomans began to develop mechanisms to regulate peace, rather than considering themselves in a permanent state of war with non-Muslim states, which had been their earlier attitude.[7] In this changing environment the relatively open borders of the Ottoman Empire, which had served well in facilitating flows of goods and people between Europe and Asia in previous centuries, became an anomaly and ultimately a liability.

The treaties the Ottomans signed in the late seventeenth and the eighteenth centuries reflected the new realities in Europe. In a departure from the earlier practice of maintaining fluid frontiers, the Ottomans now agreed to improve the visibility and security of their borders with Austria and Russia by building new citadels and repairing neglected structures in the frontier zones.[8] In addition to the special troops stationed there, the frontier zones had been routinely crossed by peasants, peddlers, and nomads in earlier centuries. Partly to fulfill the stipulations of their treaties and partly as a result of internal pressures that I discuss later, the Ottomans took steps to control and limit such movements. For example, they banned the use of forced labor in frontier regions, because this had become a key factor in pushing Christian peasants to flee their villages.[9] Moreover, the definitions of boundaries in treaties became considerably more specific than those in earlier ones. As can be seen in the following passage from a treaty signed in 1724, the Ottoman and Russian Empires tried to follow precise methods in partitioning the northwest provinces of Iran:

> Riders provided and furnished with good and accurate timepieces will proceed on horseback, at a trot, along the quickest route from Shamaki to the border of the Caspian Sea; upon their arrival at that sea the number of hours taken from Shamakhi will be calculated. That number will be divided by three; the riders will return by the same route and upon completing two-thirds of it will post a marker at that point. One-third from that post to Shamakhi shall belong to the Sublime Porte [the Ottomans]. . . the other two-thirds located between the post and the seat shall belong to His Tsarist Majesty.[10]

Building citadels and fortifying the borders did not necessarily stop the attacks the Ottomans were experiencing from their neighbors. Nor did these steps make the border areas more secure. On the contrary, instead of maintaining mobile and dynamic forces akin to shock troops, the Ottomans were now building citadels in territories that were not necessarily friendly.[11] This was because in previous centuries they had made no sustained effort to change the ethnic or religious composition of these areas and thoroughly integrate them into the empire. As long as the center was powerful, it was easy to pull the loosely aligned frontier zones into the empire's orbit. Once this pull lost its effectiveness, the frontier communities began to act independently and carve out zones for themselves. Many citadels and other markers were quickly overrun, and these regions began to resemble the moving frontiers of previous centuries, except that now the borders were retracting, not expanding.

Clear delineation of boundaries and their fortification for security were not confined to the land borders of the Ottoman Empire. The Ottomans also became concerned with the status of their maritime borders and took measures to better define and defend them as well. As part of this effort, in 1701 they prohibited Algerian seafarers from raiding the Aegean coasts, even though this had been a commonly used method of drafting seamen for both military and commercial purposes for centuries.[12] But in this regard, too, Ottoman efforts were ineffective in the long run.

INTERNAL PRESSURES

The long wars of the sixteenth and seventeenth centuries and changing relations with a new and increasingly dynamic Europe put a great strain on Ottoman society, economy, and institutions. Perhaps the most important problem was the growing shortage of manpower, because continuous war meant continuous demand for soldiers. In many parts of Anatolia and the Balkans, men of fighting age were absent from their homes and villages for long stretches of time, either fighting with the army, providing auxiliary services for it, or fleeing from their obligations. Their absence severely interrupted the cultivation and harvesting of fields. Large numbers of people who were displaced from their villages because they could no longer support themselves by farming either moved to towns, causing the urban population to rise and putting additional pressure on agriculture, or circulated in rural areas, undermining security in large sections of the countryside.[13] A survey conducted in Karasi, in western Anatolia, in the early eighteenth century found that of the 170 households previously registered there, only 56 remained, and 12 of the 54 villages that were part of the district were in ruins. In the remaining 42 villages there were no more than 144 households.[14] The French consul in Cairo described the countryside in terms of "a weakness, which he would never have conceived at a distance." It contained "desolate provinces, disconcerted people, and insufficient and undisciplined militia, which lacked leaders."[15] It was becoming difficult for the empire's peasant economy to meet the demands of both the growing population in towns and a central authority whose need for additional fighters and revenue in kind and cash seemed to be increasing without limit.[16]

Initially, the Ottoman administration tried to meet its growing need for revenue by making regular and routine the special taxes that were supposed to be levied only under exceptional circumstances. This could double and even triple the burden on peasants, who were expected to continue to pay their regular dues.[17] It led many more of them to quit their land and join the migrating groups. The Ottoman government tried to deal with the deteriorating situation through some ad hoc measures. For example, when conditions became particularly desperate in an area, the government would decree a form of universal mobilization (*nefr-i âm*), drafting most of the able-bodied males in the area.[18] This made things worse, and even more people fled their homes to avoid the impositions.

For the Ottoman rulers, being unable to collect revenue meant that in addition to having difficulty paying the salaries of soldiers and functionaries, they were losing the resources they needed to make deals with local potentates and tribal chiefs in order to maintain their allegiance to the center. Under these circumstances, local notables, tribal chiefs, members of nomadic tribes, peasants, and even local officials and Janissaries found it more beneficial to work for their own interests, often in competition with one another. Not only did they ignore the demands of the central government, but they also worked against and even challenged the state by force in order to improve their local standing. One former Janissary and his men, for example, took advantage of the absence of a local *kadı* in İzmir in 1605 and raided his home, looted his possessions, and raped his wife and children.[19] Another person of dubious background claimed to be authorized by the central government to subdue the vagabondage around

İzmir. Ostensibly to carry out this order, he gathered other bandits around him and "punished" many innocent villagers, causing them to flee their homes.[20]

Because of their relative security, most towns and cities became magnets for uprooted people in Anatolia and the Balkans. More than any other city, Istanbul was the place to which many of these people wanted to move, which created further problems for Ottoman order. Like the rulers of all other empires in history, the Ottomans tried to monitor and limit the movement of people from peripheral areas to their seat of power, Istanbul. Given the diverse relations and institutions that existed in different parts of the empire, it would have been impossible to absorb all would-be immigrants without either forcing them to change in fundamental ways or infinitely multiplying and diversifying the city's institutions to accommodate them. An uncontrolled swelling of the city's population would have had a negative effect on social order not only in the city but also in surrounding areas, which would have been forced to provision an even larger population that paid no taxes and contributed in no real terms to the empire's economy.

Being the imperial center, Istanbul represented the core of Ottoman ruling culture, which was distinct from and existed in some degree of insulation from the rest of society. For most people who made the journey, moving to Istanbul would not have been unlike moving to another country. In these times of trouble, the Ottoman government sought to make the journey even more difficult. The measures it introduced to monitor and resist such migration included checkpoints, special permits for immigration, restrictions on where, how, and with whom immigrants could live, and occasional sweeps in which people were picked up and sent out of the city.[21] Still, the lure of Istanbul was strong, especially because residents of the imperial capital were protected from constant harassment by rebel forces and corrupt officials. They were also exempt from rural taxes and from the extraordinary levies that were routinely imposed on peasants.[22]

Istanbul was not the only city that attracted displaced people from the Ottoman countryside, but other cities in Anatolia did not offer all the special privileges Istanbul did. Rather than giving refugees a degree of security, these cities became even less safe when they faced waves of uncontrolled migration. Bandits and other rebellious groups, whose pressures and demands had made it all but impossible for peasants to stay in their villages, did not hesitate to pursue their prey to the very gates of major settlements in Anatolia and even right into them. In one of many similar events, in 1688 more than 5,000 recently discharged soldiers-turned-bandits surrounded Ankara and blocked its water and provisions. The populace had to pay a hefty ransom to the bandit chief, Gedik Mehmet Bölükbaşı, and his men to persuade them to lift the siege. After leaving Ankara, the rebels robbed and destroyed other settlements in north-central Anatolia. At the end of the seventeenth century, the residents of settlements such as Konya, Ilgın, Akşehir, and Kırşehir had to dig deep trenches around their towns to protect themselves against such attacks.[23]

Partly in response to the steadily growing demand for troops, a large number of people whose status and loyalty to the sultan were unclear had begun to circulate in and out of the military ranks, creating severe problems of discipline and professionalism. Of the 28,400 troops who were ready to fight the last battle of the second attack on Vienna in 1683, only 5,000 were listed as professional Janissaries.[24] In a history of the siege of Vienna, the palace secretary described the way many of the artisans who had come to the front as soldiers were interested only in the loot. Apparently, as soon as the war was over, some of these people loaded their animals with whatever they could lay their hands on and prepared to flee.[25] In the meantime, the pay of the regular soldiers was in arrears, and their regular system of recruitment, training, and discipline had broken down. One contemporary account described the unruly behavior of the Janissaries:

> Practicing brigandage, they are not satisfied with free and gratuitous fodder for their horses and food for their own bellies from the villages they meet. They covet the horse cloth and rags of the rayas and if they can get their hands on the granaries they become joyful, filling their sacks with barley and oats for provisions and fodder. While they behave in this way and make thus a habit of ruin, setting themselves to harm and oppress, the sighs and groans of mankind attain the heavens and it is certain that they will be accursed.[26]

The increasingly chaotic situation on the frontiers became worse in the aftermath of the Austrian wars at the end of the seventeenth century. According to one source, "from Hungary, Slovenia, and those parts of the Bosnian paşalık, that by the treaty of Karlowitz belonged to Austria or the Venetians, about 130,000 Muslims sought refuge in the interior of Turkey [sic]."[27] By the time the Treaty of Passarowitz, ending another war with Austria and Venice, was signed in 1718, practically no Muslim presence was left in Hungary and Slovenia. In addition to Muslim refugees, Albanian and Dalmatian deserters from the Habsburg army were also crossing the frontier zones, making it that much more difficult to stabilize these areas.[28] The disorder in the ranks of the Ottoman military contrasted sharply with the better organization of the European armies, which were employing new methods of training and fighting. Under these circumstances, the Ottomans' clashes with their western neighbors were becoming costly. In the 1717–18 war with Austria the Ottomans lost more than 20,000 soldiers, versus 5,400 Habsburg casualties.[29]

Not only was the Ottoman Empire suffering external defeats, territorial losses, and internal disorder during these years, but the imperial center was also losing the coherence and authority necessary to plan and implement a thorough reorganization. It was probably no coincidence that the reigns of some ineffective and detached sultans coincided with these years of growing difficulties. Given their ineptitude and limited education, it was no longer possible to regard some of these sultans as the shadow of God on earth and hence infallible. On the contrary, now they could be opposed, pressured, forced off the throne, and even murdered by any one of the groups vying for power in the capital. A Prussian resident of Istanbul said that "though the form of government is despotic, it is such that when the people is enraged, the Government is no longer master and must yield to the torrent."[30] Another source described how, in a great mutiny of the army in Europe in 1686–87, soldiers "not only chose their own officers but also deposed many of the highest ranking government officials."[31] Indeed, of the five sultans who ruled between 1648 and 1730, only two escaped deposition. These were Süleyman II (r. 1687–91) and Ahmed II (r. 1691–95), who together ruled for only eight years. Although there is some evidence that Süleyman II was interested in reform, his reign was too short for him to assert his authority or control the military.[32] In the early months of his rule, military troops occupied private homes and killed many government officials in Istanbul, "burning and stealing at will."[33] Ahmed II was completely ineffectual.

A strong undercurrent of conservatism also influenced the Ottoman approach to government between the late sixteenth and early eighteenth centuries. The same worldview would become a vehicle for rebellions and other political machinations. For several decades in the second half of the seventeenth century, for example, a group of religious scholars in Istanbul known as Kadızadeliler undertook a campaign to eradicate the traces of

Sufi interpretations of Islam from government circles in favor of a more rigid and orthodox form.[34] In 1731, a group motivated in part by another conservative worldview put a violent end to another period of relative openness and experimentation, known as the Tulip Age.[35]

While the traditional core of the state was becoming weak, however, a civilian bureaucracy was beginning to be developed under the auspices of extraordinarily able and ambitious grand viziers, particularly members of the Köprülü family, who held this top administrative post during most of the second half of the seventeenth century. Köprülüs are credited with many of the steps taken that helped reinforce some of the institutions of the empire. Hence, the overall conservative aura notwithstanding, a gradual opening to the west and a willingness to experiment with new ideas could be seen among certain segments of the Ottoman ruling elite in the eighteenth century.

Along the same lines, Ottoman contact with the west expanded during this period to include not just fighting but learning from the west. The first in a long succession of European military advisers, who would keep coming until the end of the empire, arrived in Istanbul in the eighteenth century. One of the earliest and best known of these advisers was Comte de Bonneval (1675–1747), an expert in light artillery. He converted to Islam and joined the Ottoman elites under his new name, Humbaracı Ahmed Paşa. Also in the same period the Ottomans began to regulate their representatives abroad, giving them the task not only of protecting the interests of the empire but also of reporting on the factors responsible for the progress of European countries.[36] Ottoman intellectuals read European books and incorporated them into their own writings. It was now possible for these writings, which included translations of some of the European classics, to be printed, thanks to the inauguration of the first Ottoman Turkish printing press in the Ottoman capital in the 1720s. Ibrahim Müteferrika, a Hungarian convert to Islam and founder of these printing facilities in Istanbul, wrote a book in 1731 in which he emphasized the importance of military reform and pointed out Russia under Peter the Great as an example.[37]

This environment also gave rise to interesting thinkers and writers such as Katip Çelebi, who, in addition to making maps and writing books on geography that incorporated European and Islamic knowledge, worked on compiling in Arabic an annotated "bibliography of all known works, on any subject, composed in Arabic, Persian, or in Turkish."[38] In this sense, the seventeenth and early eighteenth centuries appear to have been a time not just of decline or pause but also of transformation, linking the classical empire to its aftermath.

Ottoman historians wrote extensively about the empire's problems and suggested ways of dealing with them. The question of the empire's decline occupied them with growing intensity, and in their search for answers they read sources from the west and the east. They were more or less in agreement that the Ottoman Empire was experiencing difficulties because the rulers were paying too little attention to their Islamic faith and because the bureaucracy and the professional military had become disorganized and corrupt.[39] They also agreed that to be successful again, the Ottomans had to restore the political and moral authority of the ruling elites, especially the sultan.

Striking parallels exist between the writings of the medieval Tunisian writer and statesman Ibn Khaldun and the major Ottoman historians in the way each explained the trajectories of imperial rise and decline. They used concepts such as the circle of justice and the cyclical pattern of imperial histories. Some of Ibn Khaldun's writings were translated into Turkish and read by palace historians, but in developing their arguments, the Ottomans did not just copy the medieval author. The similarities were there because the two sets of writers approached their subject matters from similar vantage points and with similar interests and concerns.[40] It is noteworthy that both Ibn Khaldun and Ottoman historians such as Naima approached history and politics not as divine creation but as subjects that could be understood and controlled.[41]

In the long period that began in the second half the sixteenth century and continued right through the eighteenth, the Ottoman government tried to act on these ideas to solve the multiple problems the empire faced. The tens of thousands of tribesmen, former soldiers, peasants, and other unattached individuals and groups who roamed the countryside in an uncontrolled and aimless manner posed the greatest challenge to the central government. Along with other unattached and unsettled groups, such as rebellious soldiers, fleeing peasants, and refugees, nomads came to be regarded as the main culprits in everything from the decline of agricultural production to the vulnerability of the borders.[42] As a result, the imperial government focused its attention and concentrated its resources on developing ways of encouraging, enticing, and forcing the thousands of nomadic tribes and other nonsedentary people to adopt a settled way of life.

The turning point in the empire's relations with nomadic tribes and other mobile groups came in 1689, during the short tenure of grand vizier Köprülü Fazıl Mustafa Paşa, when the first set of comprehensive orders to settle the nomadic tribes was issued. These were followed in 1691 with another series of directives aimed at registering as many of the nomadic tribes as possible.[43] Besides monitoring the movements of these communities, the registration drive helped create specially designated companies that were then drafted into the army.[44] Some historians argue that these measures were unique, the products of a particularly difficult period of wars and rebellions.[45] Although the urgent need to reinforce the army under these trying circumstances was an important factor that informed these measures, the policy of settling nomads did not end there. The last two centuries of the empire's history witnessed a steady stream of orders and decrees dealing with problems related to nomadic populations, migrants, and refugees and their settlement. Such orders and the underlying policy that shaped them became clearer and better focused during this period. One sees this in the increasingly uniform wording of the directives and in the growing consistency of the kinds of incentives they offered to the tribes, the specific duties that were imposed on them, and the punishments that were doled out. In the long run, standardizing the policies may have undermined their effectiveness, because the tribes and regions they targeted were vastly different from one another and needed a finer-tuned approach that took local conditions into consideration. I say more about these complexities later on, but for now it seems appropriate to think of the late seventeenth century as a period of inflection that signaled the beginning of a more sedentary approach to rule and a centralized imperial state.

Orders of settlement issued after 1689 usually began with a list of the names and leaders of the tribes that would be affected. This list could be fairly lengthy and included as much information as possible about the tribes, their origins, how they had ended up in a particular region, and the nature of their previous interactions with the central government. In one such order in 1692, the first tribe is described as "Kıcılu tribe, which is a part of the Türkman community, with an imperial land grant in Haleb, and which had been ordered to settle in Hama and Hums, and which is presently under the authority of Hamze *kethüda,* who also belongs to Turkman community."[46] The order goes on to list thirty-four other tribes similarly. The second part of most orders usually included an explanation of why the specific tribes were being required to move, settle, or both. Government officials tended to be very specific here, trying not only to convey their decree but also, and more significantly, to justify their policy. An example from 1690 reads: "Several tribes who belong to the Türkman-Danişmendlü community had been living in Adana and Haleb, but [I have been informed] that these tribes have now retreated to semi-nomadism. They are looting the towns and the villages they pass through, stealing the animals and the harvest and committing wrongful acts of violence against many individuals."[47]

After giving these reasons, the order describes the places to which this tribe will be relocated in western Anatolia. In some cases the government put forth the argument that settling was for the good of the tribes themselves. It might be that "the place where they are settled now is not airy and very unpleasant," so moving to better quarters would improve their well-being.[48]

The fact that the sultan—these orders were written in the first person—considered it necessary to explain his actions suggests that in forcing tribes to settle, the government was doing something out of the ordinary. Its actions might have been interpreted as a breach of a social compact that had existed between nomads and the central government for many centuries. In many cases questions of law, order, and security figured prominently as factors that forced the government to take the radical step of requiring tribes to relocate and settle. Typically, the reasons listed in the decrees have to do with banditry, raids on surrounding villages, and other disruptive behavior. Not only is such behavior described, but also local officials are warned to deal with the tribes carefully and not to resort to collective punishment:

> Beğmişli, Arablı, Kara Şeyhli, Döğerli, Kadirli, Simre, Boz Koyunlu, Dimlik, Çepeni, [and] Mamalı, tribes that are part of the Türkman community . . . have become bandits. It has become their habit to attack travelers, kill people, and loot the property of people in Darende. Three years ago they hit a caravan coming from Baghdad. . . . there is no end to their evil deeds and banditry. As I indicated in my previous orders, you should be using your own men and local forces to attack these bandits and demand that each tribe hand over those who engaged in banditry. . . . If they don't, make sure to punish them. While going after these bandits, you should not harm those who had nothing

to do with these illegal acts. While pursuing the bandits, you should not make demands for food or other provisions from the poor peasants.[49]

The exact location of the settlement, the size and nature of the land being given to the tribes, the exemptions from taxes and services granted to tribal members, and the specific services required of them were all listed in minute detail in these orders. In most cases, in return for the land and the exemptions they were granted, the tribes were expected to revitalize abandoned villages and land, embark on sedentary agriculture, and provide security in the area:

> A part of the tribal community [is] to be settled in the vacant and neglected lands that are in the region of Turabalı, which is near the town of Viranşehir, which is a part of the sanjak of Sığla; and another part in vacant lands known as Timur Kapı and Viran Han that are near the villages of Su Sısırlığı and Ömer Köy, which are in Balıkesri sanjak. . . .[50] On the condition that they protect the buildings and the people who reside in those places from the attacks of the bandits, they will be exempted from all regular and irregular taxes and fees.[51]

In the earlier phases of this new policy, the tribes were not necessarily expected to give up all their nomadic and pastoral activities when they settled. In many situations they could comply with the settlement order simply by expanding one part of their activities, farming, and reducing the other, husbandry, without abandoning pastoralism altogether. More typically they blended farming into their seasonal activities, gradually reducing the distances over which they traveled with their animals. Sometimes they were required to take the additional step of having only a limited number of shepherds accompany the animals instead of having the whole tribal community move with the sheep during their seasonal circulation, animal transportation, or regular grazing. "When they take their sheep to the pastures as is their custom, they should not do it themselves. They should stay with their families in the area of their settlement in the summers and in the winters, and only the shepherds should accompany the sheep."[52] These documents suggest that from the very beginning Ottoman officials were compelled to recognize the power of the tribal chiefs and negotiated with them in order to make the orders palatable, rather than pushing them unilaterally.

Many of the early directives for settling tribes were focused on south-eastern Anatolia and involved either moving people there from central Anatolia or forcing tribes and confederations whose activities had been disruptive of social order out of the area and settling them elsewhere in the empire. The reason for the central government's renewed interest in paci-fying the southeast had to do with the continuing wars with Iran, recur-rent rebellions among the local populace, and, in particular, the popularity of the Alevi and Kızılbaş orders. These factors made it imperative for the Ottoman government to exercise closer control over the region and the people in it.[53] As part of this plan, the Badıllı tribe, which had been spend-ing its winters around Ankara and Çankırı, was relocated to Syria in 1691 to counter the growing power of the Bedouin and Kurdish tribes there.[54] In order to populate the vast, empty stretches of northern Syria, 2,308 mem-bers of the Receblu clan were gathered from various parts of Anatolia and from Istanbul and were forced to settle in Rakka (Ar. *Raqqah*) between 1703 and 1728.[55] At the same time, the Ottomans did not hesitate to break up local communities and disperse them across the empire. One example of this type of decree concerned the Kurdish Mihmadlu tribe, some of whose members were moved from eastern Anatolia to the area around İzmir in 1713.[56]

If the tribes found a way of avoiding the government's orders and escaped, the government followed through by alerting local officials and asking them to reimpose the original order and bring the fugitive tribes back. The governor of Rakka was issued an order in 1698 that read in part, "The tribes that had been settled in Rakka by my previous order have escaped from the area and are now in the provinces of Haleb, Şam, Trablus-Şam, Arz-ı Rum, Meraş, Kars, Adana, Karaman, Sivas, and Anadolu, hid-ing among other tribes in these places. The agents that you will send should see to it that their families, property, and food should be moved back to Rakka."[57] In some cases parallel orders were sent to the places where the tribes were hiding, and the officials there were also asked to comply with the government's directives.[58] In 1719, in a token attempt to strengthen cen-tral control over the movement of people, the government banned all inter-nal migration, although there was no way the order could be enforced.[59]

The large amount of information these orders contain shows that in implementing its program of sedentarization, the Ottoman government was not starting from scratch. The networks used to gather the informa-tion had been set up in earlier centuries when land surveys were first conducted and registers first made following the conquest of Constantinople. For example, in punishing a tribe for trespassing, officials could be very specific:

> About fifty to sixty individuals who belong to the Akkeçülü Yürük tribe, who are part of the subprovince of Kütahya, tried to enter the local bath when women were bathing. They removed the towel from the door and attempted to kidnap some of the women. They also attacked, beat, and insulted the imperial courier Derviş Çavuş, who was coming from Rhodes. Now I order that the perpetrators of these deeds be exiled to Cyprus along with their families. As soon as you receive this order, identify the guilty parties, cut their links with the region, and move them to the port of Silifke for transportation to Cyprus. Let me know when you have carried out this order and when these individuals have been settled in Cyprus.[60]

Although the elements of a new approach to administration are discernible in these orders, it would be wrong to see them as representing a radical break with the empire's earlier practices. After all, it was not out of the ordinary for tribe members, individually or in groups, routinely to be moved over great distances. "Forcing" them to relocate from, say, central Anatolia to Syria did not always involve a major burden. Indeed, in some instances the orders were crafted to incorporate existing patterns of mobility, mandating that tribes settle in pastures they had been using seasonally for generations.[61]

It seems, however, that the kind of information the central government was seeking expanded qualitatively as well as quantitatively in the late seventeenth century. This indicates a new orientation toward a more centralized and more tightly controlled bureaucracy in the Ottoman Empire, which involved, among other things, the expansion of the powers of civilian officials.[62] As part of this new development, almost as soon as the settlement decrees began to be issued, a new Office of Settlements (İskân Dairesi) was established in the palace, and in 1693 all such initiatives were placed under its authority.[63] The subtle shift of power toward civilian authorities created a deep sense of unease among the military, which led to a series of revolts in the eighteenth century. Unlike earlier directives, the new orders required tribes to settle in order to take advantage of the state's offer of protection and the special incentives that were attached.[64] Now sedentarization was part of a bigger program that also included the incorporation of tribes and nomads into the empire-wide system of guards and into the main branches of the professional army.

NOMADS INTO GUARDS

The uprooting and migration of large numbers of people across the Ottoman Empire in the seventeenth century was hugely disruptive to communication and security. By the last decades of the seventeenth century it had become difficult to carry out daily activities or conduct affairs of state in large parts of the empire. One of the ways in which the Ottoman government responded to this situation was by expanding the empire's network of communication and security, called the *derbend* system (literally referring to the guardians of mountain passes), by enlisting into it tribal communities, fleeing peasants, immigrants, and even brigands. Ottoman officials saw this as another method of sedentarizing itinerant persons and communities while enhancing the security of roads and border areas. It was hoped that improving the conditions of roads, bridges, and commercial and lodging establishments along the main routes of the empire would reopen the networks of internal trade and relink them with their European and Asian counterparts in a steadier and more regular manner.[65] It was also expected that by obtaining land and joining the network of guards and sentries, some of the itinerant groups would acquire a stake in the social order they were expected to defend and protect.

Like many other institutions dating back to the early centuries of the empire's history, the *derbend* system had no uniform method of constitution. In some cases, people who were appointed as guards were exempted from all duties and served full-time. More typically, local communities and villages were exempted from part of their regular taxes in return for providing security at key intersections, bridges, mountain passes, and main roads in imperial territories. While performing such tasks, they continued to cultivate their land, pay their dues, and provide for their own livelihood.[66] In the chaotic conditions of Anatolia in the late seventeenth century, some villagers volunteered to become *derbend*s because this was one of the few legitimate ways to acquire weapons to protect themselves and their property. It seems that the central government considered these requests carefully and approved or denied them according to the importance of the particular pass or site over which the villagers were seeking to be appointed as guards—in addition to whether forfeiting part of the revenue from the village would harm the government treasury.[67] Some rules had to be further relaxed in order to recruit nomads.

The *derbend* organization, especially in southeastern Anatolia, received intense attention from the state. Hundreds of nomadic tribes from different parts of Anatolia were settled as *derbends* between Aleppo and Damascus in the 1690s, thereby solving both the problem of uncertainty they were creating in central Anatolia and providing security against the attacks of Arab tribes along this important commercial route. Similar decrees moved and settled tribes as *derbends* in large sections of central, eastern, and southeastern Anatolia as trade networks collapsed in the late seventeenth and early eighteenth centuries.[68] In a further relaxation of the rules, the Ottomans employed Christians for these jobs. But instead of granting them tax exemptions, the government actually paid the Christian recruits (called *pandors* and *martolos*) for their services. Christian guards were placed under Muslim commanders and tended to be concentrated in border areas, which became sources of trouble for the Ottoman state in later decades.[69] Similarly, the government paid Bedouin tribes to protect hajj caravans. But Bedouins, too, were unlikely to be reliable allies in the long run.[70]

The policy of broadening the pool of *derbends* meant that the very brigands who had wreaked havoc in the countryside were now put in charge of providing security in the same places and protecting what until recently had been their prey. Those who were assigned to protect caravans and passengers frequently turned on the travelers and robbed and harassed them instead. This points out a persistent problem of the Ottoman reform movement: when it came to implementing its many well-thought-out measures, the government had only limited methods and agents to call upon. More often than not, those who were expected to carry out the policies of enhancing the authority of the state were the very groups who had benefited most from disorder. Ottoman reform was repeatedly undermined by this factor until the nineteenth century, when a series of institutional reforms accompanied such measures, making their implementation and the realization of their goals more likely.

FROM VAGABONDS TO CHILDREN OF CONQUERORS

The Ottoman response to deteriorating internal and external security in the Balkans, unlike in Anatolia, was focused much more on counting and registering tribes and drafting them into the army than on carrying out a sedentarization program. Tribes were moved to the Balkans not to settle but to fight. When the Austrian wars were going on at the end of the seventeenth century, the central government made frequent demands on the tribes to make fighters available to be sent to the front. As part of these efforts, twenty representatives of the Boz Ulus Türkmen confederation were convened in Konya, and an order was read to them. It identified all twenty tribal leaders individually—for example, "Cafer Beğ ibni Minnet"—and ordered them to record 300 armed soldiers who would join the army. These people would have to "be removed from their homes and conveyed to their designated spots quickly and efficiently."[71] Furthermore, the twenty chiefs were required to act as guarantors for those being dispatched to war, a common policy in the eighteenth and nineteenth centuries. In an order sent to the Morea, the sultan requested 2,000 fighters for the upcoming battle in Hungary and specified that "not one of these should be under age . . . and each should be armed with two pistols and a rifle."[72] Similar orders went to other parts of the empire, requesting thousands of fighters around the same time.[73]

In 1691, comprehensive registration of the nomadic Yürük tribes was initiated in the Balkans. By identifying the tribes, determining their numbers, and formalizing their position in the army, the central government hoped to exercise closer control over their activities. It was hoped that knowing the whos and wheres of the tribes and using them to reorganize the army would help the central government not only in dealing with the deteriorating conditions on the frontiers but also in countering the lawlessness that was spreading across the frontier zones.

The registration and recruitment of tribal groups into the Ottoman army was not entirely a new practice. In earlier periods, people of nomadic origins had played a number of roles in the Ottoman army. They were part of the locally recruited irregulars, who numbered in the tens of thousands and performed mostly menial jobs. Some of these irregulars constituted the highly effective mobile units called *akıncı* in the frontier regions and served as shock troops in the empire's expansion in eastern Europe. As was the case in its dealings with the Kurdish and Arab tribes in the south, the Ottoman center took advantage of the Balkan communities' existing organization and coherence and turned them into effective tools of the empire. The legal decrees issued by Mehmed II in 1487–88 included special provisions for the registration of nomadic tribes that had crossed into Thrace in earlier centuries on their own and who had since been carrying out tasks for the army. It was common even in earlier times for the Ottoman army to follow the spontaneous expansion of the frontline tribes in pushing the boundaries of the empire in the Balkans. In addition to recording the sizes of nomadic households and their tax potential, officials grouped them into "hearths" (*ocaks*) of twenty-four each, and these became the units in which tribal members stayed when they participated in military campaigns or performed auxiliary services for the army.[74] The laws governing the recruitment and employment of the nomadic tribes were further expanded in the following years, particularly during the reign of Süleyman the Magnificent (r. 1520–66).[75]

Yet the program started in 1691 was a much more comprehensive effort to formally integrate nomadic tribes into the army. In an attempt to evoke a previous time when nomads had played a key role in expanding the Ottoman presence in the Balkans, the newly constituted Yürük companies in the late seventeenth century were given the name Evlad-ı Fatihan, or Children of the Conquerors.[76] The Ottomans tried to register as Evlad-ı Fatihan as many of the Yürük communities in the Balkans as possible, writing down their sizes, leaders, and recent histories and grouping them according to their military capabilities and the kinds of tasks they were likely to perform in the Ottoman army. It was stipulated that Yürüks who had moved from other parts of the empire and those who had been registered in other books and under different categories were to be reregistered as Yürüks in their new places, with the expectation that they would not move again. Once registered as Evlad-ı Fatihan, these communities were exempted from most tax obligations but in return were required to mobilize one of every six adult males in times of need. Those who were not drafted had to pay a special tax to the Evlad-ı Fatihan administration. In times of peace, all the Yürüks had to pay this special tax, and the money went to the treasury. For many newly settled nomads, however, this had little meaning, because wars seemed never-ending in these years. Creating the Evlad-ı Fatihan companies was a way of generating additional troops for the army, but registering tribal members as part of the tribes and keeping them as such in the army undermined the central government's long-term goals by perpetuating factors that contributed to decentralization and devolution of power.

Cognizant of established practices and expectations, and aware that the very mobility of the tribes gave them an important means of protection (and the possibility of evasion by flight), the central government approached sedentarization cautiously. Rather than relying solely on force, it tried to make the option of settlement and joining the army attractive by offering a wide range of incentives to tribes that agreed to change their status. Such tribes were exempted from all regular duties, nomadic or sedentary, for several years at a time.[77] They were granted free seeds and oxen, better access to sources of irrigation, and other encouragements and subventions tailored specially for different regions.[78] In return for these privileges the nomads were typically required to abandon their peripatetic lives and assume sedentary farming. They agreed to pay a one-time special tax and desist from attacking and harming villages in their new areas of settlement.[79] In some parts of Anatolia, nomads obtained even broader privileges if they agreed to plant certain crops that were highly valued or needed, such as wheat (and cotton in later centuries) in central and southern Anatolia.[80] The Ottoman government offered similar incentives to fugitive peasants who had quit their land and were roaming the countryside.[81]

To be sure, when conditions required—especially if a tribe was in breach of a law or directive—the government used force against it. Many times sedentarization and punishment overlapped, making it difficult to distinguish the government's main motive. This was partly because many of the tribes that were forced to settle in the eighteenth century had taken part in rural depredations and rebellions. Furthermore, places such as Cyprus and the desert region around Rakka in Syria, which the Ottoman government sought to populate with settled farmers, were also used as penal destinations for unruly tribes. Sometimes a single order included as goals both the revitalization of specific sites and the punishment of certain tribes, making it even more difficult to identify the overriding priority that motivated the center. According to an order issued in 1719, a segment of the Danişmetlu tribe, of Türkmen origins, which had been relocated in western Anatolia, was forced back to its place of origin in Rakka because of its unruly behavior: "Rather than staying at the places that were designated for them, they [were] wandering and acting aggressively and harming the farms and animals of the villages in the area." Therefore, those "who minded their own business, built stone houses in their places of settlement, became engaged in agriculture, and did not mount horses, carry weapons, or dress as fugitive soldiers, vagabonds, or brigands" were permitted to stay in the west, but only on the condition that someone agreed to act as guarantor for them.[82] Leaders of tribes that refused to go along with such orders or whose actions harmed the lives and property of villagers were punished by the central government.[83] An order issued to the governor general of Rakka in 1690 stated that as many as 1,200 persons had quit Rakka, where they were supposed to be settled and keep the area safe from banditry. The sultan ordered the governor general to "find and seize these people wherever they may have gone, imprison those who were responsible, and bring the rest to their places of settlement in Rakka."[84]

When a tribe was ordered to move and settle in a specific region, administrators in both the place of origin and the place of destination were required to make sure that the order was carried out unproblematically. If some members of a tribe or even peasants in a village that was subject to a relocation order fled, those who were left behind or who could be located and identified were forced to pay the taxes and the penalties of those who had disappeared.[85] Before the execution of an order, the leading members of a tribe were identified and forced to act as guarantors for one another and for the tribe as a whole.[86] An even more extreme measure was to take the leading members of a tribe hostage. In one such instance in 1706, twenty-eight prominent persons were arrested and taken away from nine tribes that had been ordered to settle in the Rakka region of Syria. These people were imprisoned in different parts of central Anatolia, where they were to be held until the tribes had actually moved and settled in their new places. In this case, however, the hostages were soon spirited away from their prisons. In response, the government ordered the prison guards jailed in order to "set an example to others."[87]

Although the scope of the settlement orders is impressive, in the chaotic conditions of the late seventeenth and early eighteenth centuries the Ottoman government had limited means of forcing tribes to move long distances and settle against their will. Consequently, government officials once again found themselves having to negotiate with a multitude of competing groups who were affected by the sedentarization orders, which often led to the further empowerment of the very interests these orders had targeted in the first place and the eventual dilution of the directives.[88] In other words, the officials had to rely as much on the consent of those who were the main targets of the measures as on coercion.

In many of the orders issued at the end of the seventeenth century, the central government even recognized the communal leaders who were somehow chosen (*ihtiyar* or *intihab*) by the members of the tribes themselves. Typically such figures were described as "trustworthy men who have been elected by their tribes."[89] The government held them responsible for the behavior of the rest of the tribe and expected them to act as guarantors that the tribe would comply with the settlement order. As compensation for their new responsibilities, the leaders were given more and better-quality land, which meant that their privileged status expanded under the new conditions.[90]

In identifying the leaders it would work with, the government sometimes took advantage of intra- and intertribal conflicts. Sometimes government officials employed one of the tribes, a segment of a tribe, or a confederation to police the others, as it did in recruiting the Mamali tribe to police and punish the Cirid, Afşar, and other tribes, who had been engaged in banditry around Bozok in central Anatolia in 1699.[91] On an imperial level, the Ottoman center tried to draw some of the tribes and bandits to its side by giving their chiefs official titles and appointing them to influential posts. Even the first two occupants of the office of head of settlement (*iskan başı*), which was established in 1693, had tribal backgrounds. They were the brothers Firuzoğlu Şahin Bey and Kenan Bey, of the Bozkoyunlu commune, which was of Türkmen origin.[92] This was the same Bozkoyunlu clan that in 1688 had laid siege to Maraş for forty days, killed 500 of the city's residents, kidnapped women and children, and committed other reported acts of banditry.[93]

The Ottoman government could never take it for granted that such leaders would continue to support the government unless their status and privileges were secured and expanded with additional steps. But there was always the danger that these policies would end up strengthening the very centrifugal tendencies that the government was trying to combat. This happened in 1687 when a bandit named Yeğen Osman, who had been creating havoc in west-central Anatolia, was appointed governor (*sanjak beyi*) of Afyon. In return he was required to bring 5,000 of his followers to the front and join the Ottoman army. Yeğen Osman demanded the additional title of provincial security chief (*serçeşme*) in order to comply, but after receiving the title he brought his troops not to the front but to the very center of Istanbul, apparently to threaten the central government.[94] Another local leader, Janum (*sic*) Hodja, tried to unite the principalities in Tripoli in 1720 by using the region's access to the sea. Janum was invited to Istanbul in 1722 and appointed superintendent of the imperial arsenal. He then received a commission to build two ships in Sinop, a ploy to get him out of Istanbul. From Sinop, Janum was eventually exiled to Nauplia in the Morea and then to Retimo on Crete.[95]

In all matters pertaining to the recruitment, work, or administration of tribes, the Ottoman government tried to deal with a tribe as a whole, typically through its chief, which reinforced the distinct identities of the tribes. The central administration did not interfere with the actual planning or apportioning of tasks among tribal members or subgroups, leaving these to be carried out according to the established traditions and practices of the tribes. In military matters, too, Ottoman reliance on the autonomous organization and movement of these units was strong. Hence, even at a time when the central government's attitude toward tribes was changing significantly and the reorganization of the imperial government was in the direction of creating a more centralized administration, some of its policies ended up either strengthening existing tribal hierarchies and dynasties or creating new ones.

The central government tried to regain the loyalty of even bandit chiefs and other rebels by giving them further titles and appointing them to powerful positions such as the governorships of major provinces in Anatolia. Even a rebel chief such as Gedik Mehmet Paşa, who had kept Ankara under siege, was rewarded with a prestigious position.[96] Far from serving as solutions, such steps tended to make the situation worse. Receiving new titles and recognition from the government emboldened the tribal leaders, rebel chiefs, and bandits, who used their enhanced power to put even more pressure on the peasants and to challenge the central government with a new sense of confidence. What Michael Cook wrote about the Celali uprisings of the turn of the seventeenth century applies to this period as well: "Whether or not a man is a rebel comes to depend less on what he does than on the more or less fortuitous fact that he has or has not an official authorization for his marauding."[97]

Another and even more important problem the Ottomans faced in carrying out their program of registration and sedentarization was the difficulty of identifying individual tribes and other itinerant groups beyond some general characterizations. Religion was the most common marker, but even there, for reasons mentioned in chapter 1, the outer margins of many religious orders and sects were imprecise, varied over time, and were not always useful as units of administration. Looking closely at the first series of orders issued in the late seventeenth century, one sees that especially the non-Kurdish tribes that belonged to no distinct religious order were identified imprecisely, with names that referred either to a characteristic economic activity such as hide tanning or oil making or to some notable aspect of the group's history. In the course of the eighteenth century, official decrees would become more specific, at least in terms of the areas where the tribes in question were (or were supposed to be) located, reflecting improvements in the government's ability to monitor them. One sees names such as Selanik Yürükleri (Yürüks of Salonica), Mihmadlu Kürdü (Kurds of Mihmadlu), Kütahya'ya tabi Ak Keçili Yürükleri (white goat Yürüks who belong to Kütahya), İç İl'den Çıkıp Alaiye'ye gelen Yürük taifeleri (Yürüks who moved from İç İl to Alaiyye), Halep Yeni Il Türkmenine bağlı Emir cemaati (Emir community that was part of the Yeni-Il Türkmen confederation based in Aleppo), and Karahisar-ı Sahib Piyadeleri (infantry from the district of Karahisar-ı Sahib).[98] Perhaps because of their distinct identity, which was manifested in their language and the tenacity of their organizations, Kurds were the only groups that were always identified clearly and consistently in terms of their ethnicity.[99] Ascribing ethnic content to administrative categories such as "Yürüks" would become common in the republican period, but such descriptions were without foundation and were based more on ideology than on science.[100]

POPULAR REACTION

The autonomy and freedom that were embedded in nomadism, together with the special exemptions and protections given to nomads, made this an attractive mode of existence in many parts of the Ottoman Empire. Tribal members always resisted registration and sedentarization, because these were usually followed by additional demands for taxes and military service.[101] Tribal members all over the empire also tried to ignore, deflect, or subvert the government's settlement orders by writing petitions, expressing complaints, and, frequently, organizing resistance movements. Although it was usually the tribal chiefs who complained and wrote the petitions, it was not uncommon for individual members to take the lead in such matters. The most common sources of complaint were the distance a tribe would have to travel, the size of the plot being given to it, and the limited resources being made available. Local officials reviewed such petitions and usually referred them to higher-ranking bureaucrats. Not surprisingly, the desert area around Rakka in Syria, where many nomads were forced to settle, became a particularly strong source of discontent for the tribes that were sent there. Lack of water and sparse vegetation were the main factors the tribal leaders cited in demanding a change in their orders of settlement. In many instances the tribes mobilized large numbers of their members to resist the government's order, not only by fighting Ottoman forces but also by making their places of settlement inhospitable by burning and destroying the existing fields.[102] When faced with such protests, in word or deed, it was not uncommon for the central government to agree to alter its original decrees.[103]

The Ottoman government faced particularly serious problems in trying to settle former soldiers and other young, single men who had no visible attachments and had become members of marauding bandit groups that undermined the social order across large areas of the imperial landscape. These groups were treated similarly to fleeing peasants and nomadic tribes and sometimes were given land and other privileges in return for abandoning their ruinous ways and taking up settled farming. In the case of nomads, the government still had considerable room to negotiate and apply pressure. When dealing with former soldiers and peasants who had quit their villages, however, the government had little to use as leverage. Consequently, in the last quarter of the eighteenth century, 100 years after the first orders of settlement were issued, the Ottoman government was still trying suppress "mountain rebellions" (dağlı isyanları) organized by fugitive soldiers in the Balkans.[104]

In the course of the eighteenth century, these former-soldiers-turned-bandits played an even more significant role by joining rebellious provincial notables (ayans) and providing them with fighting forces.[105] Whether tribes rebelled and whether local notables supported them depended on local conditions. Such alliances were never fixed, either. A tribe could switch from being rebellious to being supportive of the government and vice versa. The same was true for provincial elites. In general, however, the local urban elites never trusted the nomadic tribes, even after they settled down.[106]

In trying to settle the nomadic tribal communities and others, the Ottoman government also clashed with villagers whose interests were threatened by the introduction of new groups in their midst.[107] An important part of this conflict was rooted in the ownership patterns of Ottoman agriculture, which had created several distinct groups with equally strong and competing claims of rights, especially in the more fertile areas in Anatolia and Mesopotamia. These included tax farmers, absentee landlords, and the sultan's household, all of whom had become de facto landlords with the introduction of life-long leases in 1695. There were also the peasants who had been working the land. In a pattern that would repeat itself many times in the eighteenth and nineteenth centuries, the absentee landlords could agree to the government's policies of sedentarization and pacification for their own reasons while the peasants, who were the actual cultivators in possession of the land, strongly opposed the arrival of refugees and the settlement of nomadic tribes. Indeed, most of the complaints whose records have survived, revealing the processes and problems of settling nomads, were filed by villagers. Especially in western Anatolia, the common claim was that the land was already congested, and settling new groups there would make life difficult for the people who already lived in these places. It was not uncommon for the Ottoman government to heed these complaints and reverse its position.[108]

In response to the growing waves of rebellions, the Ottoman government limited the free movement of people across its imperial territories and registered ever more carefully the residents of villages in areas affected by unrest. But such policies would not become effective before the middle decades of the nineteenth century, when the Ottomans launched a more comprehensive program for reforming and strengthening state institutions. Until then, the different parts of the government and local private groups tried to deal with these conditions in different ways, making it difficult to talk about an overall pattern except for growth in the militarization of Ottoman society, a trend that continued until the centralizing reforms of the Tanzimat era in the nineteenth century.[109]

AN UNCERTAIN FUTURE

Although the government's interest in settling the tribes was becoming clear, and although it had some impressive means of articulating this policy, its actual means of enforcement remained limited in the eighteenth century. As a result, the road from issuing an order to actually seeing it through was fraught with uncertainties. Nevertheless, in the five regions the central government designated as areas of settlement, some progress was made toward the emergence of a sedentary social order in the eighteenth century. These regions were circumscribed by major rivers (from west to east, the Menderes, Kızılırmak, Ceyhan, Orontes, and Euphrates), and settlement in these parts laid the groundwork for agricultural expansion in the eighteenth and nineteenth centuries.[110] According to one estimate, more than 2,300 persons from the Receblu clan alone had been settled in Rakka by 1729. Indeed, the mountain rebellions so frequently mentioned in histories dealing with these years were, according to some writers, results of the relative stability and order achieved in the lowlands.[111] Because of settlement activities, the number of villages around Damascus rose from 15–20 to more than 300 by 1720.[112] Partly as a result of the comprehensive registration program begun in the seventeenth century, a researcher in the twentieth century could find records of nearly 7,000 confederations, tribes, and communities in a survey of the relevant archival sources.[113] Also, the first two decades of the eighteenth century were considerably more peaceful than the preceding half century, both within the empire and in the empire's relations with the outside world. This peace was accompanied by fairly strong growth in foreign trade, which brought prosperity to various regions of the empire.[114]

Yet these gains proved to be temporary. By the end of the eighteenth century, conditions in and around the empire had reverted to a state of crisis. The majority of the borders remained imprecise, and a vast portion of the empire's population was still unsettled and unrecorded in terms of geography, ways of living, and identity. The Ottoman Empire had once again been drawn into lengthy and destructive wars and was faced with rural uprisings, especially in the mountainous regions where many of the rebellious soldiers, peasants, and nomads had taken refuge.[115] If anything, the centrifugal forces that had severely undermined the empire's integrity at the end of the seventeenth century seemed to be gaining strength. Far from submitting to the priorities of the central authority, some local leaders, tribal and otherwise, took advantage of their positions as intermediaries in the implementation of reform measures. By the end of the eighteenth century they had become de facto independent, wielding extensive power in their localities and seriously undermining the power and authority of the central government. These provincial notables, with their small armies, the local peasants who were loyal to them, and the nomads whose protection they had assumed as their responsibility, became so well entrenched and powerful that the last decades of the eighteenth century have come to be designated in Ottoman historiography the "Age of the Ayans [notables]."[116]

The simultaneous strengthening of the forces of centralization and decentralization in the Ottoman Empire was a pattern that would repeat itself in subsequent centuries. Each step the Ottoman state took toward reform and centralization carried the seeds of its own undermining. Whether in provincial administration, economic reform, or the settlement of nomads, Ottoman officials had little choice but to rely in part on some of the very groups that had prospered under anarchic conditions all across the empire to become the implementers of policies aiming to strengthen the center at the expense of the peripheral groups. Hence, recognizing and giving governmental posts to the *ayans* expanded the power of these notables significantly by giving them an aura of royal support. Expanding the domains of private property and private interactions in different parts of the economy enhanced the status of private bankers, merchants, and tax farmers, making them the pivots of the changing economy but also making them averse to any attempt at central control. Finally, in trying to sedentarize the nomadic segments of the rural population, Ottoman officials had to work with tribal chiefs or ally themselves closely with one group of tribes and use them to force others to move and settle. In this way they encouraged the very mobility they were trying to contain. The permanent success of these policies of sedentarization required a much more comprehensive effort, not only in issuing orders but also in institutional reform, which came only in the nineteenth century.

4 Building Stasis

On January 15, 2003, the *New York Times* published a front-page article on a Kurdish tribe called the Hamawand that was engaged in a war of resistance against the armies of Saddam Hussein in northern Iraq and also against Ansar al-Islam, a militant group connected to Al Qaeda, in the east. On these two fronts the Hamawand fighters were led, respectively, by a father and son, and most of the fighters were either related to each other or were regarded as family by their leaders. According to the *Times*, they were all completely dedicated to their cause, and whatever the odds, they were confident of their eventual victory and vindication.

A little more than 100 years earlier, as the Ottomans embarked on their program of reform and centralization, they had to deal with the very same Hamawand (or Hemvend) tribe. After failing repeatedly to entice the tribal leaders to give up their autonomy, the Ottomans broke up the tribe, confiscated its animals, and scattered its members over a large territory in central and western Anatolia, the Balkans, and North Africa in the 1880s and 1890s. Despite the Ottomans' apparent determination to erase all traces of the tribe from eastern Anatolia and the Arab provinces, within a few decades Hemvends returned to their places of origin, resumed their nomadic ways, and reasserted their local influence. In 1908, Mark Sykes identified 1,200 families as "*hamawand*" and described them as "the most valiant, courageous, and intelligent of the Baban Kurd tribes."[1] By the turn of the twenty-first century they were perceived as potential allies in the fight again Saddam Hussein. Other tribes that, like the Hemvends, were forcefully relocated during the nineteenth century also found a way of returning home, even if it meant traveling great distances under treacherous conditions.[2]

The way the Hemvends shifted between settlement and mobility resembles the general pattern of state-tribe relations that characterized most of Ottoman history. But unlike in previous centuries, in the nineteenth century imperial officials started to pay closer attention to monitoring, counting, and identifying tribes before settling them. They created formal institutions to deal with tribes and manage their settlement. The surveys that the Ottoman state conducted for this purpose starting in 1838 fill approximately 2,100 folios.[3] Regions deemed particularly sensitive, such as the Balkans and the Arab provinces, were surveyed as frequently as every four months in the closing years of the nineteenth century. Directives of settlement, which had always been detailed, became even more so in the nineteenth century. It is obvious that the Ottoman state had become determined to create a more centralized and sedentary order in the empire. Yet despite the increasing comprehensiveness and forcefulness of Ottoman policies of sedentarization in the nineteenth century, the Hemvend and other tribes managed to preserve their mobility and continued to exert pressure on the Ottoman state to protect their autonomy.

Anatolian folklore idealizes tribal resistance to government pressure and attributes the persistence of mobile identities primarily to this factor.[4] Although resistance was important, the bigger part of the explanation for the persistence of tribes lies in the peculiar relationship that evolved between tribes and the Ottoman state in the eighteenth and nineteenth centuries. The growing power of the state in the nineteenth century was neither premised upon nor followed from the complete marginalization of tribes in the Ottoman Empire. Having little in the way of alternatives, the Ottoman government continued to rely on existing power relations in various regions as it implemented its reform policies, including its sedentarization program, while setting up an increasingly elaborate set of institutions. Some tribes even benefited from the expanded power of the Ottoman state by agreeing to enforce the policies of reform and settlement in their areas. In addition to contributing to the effectiveness of the central state, this opened new venues of power and influence to the chiefs, which they found useful in dealing with their rivals. Consequently, it became possible for tribes and the Ottoman state to grow simultaneously. Far from disappearing, the names Hemvend, Lek, Avşar, Cerid, and Taciroğlu appear with remarkable regularity in documents and writings that describe the tribal policies of the Ottoman state and its successors in the eastern provinces in the eighteenth, nineteenth, twentieth, and—as we read in the *New York Times*—twenty-first centuries.

This chapter begins with the collapse of even the degree of settled life achieved by the end of the eighteenth century and the emergence of a new pattern of collaboration between tribes and local notables (*ayans*) in which the former became a major fighting force employed by the latter. I then show how the Ottoman state responded to these increasingly potent sources of rebellion militarily and administratively. Responses included the creation of special armies and offices solely for the purposes of defeating the ayans and dealing with tribal problems. In implementing these policies, the Ottoman officials had to cooperate with some tribal chiefs in order to subdue others. Consequently, the strengthening of the Ottoman state in the nineteenth century was accompanied by the strengthening of tribal networks in some parts of the empire. Although this complex arrangement carried the empire through the nineteenth century, it could not withstand the pressures created by multiplying waves of refugees and the politicization of ethnicity, which sounded the death knell for the empire in the early twentieth century.

THE COLLAPSE OF EIGHTEENTH-CENTURY SETTLEMENT

The sedentarization policies that the Ottomans adopted in the seventeenth and eighteenth centuries did not produce a permanently settled society. In the early part of the nineteenth century the trend turned once again in the opposite direction—toward growing nomadism. Although exact numbers are impossible to come by, one contemporary account estimated that on the eve of the reform movement known as the Tanzimat ("reorganization"), which began in 1839, the province of Adana alone held as many as 56,955 nomads, versus merely 5,000 settled peasants.[5] Rather than shrinking, some of the tribes were steadily expanding their power, and some were behaving as if they had all but seceded from the empire. Some towns in the area had become fairly prosperous and prominent by drawing on the produce of surrounding communities and linking it to regional and even European markets. In the early decades of the nineteenth century, the Menemencioğlu family, which had originated in a tribal confederation, became exceptionally wealthy by allowing European ships to purchase wheat in Mediterranean ports for a fee of 46,000 *kuruş* per shipload.[6] Tribes, as suppliers of both seasonal labor and animals and as carriers of some of the local trade, were crucial parts of such networks.[7] During his travels in the 1840s, William Francis Ainsworth observed the way imports from England and France were brought to Aintab and Kilis by way of Aleppo and exchanged in those towns for fruits, vegetables, and cotton grown in surrounding areas and transported by nomadic tribes. The continuing expansion of tribal power was such that people who traveled farther south in Arab provinces during these years gained the impression that land was being lost to nomads, the number of empty villages was growing, and the desert was getting larger.

The urgency of this situation for the Ottoman state can hardly be overemphasized. Just as centralization was becoming the main theme of Ottoman reform efforts, the government's hold over large parts of the empire was once again becoming tenuous. With the decline of the empire's postal system, even the ability of the center to communicate with the far reaches was steadily diminishing. In earlier centuries the Ottomans had set up an efficient method of communication called the *menzilhane* system that extended the reach of the center throughout the empire.[8] Continuing the practices of empires that had preceded them, the Ottomans placed relay stations along the main arteries of the empire. The sites were administered by salaried officers of the government who were authorized to make impositions on surrounding villages and tribes for man and animal power and for provisions. These officials were required to procure horses and keep them fed and ready at each station. Messengers who carried government orders, letters, news, money, and other valuables rested and changed horses at these relay points and then continued their journeys. The smooth functioning of the system depended on the participation of many people, especially pastoral nomads, who were the main sources of animals in the empire. It was also essential that a certain degree of security be maintained in the rural parts of the provinces.

In the early decades of the nineteenth century, some tribes in central and southern Anatolia were already refusing to make horses available to the state, preferring instead to deal with local notables or with invading Russian and Egyptian armies. Furthermore, some tribes joined those who were roaming the countryside and began attacking and robbing messengers and carriers of the post. Often carriers had to pay huge sums of protection money to local officials and notables in order to travel through parts of the empire.[9] Some locally influential families themselves captured control over way stations and segments of the communication network and used it to exert pressure on the government and further fracture the cohesiveness of the postal network.[10]

Steady deterioration of the empire's communication infrastructure affected the quality and quantity of the information that passed through it. The system became inadequate particularly for identifying the more than 20 million people living within the borders of the empire and keeping track of those who moved within and across regions and between sedentary and nomadic lives. The extraordinary diversity of tribal customs on the local level made identifying groups especially difficult. In addition to deeply entrenched practices, reproduced over many centuries, that made each tribal concentration distinct, the popularity of Sufi orders such as the Nakşibendi, Kadiri, Rifai, and Mevlevi added another layer of complexity to the empire's rural and tribal makeup. The diversity of practices, norms, and ways of living and relating that were reported by people who traveled, lived, or worked in various provinces of the Ottoman Empire stands in sharp contrast to the monolithic portrayals of the empire that became popular in subsequent years. Particularly noteworthy in this respect was the great variation in the status of women and in male-female relations in different parts of the empire. Whereas gender segregation was strictly enforced in the big cities, rural women, especially Alevis and Gypsies, were more relaxed, some appearing before traveling strangers, including Europeans, without covering their faces.[11] Cevdet Paşa remarked that the Tecirli tribe allowed women to divorce their husbands and that the same practice could be observed among some of the desert tribes.[12]

Internal power relations and the ceremonial nature of some of the tribes' most basic activities played important roles in defining tribes and reproducing their distinctive characteristics. Tribal families and their animals moved over hundreds of miles with extraordinary precision as both family members, organized by gender and age, and goats, cattle, sheep, donkeys, and camels took their designated places in the procession.[13] Ainsworth, who was in southern and southeastern Anatolia in the 1830s and 1840s, wrote that the "march of a tribe—the slow and stately pace of the camels laden with tents and tent poles, the bullocks carrying the women and children, and the solemn tread of warriors . . .—constitutes an imposing spectacle." He also mentioned the "air of haughty pride which seems to be meant to assert that a nomadic life gives to them an immeasurable superiority over all strangers, cottagers, or tillers of soil." He went on to assert that the "Bedwin despises the . . . settled Arab, and the nomadic Kurd cherishes that indifference to tillage, which, if it does not lead to wealth, most assuredly contributes to independence of character."[14] Even as they moved, the tribes continued to orally transmit their stories, legends, and lineages, which contributed to their resilience under difficult circumstances.[15]

Even at the peak of its power the Ottoman government had to engage in a complex act of balancing the interests of bureaucrats, provincial notables, local officials, and tribes. As the center became weak and lost some of its ability to maneuver among competing groups in the early nineteenth century, the border areas especially reverted back to their status as contested zones with indeterminate demarcations. Military and civilian officials, notables, and tribal elements engaged in a complex struggle to advance their respective positions, which further undermined the status of the central government.

Under these multiplying pressures, and despite the fact that the professional army had been dissolved and a new one had not yet been formed, Sultan Mahmud II took the risky step of declaring war on Russia in 1827. This was partly an attempt on the sultan's part to strengthen his status and legitimacy by heralding the conflict as a struggle for the soul of Islam and himself as the leader of Muslims everywhere.[16] The Russian Empire responded to this challenge by attacking the Ottoman Empire in both the Balkans and the Caucasus in 1828. Given the weakness of the professional army, the Ottoman state was forced to rely on locally recruited irregulars in resisting the Russian attacks. Some of these local groups were recent refugees and had not yet been fully incorporated into Ottoman society. Many of the refugees had been separated from parts of their extended families, who had remained on the other side of the border. Consequently, the Ottoman state could never be sure of the loyalty of groups such as the Crimean Tatars, some of whom had taken refuge in the Ottoman Empire when their land was occupied by the Russian army in 1783. Although some Tatars fought on the side of the Ottomans in the 1828 war,[17] those who had stayed in Russia were mobilized as part of the 100,000-strong Russian army, which quickly occupied a large swath of territory in northeastern Anatolia, including the important city of Erzurum.[18]

The arrival of the Russian army meant that those who had previously rebelled against the Ottomans in the east now had a potential protector. Alexander Pushkin, who was staying on the Black Sea during these years and accompanied the Russian troops into eastern Anatolia in 1828, described how several hundred Yezidi families walked from Mount Ararat to Erzurum to pledge allegiance to the czar.[19] Like the Hemvends, the Yezidis figured prominently in the American war in Iraq that started in 2003, when they rallied to support the American forces. They were subsequently "disappointed" when they were confused with Kurds or were assumed to be related to them.[20]

The Russians uprooted and resettled some of the sedentary population in order to secure the territories they had just occupied. As part of this scheme, thousands of Armenian families were forced to move farther east into the Russian Empire. Russians hoped that some of these wealthy and well-connected Armenians would continue their trade and bring wealth to their new places of settlement.[21] But the massive displacement achieved little more than the creation of yet another throng of destitute refugees while impoverishing cities such as Erzurum that they left behind.[22] James Fraser, who toured the area in the 1830s, wrote that the Armenians "were suffered to remain encamped and exposed to the severities of weather, without even a provision of bread to eat, so that they died by hundreds of misery and want."[23] Robert Curzon, who traveled in Ottoman lands in the nineteenth century, described their demand to return to their homes as a desire "to return to the lesser evils of the frying pan of Turkey, from whence they had leaped into the fire of despotic Russia."[24] The Russians tried to force the Kurds in eastern Anatolia to disperse as well. They destroyed the major Kurdish towns in the area where Ishak Paşa and his descendants in the Zilanlı tribe had ruled almost like independent sovereigns since the second half of the eighteenth century. Being nomads, however, the Kurds had more ways of resisting the Russians and escaping the impositions of the Russian and Ottoman states than the Armenians had.[25]

Russia's occupation of eastern Anatolia did not last long. Russian troops had already withdrawn from Kars, Bayezid, Van, Muş, Erzurum, and Bayburt by the end of 1829, but they left behind widespread destruction, spreading chaos, and festering conflict. As he toured the region around Bayezid, Fraser wrote, "I never saw so complete a scene of ruins. Scarcely one house in a hundred was inhabited; of those inhabited, few were in repair. . . . It is a most dismal, and to Kurds and Armenians must be a most exasperating, spectacle; but this is what they owe to the tender mercies of Russia." Bayezid, he said, was left "so bare of subjects and resources that the Pasha can now scarcely collect enough of means to defray his private expenses."[26]

The end of the fighting and the eventual withdrawal of Russian forces did not bring order and stability to these parts. The Treaty of Edirne, which ended hostilities between the two empires, prohibited the Ottomans from building castles or citadels to better define and protect their borders.[27] The Ottomans' inability to fill the vacuum left by the Russians and to restore order left the local notables and Kurdish chiefs free to expand their power in these regions. Some Kurdish tribes quickly gained control of a series of citadels in the border areas of eastern Anatolia, creating a region that was effectively cut off from the rest of the empire. They used these citadels as bases from which to attack travelers, traders, and peasants.[28] One of the Kurdish chiefs, Badr Khan, ended up controlling the entire region between Diyarbakır and Mosul. Badr became so powerful that he even issued coins in his name in the 1820s and 1830s.[29] Even though they were expanding their power, building palaces, maintaining armed forces, and even establishing dynasties, the Kurdish tribes never abandoned their pastoral nomadism completely. They continued to circulate in and around their regions and fought with each other to gain advantage and keep alive their tribal identities. In this way they could also keep the center at bay, being always prepared to revert to their nomadic lives if conditions changed. This made it nearly impossible for the Ottoman Empire ever to completely subdue and control the Kurdish tribes in the east.

The growing power of the nomadic tribes and their ongoing conflicts made life particularly difficult for peasants in the east. They were powerless to protect their cattle, crops, or lives in the face of the increasingly powerful tribes. According to a report written by representatives of the Ottoman government, the Arab tribes of Shammar, Al-Cerba, Cubur, and Al-Bu Hamned stole more than 3,000 animals and a variety of weapons, farming implements, and household items around Mosul between September 1848 and August 1849.[30] "Throughout the summer and autumn, not a day passed without the occurrences of murders and robberies in the neighborhood," reported the British consul in Erzurum.[31] When such conflicts became particularly acute, or whenever conditions became intolerable in general, it was not unusual for whole villages to empty out and thousands of people to move across the borders. During one such period, as many as 5,000 families were driven from Muş to other parts of the empire and to Georgia, Russia, and Iran.[32] Such mass migrations stripped the border areas of whatever sedentary order had existed there and rendered them even more open to the depredations of tribes. With large numbers of nomadic Kurds in both Ottoman and Iranian territories, the region that cut across the borders of the Ottoman and Russia Empires and Iran became subject to repeated raids from multiple directions. Hundreds of people were killed, property was stolen and destroyed, and people were kidnapped to be sold as slaves.

In the 1828–29 war, the Russians attacked the Ottoman Empire from the west as well. They occupied Moldavia, Walachia, and a string of towns on the Danube, took Edirne, and advanced all the way to the suburbs of Istanbul. Russian occupation was not long-lived in these parts either, but it still undermined and upset local conditions in significant ways. In a repetition of their relocation of Armenians in the east, the Russians forced the inhabitants of the Balkan territories to resettle in different parts of Russia. Those who refused were required to pay new taxes and forced to perform additional labor. Many among the local population took to the mountains rather than comply with Russian demands. Others escaped from the frontier to other areas, joining the refugees who were moving into the shrinking Ottoman Empire. In the rest of the nineteenth century this phenomenon continued with growing intensity, forcing the Ottoman state to deal not only with sedentarizing the unruly nomads but also with finding land and settling war refugees. With the cessation of hostilities, Russian forces withdrew from most of these territories, but they were allowed to maintain a presence in the area and exercise protection over local communities, especially in Moldavia and Walachia. The Russians prevented the Ottomans from building fortifications along this border, too, so that they would have easy access to the area.[33] These new conditions did not soothe the fears and concerns of local communities. According to one account, as many as 12,000 families from this region moved to Transylvania, 40,000 to Serbia, and 10,000 to Thrace, preferring to live under Habsburg or Ottoman rule than be protected by the Russians.[34] In the meantime, the onset of the Greek Revolution and the establishment of the independent Kingdom of Greece altered the situation further. This new state would attract many ethnic Greeks from a large area extending from the Black Sea to the southern shores of the Mediterranean.

Just as the Russian incursions upset local balances in eastern Anatolia and the Balkans, so the rebellion by the Egyptian governor Mehmed Ali and his occupation of a significant part of southeastern Anatolia and the northern sections of the Fertile Crescent created new networks and new relationships that challenged the Ottoman Empire in the 1830s and 1840s. The specter of Russian forces occupying Istanbul, coupled with the quick advance of Egyptian forces, compelled the Ottomans to focus more closely on reforming their military, reinforcing and protecting their borders, securing the loyalty of local communities, and establishing order in the Balkans and the Fertile Crescent. In Egypt, it was clear that the Ottomans faced a force that was much better organized and effective than the Ottoman army.[35] As part of their vision of creating a strong Egypt, Mehmed Ali and his son Ibrahim Paşa promoted settled agriculture and emphasized centralized administration from the very beginning. They conducted land surveys and censuses in the territories they occupied and offered land grants to tribes who cooperated with them. Underlying many of the policies of Mehmed Ali and his sons was a desire to create a more sedentary society, but the implementation of some of the measures also had the unintended consequence of starting seasonal labor migrations in addition to expanding the scope and intensity of existing patterns of mobility. Particularly significant in this respect were developments associated with the introduction of cotton, which quickly made the region around Adana a magnet for migrant workers from surrounding areas, a pattern that continues to this day.[36] Sedentarization policies in other parts of the empire led to similar developments, whereby networks of migration expanded in concentric circles starting in the core areas of settlement. A good example of this can be found in Arab provinces where the imposition of sedentary order by the Egyptians led to the displacement of Bedouin tribes who moved north, away from their traditional areas of circulation in the Syrian desert.[37]

NEW CENTERS OF POWER: *AYANS* AND TRIBES

While the Ottoman state was finding it difficult to balance a multitude of competing interests and was being attacked and occupied by foreign armies, the tribes and provincial families that had acted as agents of the central government in earlier centuries found new opportunities to assert their freedom. They could continue siding with the center and benefit from the expanded power of the state, or they could shift their allegiance and cooperate with the invading Russian or the rebellious Egyptian army and guarantee privileged positions for themselves in the territories occupied by those states.[38] Although some local notables and tribes tried either or both of these routes, the most significant development of the era was a third option, which involved the emergence of strong alliances among tribes, tribal confederations, and provincial notables. These alliances created new and potent loci of power that challenged and effectively constrained the power of the central government in the nineteenth century.

These new alliances were beneficial to both the notables and the tribes. By cooperating with tribes, locally influential families gained access to new sources of manpower and animals. The tribes gained protection from hostile elements and strengthened their bargaining power vis-à-vis the state.[39] When a local Türkmen chief refused to provide fresh camels to Ainsworth's expedition in the Taurus Mountains in the 1830s, Ainsworth surmised that not knowing how long or how effective the Egyptian occupation would be, the local chiefs were playing it safe and saving some of their animals for the Egyptians.[40] In this case the fact that the expedition had a decree from the sultan ordering that such help be extended made no difference. Charles Fellows also had difficulty obtaining horses in 1838 around Milas in western Anatolia. He could not even present the governmental order he was carrying, which required the local residents to help him. The members of a local tribe claimed that only their chief was authorized to receive such an order, but then they simply refused to identify who their leader was. Farther east, in Basra, Sheikh Zubair of the Türkmen Tajiboğlu tribe had been ignoring the central government for some time. He had allowed a large smuggling network to develop in his region in the 1840s and 1850s. He was also working closely with the French and undermining British interests in the area, partly because the British had become allies of the Ottomans during these years. In the end, the Ottoman governor could deal with this problem only by plotting with other Arab tribes to lure Zubair under false pretenses to a meeting in Basra, where he was summarily shot and his body thrown to his followers.[41] Finally, in the marshlands of southern Mesopotamia, the Arab Müntafik tribe had developed exclusive control over an area that was well known for its dates, buffalo, and especially horses, which the members of this tribe traded with India. Unlike their fierce rivals, the Shammars, the Muntafiks had already abandoned much of their predatory practice and were in a state of semi-settlement in the 1840s. But this was not necessarily good news for the Ottomans, because the tribe had also converted to Shi'ism and developed close relations with Iran.[42]

In the aftermath of the Russo-Turkish War of 1828–29, the Black Sea gained new significance as the buffer zone between the two empires. But the determination of where Russia ended and the Ottoman Empire began became no easier, because of the continuing cross-migrations of the Laz and Pontic Greeks. Under these conditions of uncertainty in the Black Sea region in the 1830s and 1840s, the Tuzcuoğlu and Hazinedaroğlu families competed with each other and with the central government to expand their local power.[43] For a while the Ottomans appointed members of the Hazinedaroğlu family as governors of Trabzon, on the condition that they not contest the hereditary authority of the Tuzcuoğlu family in the area. But when Hazinedaroğlu Osman tried to suppress his rivals by using Ottoman reform as a pretext and acting as tax collector and enforcer of reform in the 1830s, Tuzcuoğlu led an armed rebellion against him and the Ottoman center. Hazinedaroğlu suppressed the rebellion by force and dispatched Tuzcuoğlu's severed head to Istanbul.[44] Many other families were also now in positions to mobilize significant numbers of fighters in different parts of the empire, thanks primarily to the presence of disaffected tribes in their regions. The Ottoman government extended official recognition and titles to many such families. One of these was the Çapanoğlu, whose chief, Mehmet Bey, was appointed governor of the newly created province that combined Yozgat and Kayseri in 1843.[45] At its prime, this family alone could summon as many as 40,000 fighters in its defense.[46]

Farther east, almost the entire area around Ardahan was owned by four sons of a former notable in 1841. They had inherited most of this land from their father. The rest were given to them by the imperial center. The British consul described them as the wealthiest persons in this part of the empire.[47] In the early 1850s, during his travels in eastern Anatolia, Robert Curzon spoke with some Kurdish chiefs and discovered that some of the tribes had kept the chieftainship in one family going back seven generations.[48] Similarly, Cevdet Paşa described how the Ulaşlı tribe was divided into five groups governed by different chiefs who held their positions hereditarily.[49] Perhaps most important, even when they were settled and dispersed, the tribes were able to maintain a degree of tribal solidarity and identity that proved powerful.

Also in the 1840s, twelve tribes in south-central and southeastern Anatolia combined forces and created a formidable alliance against the authority of the Ottoman government. The Arıklı tribe, consisting of about 300 households and ruled by the Kozanoğlu family, rose above the others and became the supreme ruler not only over this confederation but also over a large area bounded by the Mediterranean in the west and the beginnings of the Kurdish region in the east.[50] The Kozanoğlu family got its name from its village of origin, Kozan, near the city of Ayıntab. There were other tribes as well as Muslim, Greek, and Armenian villages in and around southeastern Anatolia. The chiefs of these communities also wielded extensive power over their regions and tribes, and some of them held hereditary positions handed down for generations. But through a series of battles and successful resistance to Ottoman incursions, the Kozanoğlu family prevailed over most of the other tribes and their chiefs. So great had the Kozanoğlus' reputation become by the mid-nineteenth century that part of the Taurus mountains around which they were settled came to be called the Kozan Mountains.[51] In 1849 the British consul estimated the number of tribes under the control of the Kozanoğlu tribe at 12,000.[52] Even if they did not submit completely, other tribes in the region were obliged to share their wealth and loot with the Kozanoğlu family and to supply animals and fighters when they were needed. In a clear sign of the strength of the horizontal ties that were developing in this area, the Kurdish tribes Lek and Kırıntılı informed the representative of the central government in 1849 that they could not agree to submit to the sultan before first consulting with Kozanoğlu, whom they regarded as their supreme chief.[53] The Kozanoğlus' relationship with the Lek tribe was particularly strong. A long tradition existed in which Kozanoğlu men married Lek girls "in order to have courageous sons."[54] No one dared to speak ill of this family, especially in provincial councils where other families and the Ottoman government were represented. In one instance, in the presence of the governor, the highest-ranking representative of the central government in the province, one of Kozanoğlu Ömer's followers described his rise to the position of chieftain as his "coronation" (cülus). Although this was a clear insult to the absolute authority of the sultan, no one, including the governor, dared to object to it, and nobody was punished or even chastised for this expression of disrespect.[55]

Through its paramount position in the region, the Kozanoğlu family also controlled the overland access to eastern Anatolia, northern Syria, and Iraq. Members of the family worked with others in the area, such as the Armenian merchants who became the main intermediaries in interregional trade and finance. Pilgrims who had to pass through the area while making the hajj to Mecca became another crucial link between Ottoman territories and the outside world. Typically, Armenian merchants would purchase, in nearby towns such as Adana and Kayseri, the clothing and other household and consumption items needed by the families and tribes who lived in the mountains. They then exchanged these items with the Kozanoğlu chiefs for the rights to the tithes of specific settlements under the control of the Kozanoğlu family. After collecting the taxes in these places, a merchant would present the Kozanoğlu chief with his accounting of what he had spent and how much he had collected. According to Cevdet Paşa, the local chiefs relied completely on the merchants' presentations in settling these accounts, because they kept no books and had no way of checking the merchants' declarations of price, value, or distance.[56] A significant part of such exchanges was managed verbally and on the basis of local customs of trust that bound these communities to each other.

Although such relationships linked the higher echelons of the administrative hierarchy to the outside world, lay members of the tribes who lived in this area were isolated and confined there during most of the first half of the nineteenth century. No one was allowed in, and residents of the area were not permitted to leave without the explicit consent of their tribal chiefs. Even the provincial officials from Adana had to wait to be escorted into the region when they had business to conduct there. The escorts deliberately took circuitous paths, preventing the officials from gaining a realistic understanding of conditions in the region.[57] In places such as this, the Ottoman government was known not for its heavy-handed administration but for its absence. It is surprising to discover how light the Ottoman presence was in such parts of the empire. As was typical in some outlying provinces of the empire, the Ottomans never conducted a survey or recorded the extent and potential of the land here, even though it had been part of the empire since the early sixteenth century. Later in the nineteenth century, when the Ottoman government intensified its efforts of reform, it relied on surveys that had been conducted by the occupying Egyptian administration.[58]

Although the Kozanoğlus' influence was unlike that of any other family in the region, this did not mean that the family was unified or coherent or that its control went unchallenged. Kozanoğlu Yusuf, who was the chief in the 1840s, divided the area he controlled between two of his sons, Samur Bey and Ali Bey, starting two dynastic lines, Kozanoğlu Garbi and

Kozanoğlu Şarki.[59] Different factions within this large family, as well as other families in the area, always sought opportunities to expand their power and influence at the expense of others. The government took advantage of these divisions, supporting one or another of the factions according to circumstances. What is important is that for the most part the divisions were based on pragmatic concerns and had no relationship to any deep sense of identity based on attributes such as religion and ethnicity. One result was that far from being tranquil, the area in which the Kozanoğlu family exercised its power was at best unpredictable. Cevdet Paşa lamented in the early 1860s that it had become impossible to travel farther than a two-hour distance from the town of Adana without risking one's life or property.[60] Passengers who landed at Iskenderun on the eastern Mediterranean en route to provinces farther east chose to bypass the entire Kozanoğlu domain and followed the circuitous and considerably longer route through Aleppo in the south and then a turn north again to reach their destinations. Likewise, the pilgrimage caravans preferred the southerly Beirut-Damascus route to the treacherous mountain passage that linked Iskenderun, Belen, and Antakya, and even then they had to travel with as many as a thousand mounted escorts.[61]

While the notable Muslim families were deciding how to position themselves vis-à-vis the central government, the non-Muslim communities, too, discovered that they had some room to maneuver in the face of the government's growing interest in reform and reorganization. It seems that decisions about which direction to move in and what alliances to build were made not on the basis of ethnic or religious identity but according to specific conditions. This was true for both the various communities within the empire and for the Ottoman government. For example, when a serious rebellion broke out in the predominantly Armenian town of Zeytun in the early 1860s, half the police force that was sent to establish control consisted of Armenians.[62] Elsewhere among Armenians, serious concern existed that reform and centralization could undermine the power of local notables. Nevertheless, the promise of better administration was sufficient to lure most of the local Armenian notables to the side of the Ottomans. Three Armenian notables from Haçin received medals, and a fourth, an award of 5,000 *pisatres*, for the support they rallied in 1864 when the Ottomans staged a campaign against the tribal chiefs of the Kozanoğlu alliance.[63] When the spiritual head of the Armenian Orthodox Church, Kiragos, died two years later, he was buried with full military ceremony and honors, mainly because of the services he had rendered to the central government.[64]

The Ottoman government was not in a powerful position to deal effectively with external attacks or internal unrest in the early nineteenth century. Its army was in disarray and its institutions had lost the flexibility needed to respond to the fast-changing circumstances of the period. As a first step toward repairing these conditions, in 1831 the Ottoman government conducted the first ever empire-wide census, partly to identify and draft eligible soldiers and begin rebuilding the professional army.[65] Especially in the outlying provinces and in regions where *ayan*s and tribes were influential, these steps were met with deep skepticism, if not outright hostility. In Mosul, people marched in the streets and attacked and killed the government official who had been sent to conduct the census. The government reestablished control there only after a major show of force that included firing cannons into the city.[66] The Ottomans had limited means of imposing their will without empowering the very elements they were trying to displace. As they had always done in the past, the local potentate and tribal chiefs exacted a high price for their cooperation.[67] Typically, the tribal chiefs demanded blanket amnesty for their past illegal activities and tax exemptions and other favors before agreeing to the government's demands.[68]

While the new army was taking shape, the Ottoman government used a combination of professional soldiers and local irregulars to carry out campaigns in the 1830s, 1840s, and 1850s to pacify the border areas. These campaigns targeted the local notables of the Black Sea region, the rebellious tribes in Libya, the Kurdish emirates in northern Iraq, the Kurdish families in eastern and southern Anatolia, and the Bedouins who had been pushed north into Syria during the Wahhabi uprisings of the eighteenth century and the campaigns of the Egyptian armies.[69] In the course of the Ottoman campaigns, many tribal chiefs were defeated and forced into submission. Some of them, along with large numbers of their followers, were exiled to distant parts of the empire. These were significant accomplishments, but they did not necessarily mean that Ottoman control over these areas became permanently secure. Especially in the east, the government had to rely on some of the Kurdish chiefs to fight against other, rebellious Kurdish tribes.[70] For each tribal chief who was defeated, there were others who lay low, only to move in and take over the territory vacated by deported tribes when conditions were right, or who cooperated with the Ottoman government during the campaign in an attempt to secure and even improve their own positions.

Although the Ottomans created five new territorial armies by 1843 and passed an empire-wide law of conscription that applied to Muslim subjects, local forces continued to bear the major share of the fighting in these campaigns. Of the 3,830 troops sent to deal with the Avşar tribes around Kayseri in central Anatolia in 1849, all but 750 were described as irregulars coming from the same region. Predictably, this created problems, because the recruits were reluctant to act against their own people.[71] In the campaigns in which the Ottomans participated during the first three decades of the nineteenth century, consistently about half of the Ottoman army consisted of locally recruited irregular troops.[72] Sultan Mahmud II reconstituted the tribal Evlad-ı Fatihan troops in the 1830s and integrated them into the new modern army he was building. These troops would play an important role in pacifying northern Albania.[73] The continuing prominence of these local groups in the Ottoman campaigns enhanced their power and allowed them to play pivotal roles in some of the crucial conflicts of the last years of the empire, especially in the border regions. With names such as *bashi-bazouk, komitadji, andarte, zeybek,* and *efe,* these irregular fighters became one of the most influential and least predictable elements in the many-sided conflicts that were developing on the empire's frontiers.[74]

As the Ottoman government became confident in the capacity of its new army and institutions, it began to act more forcefully and confrontationally toward the tribes. Some chiefs and members of notable families who defied the central government were taken hostage and held until their followers joined forces with the government. Local officials made some of the customary routes of tribal migration impassable by setting up roadblocks and organizing raids against migrating tribes. They went so far as burning tents, houses, and even entire villages to enforce the new regulations.[75] Sometimes the government targeted specific tribes, restricted their access to water, required them to thin their herds so they would have less need for pasture, and compelled them to begin transitioning to settled life.[76] Some measures were harsh. For example, the Afshar chiefs, whose cooperation the government needed in subduing their areas, were lured to a meeting only to be kept in what the British consul described as "ignominious and severe confinement." They were "chained by their necks and legs without being allowed to stir except under a guard. In this condition . . . they [were] kept for more than six weeks crowded in a small tent under a scorching sun."[77]

In dealing with the large confederation of tribes dominated by the Kozanoğlu family, the Ottoman government had to be particularly comprehensive and forceful. It created a special fighting force called the Fırka-i Islahiyye (Army of Reform), consisting of professional soldiers and Albanian, Zeybek, Georgian, Circassian, and Kurdish fighters who were recruited locally.[78] One of the most respected scholar-statesmen of the era, Ahmet Cevdet Paşa, was put in charge of this army.[79] On May 8, 1864, Ahmet Cevdet, his military commanders, and approximately 17,500 troops (7,500 infantry and 10,000 cavalry) belonging to this new army set sail to the port of Iskenderun on the eastern Mediterranean.[80] Cevdet Paşa and the other officers in charge of the Fırka-i Islahiyye were granted wide latitude in the organization and operation of the army. The troops were equipped with modern weapons such as rifles, and the officers had access to the newly set-up telegraph, which they could use to communicate with Istanbul and request new troops if needed.[81]

Although it was set up as a military operation, the Fırka-i Islahiyye's campaign was carried out as a comprehensive program of pacification and sedentarization. As part of his plan, Cevdet tried to draw to his side as many tribal chiefs as possible, using both inducements and threats. Tribes that refused to submit, such as the Çerçili tribe, which Cevdet Paşa referred to as the "bandits of Çercili," were forcefully dispersed as far away as Egypt and the Balkans. Their houses were destroyed and their property was confiscated.[82] Tribal chiefs who wished to avoid the new army's wrath were required to submit to its wishes by providing fighters, animals, shelter, and other resources. They also had to agree to settle a certain number of their people.[83] Of the many groups the Fırka encountered, Türkmen tribes were particularly eager to side with the Ottoman government. In this respect the Reyhaniye confederation, which had been circulating between Maraş and the Amık Valley, proved especially helpful. The leader of this community, Mürselzade Mustafa Şevki Bey, provided security for the Ottoman troops between Iskenderun and Aleppo as the Fırka first arrived. He and other Türkmen leaders would remain strong allies of the Ottoman government in implementing the sedentarization policies of the later years of the nineteenth century.[84] The Fırka was able to find support even among some Kurds, whose tribal divisions offered many opportunities for exploitation.

Fırka-i Islahiyye commanders also spent large amounts of money to lure the tribes from their local allegiances. Instead of confiscating crops, as the Ottoman government typically did, the Fırka purchased them from the peasants. They also paid money to some of the tribes if they agreed to go along with the central government's directives.[85] In one instance, local communities were even compensated for the damage caused by the Reyhanlı tribe as it moved to help Ottoman troops in the Amık region.[86] In his report, Ahmet Cevdet went to some length to describe how important it was for the Ottoman government to be fair so that the army would have credibility and succeed in its mission.

In the course of its operations to stabilize southern Anatolia, the Fırka-i Islahiyye created new settlements as well as consolidating and expanding some existing villages and towns. The towns of Hassa, Izziye, Osmaniye, and Reyhanlı were created in this way in the 1860s and became important places of settlement for tribes and refugees in subsequent decades.[87] Farther east, in Gavur Dağı, the Fırka-i Islahiyye built another 3,800 houses in 35 villages.[88] The government created administrative councils, built schools and government offices, paid the salaries of teachers and *müfti*s, and set up a defense force in each of these towns. The councils reflected the composition of the area's population. The town council of Hassa, for example, had both Kurdish and Armenian members, whereas that of Izziye consisted entirely of Kurds.[89] Finally, and most important, once constituted, these towns were required to record the kinds and extent of landholdings in the area and start procedures for registering the male population for military service. In addition to building settlements and creating alliances to strengthen the position of the Ottoman government, the Fırka-i Islahiyye used its resources to expand and repair roads, lodgings, citadels, and observation towers, especially in and around the new settlements.[90]

The administrative reform and new institutions that accompanied the operations of the Fırka should not cloud the fact that this was primarily a military organization. Its commanders forced their way into the region, confronted the rebellious chiefs, and defeated, pushed away, and marginalized many of them in 1864 and 1865. Particularly significant in this regard was the Fırka-i Islahiyye's success in forcing into submission the Kozanoğlu family itself. In the end, the family's leading members and their families were dispersed to Tripoli, Damascus, Istanbul, Sivas, and Yozgat.[91]

Many other members were given official titles and "appointed" to faraway places or forced into retirement with large land grants.[92]

Military campaigns using special troops were only one part of the Ottoman response to the growing power of tribes and local families. Over time these were accompanied by new laws and institutions that gave the military actions and other steps greater consistency. A government publication summarizing all the laws and regulations issued between 1841 and 1867, for example, stated that all the nomadic tribes in Anatolia would henceforth be settled in their winter pastures and included in imperial censuses. From then on the tribes would be expected to engage in agriculture and pay taxes accordingly.[93] In 1854 the government deprived the tribal sheikhs of the official recognition they had previously been accorded. After losing its special status, the title "sheikh" was incorporated into the provincial administrative hierarchy along with titles such as *kaymakam* and *mutasarrıf.*[94]

The regulations concerning nomads and tribes were accompanied by several new laws designed to strengthen the overall institutional framework of the empire. One of the most important such initiatives, which aimed both to enhance the power of the central government and to protect settled peasant agriculture, was the land code enacted in 1858. Although the overall thrust of this law was to undermine the large landholding notables and undo the harmful effects of the tax farming system, it was also a clearly and strongly anti-tribal measure.[95] In a direct blow to the foundations of tribal life, the 1858 law replaced communal property and identity with the principle of individual ownership. Individual households could take advantage of this to acquire the land they had already been cultivating, simply by registering with the central government. But as happened with so many other reform measures, the actual implementation of the land code did not go exactly as the central government planned. People feared that if they registered with the authorities, they would face new taxes and conscription into the army. The tribal chiefs and the sheikhs took advantage of the fears of the rural population. Especially in southern Anatolia, they stepped into the vacuum and registered tribal land in their own names. Consequently, tribal chiefs, who had been the main targets of this law, ended up benefiting from its implementation. In addition to becoming landlords and hence acquiring some stake in the success of sedentarization, the tribal leaders maintained their traditional authority over their communities by reinforcing their role as protectors of the tribe and intermediaries in dealings with the state. This was a major blow to the government's plans to break up tribal communities. In subsequent years the Arab and Kurdish landlords, especially, became more adamant in resisting any effort by the Ottoman government to undermine their status or strip them of their new-found wealth.[96]

Other problems with the implementation of the code limited its effects in tribal regions. In devising its general rules and categorizations, the government paid little attention to local practices, especially the elaborate rhythms of circulation of the tribes. Consequently, land that might have been part of the seasonal migration of tribes could be declared empty and given either to the sultan, to local tribal and other notables, or to newly arriving refugees.[97] In many instances, those who were given title to land ended up displacing the tribes that were periodically cultivating it, even within the context of their settlement plans. Some of the tribal attacks that are generally presented as signs of primitive banditry were in fact responses to such intrusions on local practices. The cumulative effect of these shifts was a net deterioration in the status of individual part-time pastoral cultivators, who were forced into landlessness and further subjugation to local chiefs in central and eastern Anatolia and the Arab provinces. But although the long-term effects of these changes were important for the people involved, for the region, and for the empire, they did not necessarily undermine the tribal order in a significant way in the nineteenth century.

The other important legislation intended to reinforce the power of the center at the expense of localities and tribes was the provincial law of 1864, which created a highly centralized and hierarchical system of administration in which all holders of office except for the governors of subdistricts (*nahiye müdürü*) were to be appointed centrally. Paralleling the spirit of the land code, the provincial law emphasized the importance of individual, not communal, responsibility to the state.[98] It is a sign of the government's seriousness about creating a centralized administration that this law was first rehearsed in 1861 in the all-important frontier province of Danube under the governorship of the key reformer and author of the empire's first constitution, Midhat Paşa. In terms of creating an institutional framework for the integration of tribes and other local centers of power into the empire, the provincial law was more effective than the land law. But without the latter, the new institutions lacked the substantive basis to be effective in breaking old loyalties in the provinces.

In the 1840s and 1850s the government also initiated a series of regional plans that targeted special tribes and their areas. A particular target was the Avşar tribe of central Anatolia, against which a massive campaign was organized that included raids to disperse the tribe's members and forced relocations and mixing with other tribes.[99] A Hungarian officer was hired in 1852 to design settlements in south-central Syria, with detailed plans for building villages and using them to attract specific tribes. Although this plan was never fully implemented, the area became recognized as a place of settlement, and a number of tribes were in fact given land and settled there.[100]

After the Fırka's operations concluded, Cevdet Paşa was appointed governor of Aleppo in 1866, which allowed him to continue the work he had started during the campaigns. Partly because of his policies, the second half of the 1860s turned out to be prosperous years for Aleppo. Among his innovations was the creation of a mobile desert police force, primarily to protect crops from Bedouin raids.[101] Tax collection became more efficient, new roads were built, and the overall number of settled villages grew under Cevdet's governorship. He also oversaw the publication of provincial yearbooks and the official newspaper, *Fırat*, in Turkish and Arabic. In a further effort to solidify the links between the border regions and the center, Midhat Paşa was appointed governor of Baghdad in 1869. His mandate was to rebuild the city to reintegrate it and its surroundings into the empire and to recharge the authority of the central government in this important region bordering Iran. In addition to rebuilding the area's infrastructure and institutions, Midhat Paşa made tribal settlement a central element of his administration in Baghdad. His years have been described as the "years of most intense settlement" in the area.[102] In a continuation of the official anti-tribal sentiments that had begun in the 1840s, Midhat freely expressed his conviction that tribal life was fit only for primitive creatures and animals, and he said as much in negotiating with Arab and Kurdish chiefs.[103] Such sentiments would become increasingly common in the later decades of the nineteenth century.

The Ottoman government also expanded its system of information gathering significantly in the nineteenth century. In earlier centuries it had relied on a vast but diverse and inconsistent network of local officials to gather and transmit information. The effectiveness of this network depended to a large extent on local power relations and the qualifications of the officials who worked in the provinces on behalf of the Ottoman center. Sometimes travelers met local officials who were well informed about the empire, Europe, the sciences, and literature. For example, Governor Necip Paşa of Antalya, who hosted Charles Fellows in 1838, impressed his guest with his vast knowledge of minerals and his deep interest in the possibility of discovering coal in his district. Necip had several samples of minerals in metal vases, which he asked Fellows to examine.[104] It was equally likely, however, that travelers would encounter officials who were ignorant even of their immediate surroundings, let alone the broader region or the world.

As part of its effort to improve the volume and quality of information it gathered, the Ottoman government conducted a plethora of surveys to monitor all kinds of mobility within the imperial domain. In the Ottoman archives are more than 2,000 booklets containing the results of these surveys, dating from 1831 to 1914.[105] Although surveys appear to have been taken at different intervals, they typically reflect the results of six-month counts. Most of them reported on people who "come, leave, visit, die," or are "born, somewhere else, or abroad," with differences from one count to the next duly noted.[106] In addition to local surveys, the government continued to pay attention to empire-wide flows. Movements in and out of the capital city were of particular concern, because of the special privileges accorded to people who lived in Istanbul. Places such as medreses (madrasahs), Sufi lodges, lodging quarters, drinking establishments, and coffee houses in Istanbul were surveyed in order to identify unattached bachelors or vagrants who might be living there. Some of these periodic surveys were designed to monitor the movements of Jews, Greeks, Armenians, and Gypsies in order to make sure they did not escape their tax liabilities (cizye) by changing location. The government was particularly interested in finding out whether individuals had already paid their taxes before moving or whether they were supposed to be assessed and taxed in their new places.[107]

Looking at the results of these surveys, one gets the impression that this was still an empire in motion in many ways. All across the empire there were tribes, individual laborers, students, and merchants—not to mention administrators—who were constantly on the move. The key difference in the nineteenth century was that now they were faced with a burgeoning state that was keenly interested in their movements. These surveys also counted the members of particular tribes, paying close attention to matters related to taxation and employment in farms or towns.[108] They monitored recent refugees from Crimea and elsewhere.[109] They followed the itineraries of tribes that had been forced to relocate.[110] They recorded eligible draftees and tracked foreigners, especially Russians in the east.[111] They also reflected interest in the number and status of non-Muslims residing in various towns and cities and living with tribes, which was not an uncommon situation, especially in the east.[112]

Overall, taxation, security, and conscription seem to have been the three most important concerns shaping the government's interest in collecting information through these surveys. People who were counted were listed according to their tax liabilities, and potential draftees were identified. Places such as the Balkans, the shores of the Black Sea, and other frontier areas that had been witnessing external attacks or internal unrest received particular attention. In all the surveys, nomads were registered with as much information as possible, including not only their names and the reputations of their chiefs but also the boundaries of the areas in which they circulated and the names of the local officials who would be responsible for them.[113] Such information, which was compiled in an increasingly specific and systematic manner during the nineteenth century, became the basis for the increasingly detailed and accurate maps of the empire, empire-wide censuses, and provincial almanacs.[114] As one moved farther from the center, the methods of information collecting became less direct. Few surveys from Arab or North African provinces exist, reflecting the central government's continuing reliance on local representatives for information about these regions.

The government used its new institutions and laws and the information it was collecting not only to enforce its settlement orders but also to undermine ties between local notables and tribes and to break the authority of both notables and tribal chiefs. In particular, the purpose behind identifying tribes and tribal members was to recognize them as individuals. The government then tried to reinforce the separate status of each member of the tribe with land grants and other awards. From the perspective of the central government, these were initial steps that would eventually culminate in a more systematic and comprehensive program integrating the subjects of the Ottoman state as individuals under a centralized and powerful administration. The strategy signaled a significant departure from the way the empire had previously approached the task of governing, in which the focus had always been on communities and communal responsibility.

In some parts of the empire the reforms were greeted with enthusiasm because of their promise to liberate tribal members and villagers from the arbitrary demands of local notables and tribal chiefs. More typically, local communities greeted these steps with suspicion and saw them as unwelcome intrusions into established local practices.[115] Sometimes even local officials, who were used to the older arrangements, refused to implement the new rules, leaving the government in the awkward position of having to govern in spite of its own representatives. In 1840 the governor of Denizli was forced to flee the town after he refused to act according to the stipulations of the reform order and tore up a petition signed by thousands of inhabitants.[116] In Erzurum, on the other hand, local Kurds prevented the government's representative, who had come to issue the new reform edict in 1845, from entering the city. A deputation from Van informed the government representative that they would not permit the introduction of reforms and demanded that one of their own chiefs be appointed governor. Neither would they supply troops to the army or permit Ottoman troops to be quartered in Van. There was little the Ottoman administration could do to respond, because the overwhelmingly Kurdish residents of the district were likely to escape to Iran if they were pressured too much.[117] In Diyarbakır the Ottomans redrew the boundaries of the province and stationed permanent troops in order to pacify the area in 1847.[118]

SETTLING REFUGEES

The Crimean War of 1854–56 represented a major turning point in the Ottomans' efforts to sedentarize and centralize their empire. The war itself occupied the bulk of the Ottoman army for two years, which meant that the campaigns against local notables and their tribal followers had to be suspended. Once again, however, it would be wrong to assume that all the tribal leaders and provincial notables rushed to take advantage of this distraction to expand their local power. As in previous cases, some tribes supported and fought on the side of the Ottoman army. Among those was the Caf (Jaff) tribe, which, with more than 10,000 households at the turn of the twentieth century, was one of the largest Kurdish tribes in southeastern Anatolia and northern Iraq.[119] Another was the Cerid tribe, which went to the front under the leadership of a woman named Kara Fatma, who was awarded a silver medal and a monthly salary of 100 *kuruş* upon her return.[120]

But the key effect of the war for the government's program of settlement was the waves of refugees it instigated. What had started in the late eighteenth century as a stream of people and had picked up somewhat during the 1828–29 Russo-Turkish War became a tidal wave of migration in the aftermath of the Crimean War and continued through the end of the empire.[121] By some estimates as many as 900,000 people were forced to leave Crimea and the Caucasus for the Ottoman Empire in the eight years following the Crimean War.[122] Although the overwhelming majority of these people were Muslims, Russia took advantage of the war conditions and expelled Jews from the border areas, most of whom sought refuge in Ottoman lands.[123] The sudden arrival of large numbers of people clashed with existing institutions and practices in the Ottoman Empire in three ways. First, under the prevailing conditions, it was challenging if not impossible for the Ottoman state to absorb the refugees. Second, and related to the first, were the complications these new arrivals presented to ongoing plans for settling the nomadic tribes who were already in the empire. Even though land was plentiful and available in most parts of the empire, the question of who came first and had which rights to which property became contentious, especially in the fertile lands of western and southern Anatolia. Finally, the refugee flows made it clear that the Ottoman state could no longer afford to manage its population without a clear policy on immigration and citizenship.

Rather than dealing with the newcomers as a separate problem, the Ottoman government used the refugees as a means of bolstering its sedentarization program and as an excuse for building new and powerful institutions to control its population. Most of the refugees who came from Russia had been sedentary farmers or urban dwellers at home, and they expected (and received) similar status in the Ottoman Empire. Also, because the refugees were not parts of already established tribal or other hierarchies, the government could easily treat them as distinct households and give them parcels of land of equal sizes, although the size for each household declined significantly between the 1850s and the 1870s.[124] In dealing with the settlement of tribes, on the other hand, the government was often forced to favor the tribal chiefs and other leaders, who demanded more of the best land in return for their cooperation. This was an important factor that perpetuated tribal hierarchies even in the midst of the government's campaign of sed-entarization and individuation. In addition to bolstering sedentary farm-ing, the arrival of refugees provided the government with a new means of fighting the rebellious tribes and undermining the authority of the chiefs. Some of the new *muhajir* (immigrant) villages in central Anatolia were designed in a way that formed ribbonlike patterns around the lower reaches of the mountains, so that the migration routes of the local tribes would be blocked and the tribes would have to alter their nomadic lives.[125]

Not surprisingly, some among the local communities saw the insertion of refugees in their midst as yet another intrusion by the central govern-ment, disrupting their region's moral economy. In several instances the central government had to dispatch armed guards to protect refugees from nomads who tried to force them out of the area. At the same time, some tribal leaders were appointed chiefs of irregular cavalry units and were paid salaries, another attempt to incorporate tribal authority into the imperial bureaucracy—with uncertain results.[126] Indeed, such interven-tions sometimes had the effect of reversing gains in sedentarization. This was the case with the Alevi Avşar tribes, which had been settling and devel-oping complex relationships with the central government and with local groups but which resented the government's heavy-handed tactics. Avşars stopped complying with the central government's orders and returned to their nomadic lives in the mountains around Kayseri in the 1850s.

To process and move the refugees, the government initially relied on local municipal authorities. When the numbers became too large for local authorities to deal with, the government responded with ad hoc steps such as launching aid campaigns to which local officials and military personnel were obliged to contribute.[127] Then in 1857 the Ottomans passed their first ever immigration code, attempting, among other things, to regulate their policy of citizenship for the first time. Parts of the law consisted of no more than codifications of existing practices. The central government continued to accept into the empire anyone who agreed to become the sultan's subject, provided he or she was not a criminal. The only other requirement was that each household have capital of at least 60 *mecidiye*, but this was not an easily enforceable rule, especially under the conditions that had cre-ated the refugee flows in the first place. The immigrants would be given the best available land and be exempted from all taxes for six years in Rumelia (Rumeli in Turkish)—that part of the Balkans generally including Albania, Macedonia, and Thrace—and for twelve years in Anatolia. They could not sell their land for twenty years, however, and would be required to return it if they decided to leave the country.[128]

In 1859 the government took one more step and established a special commission under the title Muhacirin Komisyonu to deal with the problems of immigrants and refugees. The membership of this body was drawn from senior officials in the government, and it was charged with coordinating and regulating settlement.[129] The commission divided Anatolia into seven regions of settlement and sent officials and translators to each in order to help settle the new arrivals.[130] In the course of the nineteenth and early twentieth centuries, the power and responsibilities of this commission would be expanded significantly. By the final years of the empire it would be the key office overseeing not only refugee matters but also questions of citizenship and thus identity in the empire. In this way, the settlement of refugees became the venue for the creation and strengthening of some key institutions and practices that would play a central role in both the reform and centralization of the empire.

Nevertheless, a significant part of the burden of dealing with refugees and other internally displaced people continued to fall on local administrators, who had very limited resources throughout the rest of the nineteenth century. Money such as that in local aid funds (*menafi-i umumiyye sandıkları*) under local control was not made available to refugees because it was collected by and for the residents of the area.[131] Governors in some of the major refugee-receiving regions, such as Syria, ended up levying special taxes on the settled population to defray the costs of dealing with the waves of new arrivals, which made them even less popular. That some of the newcomers, such as the Circassians and Chechens, were not Arabs became an additional cause for discontent among the settled population in places like Syria.[132]

The Ottomans tried to come up with a clearer definition of Ottoman nationality and citizenship in order to better manage the absorption of refugees. A new Law on Nationality was drafted in 1869, partly to protect Ottoman citizens against neighboring states that were passing their own regulations of citizenship. The same law regulated the issuing and control of passports.[133] Although it reflected some of the limitations inherent in Islamic law, which continued to provide the main framework for all laws in the Ottoman Empire, the 1869 code was liberal in granting and recognizing citizenship. According to it, all persons who lived in the Ottoman Empire were considered Ottoman subjects unless they claimed or could prove otherwise. Anyone who lived in the empire for five years could become a citizen. Muslim refugees were granted citizenship immediately upon their arrival. Others who performed services to the Ottoman state could acquire citizenship easily, as could foreigners who were escaping from other countries. Conversely, Ottoman subjects who moved to other lands with no intention of coming back, and those who served a foreign power in a military or other capacity, lost their citizenship. Even though some elements of this law suggest an emphasis on bloodline, on the whole the 1869 law was based on the principal of territorial definition of Ottoman identity, in which citizenship derived from residence in what were considered to be Ottoman lands. To be sure, this was not an easy principle to apply at a time when the boundaries of the territory were constantly changing.

Nevertheless, the approach taken in the 1869 law represented a significant departure from that of earlier laws. Previously, Muslims, non-Muslims, and foreigners had been subject to separate Ottoman laws, regardless of where they lived. The 1869 law based its specifications primarily on the status of individuals and not necessarily on their membership in groups or communities. The two main targets of this approach were the tribal communities and non-Muslims, both of whom had special rights and privileges determined on the basis of group membership. In their new roles, tribal chiefs were no longer seen as organic representatives of tribes but as intermediaries between the members of the tribe and the government, with the primary duties of transmitting and enforcing governmental decrees. The leaders of non-Muslim "millets" found themselves in a similar situation as a result of the reforms of the nineteenth century. Another important result of these changes was that they opened the possibility that tribal members could now be taken to court as individuals if they violated the law or the settlement directives, and they could, in return, petition the state.[134]

Although the 1869 law represented a significant shift in each of these areas, and the rules included in it became increasingly specific in subsequent decades, the Ottoman laws of nationality continued to contain some group-based exceptions and rules, mostly carried over from Islamic law. These were particularly important in questions having to do with gender and religion. For example, Muslim women were not permitted to marry non-Muslims, whether Ottoman or foreigner. They were not even allowed to marry Iranians, because of the suspicion with which the Ottomans continued to regard Shi'ism and the danger that an Ottoman woman who married an Iranian would become a conduit for the spread of that sect.[135] A turning point in identifying the subjects of the Ottoman state and regulating the relations between them and the government was the promulgation of the 1876 constitution, which formalized these relations, set down rules about law-making, and paved the way for elections and representative government in the Ottoman Empire.

For most of the nineteenth century, Ottoman officials expected that a sense of Ottomanism would develop if people of different ethnic and religious backgrounds were provided with space and opportunity to interact and cooperate with one another. For example, non-Muslims were no longer required to convert before they could enroll in military schools and serve in the Ottoman army. This created an institutional context in which people of different faiths could be trained to serve and even fight for the Ottoman state. Non-Muslims also became eligible to be appointed to some of the highest posts in the government without having to change their religion. Starting as early as 1845, a succession of representative assemblies and other elected bodies was convened to help govern the empire. Non-Muslims were part of these experiments as well. It would be wrong to think of these policies as steps toward creating a multicultural or federal structure in the Ottoman Empire. Underlying these citizenship policies, which continued through the end of the empire, was a strong push toward assimilation, first to an Islamic community and then increasingly to an ethnic-nationalist one.[136]

The establishment of tribal schools to educate the children of Arab and Kurdish sheikhs provides a good example of the way this approach worked in practice. The founding of these schools reflected the growing recognition on the part of some reforming bureaucrats that unless steps were taken to transform disparate subjects into a more closely integrated society consisting of citizens with individual, not communal, rights, the empire had little chance of survival in the modern world. At the same time, the Military Academy and the School of Political Sciences designed special courses for the children of Arab sheikhs.[137]

This assimilationist outlook can also be seen in the pejorative and hostile language that bureaucrats began to use when they referred to nomads and tribes, who were now seen as living in a state of "heresy, savagery, and ignorance."[138] Midhat Paşa, who, as governor first of Danube province and then of Baghdad, put particular emphasis on the settlement of tribes and refugees, described nomadism and tribalism as primitive and "fit for animals."[139] Norman Lewis has noted a general belief among officials that the Syrian desert was not necessarily arid and uncultivable but had been destroyed by nomads and their animals. According to him, the view that "the barbarous nomads should be subjugated and pushed back to the desert" was widely shared by Ottoman civilian and military office holders.[140] Ottomans also used terms such as *primitive, hoodlum, raider,* and *wild* to describe nomadic tribes. They were seen simply to be incompatible with the new institutions the Ottomans were creating. Earl Percy, in his travels in the Ottoman Empire, heard people describing the Kurds who were brought to Istanbul for the tribal school and the military as "savages." One *paşa* remarked to him that "it took the Russians nearly a hundred years to make anything of the Circassians, and they are not up to very much even now.[141]

In the Ottoman officials' changing discourse about tribal groups, and especially in the ramifications of their policies for the Arab provinces of the Ottoman Empire, one can see an attempt not only to recharge the empire but also to redefine it along the lines of the western European empires of the nineteenth century. Under this new alignment, the imperial center would be much more powerful, physical and social mobility across the ranks of the empire would be much more restricted, and the center would assume its own *mission civilisatrice* toward the backward peoples of the periphery.[142]

The Ottomans continued to empower the central institutions of the empire during the rest of the nineteenth century and create more specialized branches that dealt with questions of sedentarization and refugee settlement. Following his services in the Fırka-i Islahiyye and at Aleppo, Cevdet Paşa was appointed to the post of extraordinary reform commissioner to help settle tribes.[143] The commission on refugees that had been set up in the 1860s was expanded and given new powers under the name General Administration of the Commission of Refugees. A specially created office was attached to this body and given responsibility for dealing with new refugees.[144] The commission would determine where suitable vacant land was available, the extent of seed and other help the newcomers would need, and where such resources could be obtained. While settling tribes, the government tried to disarm and disperse them.[145]

The state was acquiring much more advanced and effective means of monitoring the implementation of its orders, to a degree hitherto unknown. Once refugees were directed to a place, delegations were dispatched from the center to make sure the overall process worked as planned.[146] When tribes were relocated across long distances, officers in both the place of origin and at the destination were enlisted to implement the order. In another marked departure from earlier practices in which petitioning the state was a widely accepted and effective way of seeking redress for peasants, the central government became unresponsive or dismissive when either peasants or tribal members complained about their settlement or relocation. In 1907, when a newly settled refugee community around Adapazarı filed a complaint because its rifles had been confiscated by the Public Debt Administration, the central government issued a blistering response that, instead of dealing with the question at hand, scolded the petitioners for presuming that they could address the government as a group. The response went on to describe the requirement that they would have to legally constitute themselves before they could act as a group, but it added that because the government was already acting as their representative, they did not need to create yet another intermediary body to protect their interests.[147] In the same year, when villagers around Adana protested the arrival of new refugees in their midst and their loss of land as a result, the government was unmoved. The petitioners were reminded that the land allocated for the refugees had been identified after lengthy inspections, and the region had plenty of arable land.[148]

The central government also requested reports about the behavior of tribes following their resettlement. If the tribes continued their unruliness, they were moved farther away and punished in new ways. The Kurdish Hemvends, with whom I opened this chapter, were one community subjected to repeated government orders and attention, especially in the last quarter of the nineteenth century. After causing numerous problems in the region between Baghdad, Mosul, and the Iranian border, and after some of their leaders escaped from Yemen, where they had been imprisoned, the Hemvends were divided into groups, and one part was forced to move to İşkodra (Scutari), in Albania, in 1886.[149] Those who remained in the area but refused to settle near their places of circulation around Mosul were pushed toward Adana, Ankara, Sivas, and Konya.[150] At the same time, orders were given for the confiscation and selling of their animals, so that they would have nothing to come back to.[151] Another group of Hemvends that continued to organize raids between Mosul and Kerkük was ejected and settled partly in İşkodra and partly in Benghazi, in Libya.[152] In the execution of this last order, the central government kept close watch as the Hemvends moved from around Mosul to Albania and Libya by way of İzmir.[153] In 1887, because of the growing cost of moving the Hemvends around the empire, the government ordered that some of their animals be sold and the money used to meet some of the expenses.[154]

Other Kurdish confederations that played prominent roles throughout the modern history of Iraq were also sources of concern for the Ottomans in the nineteenth century. In 1886 the vice director of the Ottoman Military Inspectorate (Teftiş-i Askeri Komsiyonu), İsmail Paşa, was given special powers, and the public prosecutor in Mosul was ordered to work with him to force the Berzenci and Talabani tribes to cease attacking each other and to quell banditry in the region.[155] Several months later the central government was alerted once again to conflict between these two confederations.[156] Two months after this, İsmail Paşa reported that the trial of the leaders of the two confederations was completed. Their weapons had been confiscated, and they had been ordered to abandon their nomadic and bandit ways.[157] In executing this order the government continued to use force. According to one estimate, 20,000 tribal members were killed between 1868 and 1890 as they were pushed to settle across the empire, giving rise to a rich folklore of pain and persecution at the hands of the state that became a central motif in the culture of these tribes long after they took up sedentary life.[158]

END OF NOMADISM, SURVIVAL OF TRIBALISM

Available data suggest that the number of settlements in tribal areas and villages associated with specific tribes steadily increased during the nineteenth century.[159] It also seems that the central government took special care to create as many mixed villages as possible, in order to break the cohesion of tribes as they took up settled life.[160] As a corollary to this trend, the data also show that the nomadic population in the Ottoman Empire declined during the same period—in Anatolia, by 26 percent between 1840 and 1890.[161] The Arab provinces underwent a similar decline. Around the province of Basra, the percentage of nomads declined from 50 to 19 between 1867 and 1905. Around Baghdad the decline was from 23 to 7 percent.[162]

The success of military operations, the pacification of the countryside, and the growing effectiveness of the new institutions led to periods of tranquility and even economic expansion in parts of the Ottoman Empire. The years between the end of the Crimean War and the late 1860s were one such period. Former chiefs and notables who had acquired title to large landholdings, as well as newly settled nomads and refugees, contributed to and benefited from the spread of these conditions. Economic opportunities provided further incentive for "self-settlement" as nomadic tribes sought to take part in the cultivation and trade of lucrative crops such as cotton and tobacco. In general the government played a supportive role in this regard by pushing tribes toward specific areas such as the wheat- and cotton-farming regions of central and southern Anatolia.[163] Even when the central government did not intervene, local practices were flexible enough that settled agriculture could expand fairly quickly by absorbing itinerant, migrant, and refugee workers. The *mush'a* system of landownership in the Arab regions was particularly conducive to such expansion, because it allowed for the allocation of parcels of land to newcomers as a way of incorporating them into local communities.[164]

By the early 1870s the empire was already facing difficulty in continuing the relative success of previous years. A decline in world prices for cotton, coupled with repeated occurrences of cholera and widespread malaria, severely affected the area around Adana, which had been one of the major areas of settlement for both nomads and refugees. It is estimated that as many as half the nomads who had been settled there died in the malaria epidemic of 1869.[165] The new institutions of the empire were further tested by the continuing stream of refugees from Crete, Serbia, Bulgaria, and the Caucasus. This stream gained momentum in the 1870s and became particularly large following the Russo-Turkish War of 1877–78. As many as 2 million Muslims left Russia and the Balkans for Ottoman lands after this war.[166] The effects of the sudden increase were truly chaotic for the Ottoman Empire. For most of these people, the first stop was Istanbul, where they had to wait—poor, hungry, and wounded—before permanent places could be found for them. The Turkish writer Halit Ziya Uşaklıgil described the heartbreaking scenes of cold and poverty that engulfed these refugees in Istanbul: "Mosques, prayer halls, lodges, and ruins were all filling slowly; death was persistent in claiming chunks of this humanity, but the spaces left behind were nowhere close to being sufficient to absorb the newcomers. Wherever there was a hole or a ditch, there went mothers hugging their babies, sick old people, and children crying and holding onto their mothers' legs—all Turkish Muslims refugees from the fires of war."[167]

The Russo-Turkish War of 1877–78 also created a secondary wave of migration of Circassians and Chechens who had been settled in Rumelia earlier in the nineteenth century. Claiming that they were creating transborder problems and disturbances, Russia insisted that the Ottoman government remove these communities from the Balkans. Between February and August 1878 the entire Circassian and Chechen populations of Thrace and Macedonia were dispersed into Anatolia and the Arab provinces.[168] The arrival of tens of thousands of Circassians and Chechens in their midst aroused deep resentment among the local groups, who were unhappy with the support the refugees received from the central government and saw them as little more than agents of the Porte.[169] In reality, like many other communities that became part of the empire's policy of settlement and sedentarization, Circassians presented a more varied and complex picture. Many of them resented their new places and claimed that the land and resources given to them were insufficient. In time, some of them became famous for their fierce independence and banditry, generating a strong reaction from the central government.[170] The most significant outcome of the chaos following the 1877–78 war was the return to their homes and property of the tribal chiefs who had been exiled to the Balkans. They reassumed leadership, and some of them took up arms against the central government.[171]

While the war was a decisive blow to the order established earlier in the nineteenth century, the other factor that undermined centralization was the persistent strength of tribal relations, which continued to concentrate power in localities. The ties that connected tribal members to one another proved to be expansive, flexible, and adaptive to the requirements of the centralizing Ottoman state. The result was that economic growth achieved during periods such as the mid-nineteenth century unraveled easily when conditions changed or new elements such as wars entered the picture. Under such circumstances, the tribes could rally their people and even restore some of their nomadic practices, so that no linear or definitive transition from nomadic to settled order took place in any part of the Ottoman Empire. More typically one sees a cyclical alternation between nomadism and sedentary life, sometimes involving the same communities. These patterns and transitions were supported by the continuing strength of tribal relations.[172]

The reasons for this fluctuating pattern of sedentarization lay in the policies of the Ottoman state, which continued to rely on tribal leaders for their implementation. In essence, Ottoman officials were forced to negotiate with the very elements whose power they were trying to curb. It almost always fell on the tribal chiefs, for example, to guarantee that their tribes would stay in their designated places of settlement.[173] If they did not, the chiefs would bear the brunt of punishment. In return the chiefs were given better-quality land, were granted privileged access to higher echelons of the bureaucracy, and were rewarded with posts, salaries, medals, and lump-sum payments. Allowing tribes to settle on familiar ground around their winter pastures and to continue practicing animal husbandry were other concessions the central government made in its dealings with tribes. Sometimes the very act of settlement helped reinforce tribal organization and identity, because now a tribe had to deal with new contingencies such as gaining access to water, which could be achieved only as a group and even in cooperation with other tribes.[174]

A well-known example of the Ottoman policy of using some tribes to suppress, punish, and settle others is the constitution and operation of the Hamidiye regiments. These were formed in 1892 and were staffed exclusively by Sunni Kurds, who were given a free hand and strong government backing to pacify Alevi Kurds and Armenian and other non-Muslim minorities in eastern Anatolia. The tribes that were recruited into the Hamidiye stayed together as tribes and were led by their own chiefs. Their number increased from about forty regiments in 1892 to sixty-three in 1899.[175] During the late nineteenth and early twentieth centuries the Hamidiye became well known for their brutality. They raided the property of rival Kurdish tribes and especially of Armenians and pushed them out of their land.

In this and other instances, instead of being subsumed under the centralizing power of the state while serving the government, tribal chiefs enhanced their positions and became even more powerful and indispensable. Some of the chiefs created local networks of administration that looked like replicas of the imperial institutions. Ibrahim Paşa of the Milan tribe, who was made a Hamidiye commander, became so powerful that he was referred to as the "uncrowned king of Kurdistan." In the course of his depredations, when he laid siege to the city of Diyarbakır, the local population reacted by occupying the post office and staging a demonstration to force the central government to move Ibrahim's troops to Hejaz.[176] Indeed, with the growing power of the Hamidiye, it was as if a parallel power structure had been inserted into the provinces, one that received its authority directly from the sultan and whose operations undermined the work of the newly reformed civilian judicial structures.

Hence, to a large extent it was the bonds of mutual help and cooperation that the central government forged between its new institutions and some of the tribal chiefs that made tribalism so resilient. Until 1852 governors regularly invited Kurdish and Arab tribal sheikhs to provincial centers and gave them gifts and money in special ceremonies held in their honor. The tribal leaders freely used the fact that they were recognized by the central government to further their authority over their followers.[177] Although this practice of recognition was formally abolished in 1852, local governors continued to use it, with the knowledge of the imperial center.

In many other ways the central government helped strengthen the power and prestige of tribal leaders in order to use them as allies in furthering its reform agenda. For example, Sultan Abdülhamid gave a large portion of the land around Sülaymaniye to two brothers who were among the leading sheikhs of the Kurdish Caf tribe, which had been particularly loyal to the central government. In the course of the nineteenth century, and especially during the long reign of Abdülhamid, the government became particularly keen on courting the Nakşibendi Kurdish sheikhs, who had large followings and were active in educating and providing social services in their regions. The Ottoman government hoped the religious orders, or *tarikats*, would cut across tribal identities and unify the populace. In order to help them along, the imperial center set up endowments, provided food aid to these religious communities, and even paid their leaders salaries. In 1880 the sheikh of the Kadiri *tarikat* in Kerkük, Abdülbaki efendi, received, as an endowment for the benefit of his order, the revenue of eleven villages.[178] When the Persian state tried to lure some of these communities away by providing similar enticements, the Ottomans expanded their own help and support.[179] In 1892 the leader of the Ravala tribe in Syria was rewarded with an audience with Sultan Abdülhamid in Istanbul and was given a decoration and the title of *paşa* in return for his services.[180] Even the Hemvends, who never ceased being a source of trouble for the central government, were allowed to import agricultural machinery without paying customs duties. Their chiefs were paid salaries, and they were employed as armed guards.[181] According to Andrew Gordon Gould, as of 1881, 34,775 *kuruş* a month was being paid in salaries to 140 tribal and other notables.[182]

From the long-term perspective, there is little doubt that the Ottoman state became formally more centralized and more powerful, and the Ottoman landscape became more orderly and settled, in the course of the nineteenth and early twentieth centuries. But the formal strengthening of state institutions went hand in hand not only with the survival of tribes but also with the reinforcement of tribal identities among Kurdish, Arab, Türkmen, and other tribes in the Ottoman Empire.[183] Indeed, it can be argued that the breaking of the emirates—the large tribal conglomerations and confederations—paved the way for the reemergence and restrengthening of lower-level tribal identities across the empire. What is interesting about groupings and sentiments on this level is that they were locally focused. Mark Sykes, who traveled in the Kurdish areas with the goal of describing the lives and work of as many of the Kurdish tribes as possible in the early twentieth century, found a broad spectrum of communities. He described tribes that were sedentary, nomadic, and in-between, and tribes that were Christian, Sunni, and Alevi. Some Türkmen tribes spoke Kurdish, and some Kurdish tribes spoke Turkish. Different Kurdish tribes spoke dialects that were not always mutually comprehensible. Some tribes, especially Armenians, were in close relationship and interaction with other groups in the area; others were completely cut off from each other and the outside world. Some maintained close connections with people in neighboring countries. Most of the tribes were well armed, defending themselves not only against the incursions of the central government but also against each other. Among the communities in the mountains around Hakkari, the Süryani tribes were well known for their fierceness and warlike qualities. At the same time, the Süryani communities, along with the Chaldeans, maintained some of the strongest ties with the outside world.[184] Earl Percy even wrote about the chief of the Süryani Jelu tribe, whose son had traveled to Europe and could speak six languages.[185] Descriptions also exist of "mixed" tribes that had become so as a result of marriages across ethnic lines.[186] Such crossings and interpenetrations were particularly typical of Nakşibendi Sufi communities, which were widespread among Kurds.

What is perhaps most remarkable is that many of the Kurdish tribal figures Sykes spoke with insisted on their rights to their land and to various exemptions by referring to the dispensations they had received from Sultan Selim I in the sixteenth century. In a culture with little written tradition, it was only in tribal oral traditions that such knowledge was transmitted across the centuries, and this only strengthened the ties that bound tribes as units.[187] There was little possibility for alliances among such disparate groups. If anything, intense rivalries set them against each other, rivalries shaped by the new opportunities being offered by the newly reformed and centralized Ottoman government. Alliances across tribal lines were formed only along religious axes facilitated by the religious orders, and these turned into social movements not for clearly defined Kurdish national reasons but for more specifically focused religious purposes. Over the rest of the nineteenth and twentieth centuries, what survived and became even more vivid was not a clear and coherent sense of Kurdishness but tribes such as the Hemvends, Talabanis, Barzanis, and Arab Shammar, who were still forcing powerful countries such as the United States to work and negotiate with them in the twenty-first century. The Ottoman policies of not always disarming the Kurds, preferring to rule large sections of Kurdistan through local tribal leaders, and recruiting Kurds into the Ottoman army as tribal regiments or rural guards contributed to the survival of these units. In addition, the powerful pull of the familiar kept tribal communities together. This close and powerful sense of community survived even the Ottoman government's most persistent attempts at dispersal—as in the case of the Hemvends, some of whom found a way of trekking back to Mosul from Benghazi in the closing years of the twentieth century.[188]

5 The Immovable State

In the history covered in the previous chapters, Ottoman state policies toward mobility changed from being supportive and protective of nomads, migrants, and refugees to being restrictive and even antagonistic. The official policy of upholding the empire's heterogeneous social structure through institutional reform, selective sedentarization, and the crafting of an Ottomanist worldview clashed with the narrowly conceived nationalisms that enveloped and divided many communities in the Ottoman Empire in the eighteenth and nineteenth centuries. Like all other modern states, the Ottoman-Turkish state preferred to anchor its institutions in stable social structures. In a world of nation-states, census taking, conscription, taxation, defense, and the maintenance of security could be carried out only by working with an easily identifiable and classifiable population within well-defined borders. On a general level, the move from empire to modern state involved a shift from a society that was highly mobile and open to one that was sedentary, increasingly fragmented, and closed.

Still, it is inaccurate to posit a sharp divide between empire and modern state in terms of the degree to which cosmopolitan imperialist and ethnically pure nationalist sentiments prevailed in each or the extent of mobility that characterized the two. Many urban notables, merchants, and intellectuals from different ethnic and religious backgrounds participated in the reforms of the nineteenth century that sought to centralize and strengthen the imperial government. They took part as delegates or electors in the six parliamentary elections held in the Ottoman Empire between 1876 and 1919.[1] In the parliaments elected in 1908, 1912, and 1914, 30 to 40 percent of the delegates consisted of Greeks, Armenians, Jews, Arabs, Kurds, and Albanians.[2]

As for the mobility of various communities, I have shown in previous chapters that as Ottoman officials developed new ways of containing the mobile populations, they met with resistance from these groups. More often than not officials had to collaborate with nomadic tribes and other migratory groups in order to carry out their reform policies. Without the help of these groups, it would have been impossible for the new institutions of the Ottoman state to extend their reach into the far corners of the empire. As a result, the Ottomans' sedentarization policies entailed the further empowering and entrenchment of some nomadic and other migratory communities in various parts of the empire. The interests of these groups came to be embedded in the institutions and practices of modern states in the late and post-Ottoman world, making these societies particularly open to resuming migratory patterns and connecting with regional and global flows depending on shifts in prevailing conditions.

In addition to long-term patterns of internal migration, which were never completely contained, the Ottoman Empire experienced one of the largest movements of people in human history during the creation of new states in the Balkans and the Middle East in the 1910s and 1920s. In the decade between the First Balkan War in 1912 and the end of Turkey's war with Greece in 1922, as many as 3.5 million Christians (Greeks, Bulgarians, Armenians) and Muslims in the affected areas were forced to leave their homes.[3] These migrations involved the "unmixing" of populations, whereby a large part of the Ottoman (as well as the Austro-Hungarian) Empire was divided into nation-states.[4] With the encouragement of intellectuals and some clergy, political leaders tried to remake these lands and societies so that people who lived in any one of the newly created entities were as "ethnically pure" as possible. What this meant and how it would be achieved was not clear to anybody involved in the process. In the end, largely through arbitrary measures and accidental means and dependent upon contingent factors, people who lived in this part of the world were defined as belonging to different nationalities. Drawing such political and ideological boundaries inevitably excluded some people for reasons having to do with their religion, ethnic background, or other factors that were neither clear nor consistent.

The consequences of these interventions were disastrous for those who found themselves on the wrong side of a real or imaginary line of demarcation.[5] They were expelled, destroyed, or forced to submit to the priorities of dominant groups. The massive movement of populations that took place at the end of the empire resulted for the most part from these measures. Unlike earlier population movements, which had no clear ethnic pattern and were integral to the organization and functioning of the Ottoman Empire, the migrations of the late nineteenth and early twentieth centuries were based almost exclusively on some aspect of the identity of the people involved. They portended the end of the empire. This great shuffle of population would leave an indelible mark on the people and institutions of the new Turkish and other states in the region.

Even as the Ottoman Empire was undergoing partitioning and forced migrations, the circulation of people within its borders continued. Workers, especially Greeks, moved back and forth between parts of Anatolia and between western Anatolia, the Aegean islands, the Greek mainland, and places beyond. Nomads and other rural people traveled long distances to work in harvests in southern Anatolia, and itinerant merchants continued to conduct business straddling the rapidly changing borders of the old and new states.[6] Despite 200 years of effort to create a sedentary order, people in the Ottoman Empire appeared to be even more mobile than ever at the turn of the twentieth century. Indeed, some reforms, such as the abolition of corvée, made migration even more likely for certain people. As Gersaimos Augustinos summarized it, "Asia Minor, for both Muslim and non-Muslim, had become a land full of human wandering in the late nineteenth century."[7]

In the following pages I briefly review the three big waves of population movement of the first decades of the twentieth century: refugee movements during and after the Balkan Wars of 1912–13, the expulsions and exchanges of World War I, and refugee flows and the exchange of Greek Orthodox and Muslim populations during and after the Second Greco-Turkish War of 1919–22. I discuss the role of states in each of these waves, as well as their implications for the rise of new states in the Balkans and the Middle East. What follows is not an exhaustive account of these migrations but an overview highlighting differences between the population movements that made the Ottoman Empire and those that unmade it.

The Balkan Wars were a many-sided conflagration of persecution, punishment, and bloodletting that involved Greeks, Bulgarians, Albanians, Serbs, and Muslim Turks. Hundreds of thousands of terrorized civilians in the Balkans were subjected to unprecedented violence in 1912 and 1913 by the many armies either occupying their land or retreating through it and by their local supporters and enablers. Intertwined with deportations and mass killings intended to serve nationalist causes by creating homogeneous communities were many instances of everyday violence. Men, women, and children were killed so that their property could be stolen, old scores settled, or others frightened into leaving. In this violent entanglement, no group can consistently be identified as either the victim or the perpetrator. Muslims, Bulgarians, and Greeks went after one another using exactly the same tactics. And no group or even the armies that confronted each other were homogeneous or "national," because their respective states were undergoing their own processes of separation and unmixing. Often, people of the same ethnicity found themselves on opposite sides of a battle line, fighting each other in different armies.[8]

The ultimate outcome of the Balkan Wars was the ungluing of a society that had been held together with the help of multiple local alliances and the supervision of a powerful state for many centuries. This disintegration took place in several steps. First, the Muslim population in Macedonia was pushed toward Salonica by the advancing armies of the Greeks, Serbs, and Bulgarians in 1912. After Bulgaria quit the alliance, fought its erstwhile friends in 1913, and lost, the Bulgarian population had little choice but to follow the retreating Bulgarian army. Following this, the Greek population was expelled from areas ceded to Bulgaria with the treaty of Bucharest in 1913. Within less than a year, a refugee problem on an unprecedented scale had developed in the Balkans. A special commission convened by the Carnegie Foundation counted 135,000 Muslim refugees in Salonica, 111,500 Bulgarians escaping the Greek army in Thrace and Macedonia, and 100,000 Greeks escaping Bulgarian rule in 1914. According to the commission's report, the situation was one of "real exodus," in which "the Turks are fleeing before Christians, the Bulgarians before the Greeks and the Turks, the Greeks and the Turks before the Bulgarians, the Albanians before the Servians."[9]

Migrations that began during the Balkan Wars reached even greater levels during World War I. The Ottoman government expelled more than 100,000 Greeks from the Aegean littoral to the islands and to Greece in 1914. Of the remaining Greek population, some of the men were sent east to work at road construction and other hard labor. In the following year, as many as 1 million Armenians were forcefully removed from their homes all across Anatolia to be resettled in northern Syria. Most of them were murdered on their way to Syria by the regular and irregular troops of the Ottoman army.

The uprooting of the Armenian population of Anatolia was a policy unilaterally conceived and implemented by the Ottoman government. It resulted in the destruction of the entire Armenian population of Anatolia, which had stood at more than 1 million before World War I.[10] But although the events of 1915 marked the end of Armenian life in Anatolia, the persecution of Armenians in the Ottoman Empire had begun earlier, in the nineteenth century. Waves of mass killings in the second half of that century, which claimed the lives of tens of thousands Armenians, were linked more to the Islamist than to the Turkish-nationalist turn in Ottoman policy.[11] In comparison with the mass killings of 1915, the earlier episodes were more contained, both temporally and regionally. Nevertheless, the 1894–96 events paved the way for subsequent persecutions and massacres, and as such they represent a turning point in relations between Armenians, their Ottoman rulers, and the Muslim groups of the Ottoman Empire.[12]

Several types of sources that have become available provide a clear picture of what happened in 1915. Among these are the reports of American missionaries who were active among the Armenians in eastern Anatolia.[13] Representatives of foreign governments, especially the American consuls in the area and the U.S. ambassador, Henry Morgenthau, also tried to publicize the suffering of the Armenians and intervene on their behalf. Morgenthau in particular was relentless in pleading with Ottoman officials and trying to rally public support in the United States.[14] Although access to official records of the Ottoman government remains restricted, some government officials and other observers published their observations and experiences during those years.[15] A growing body of writings reflects the firsthand experiences of survivors, either directly or through their children and grandchildren.[16] Finally, in recent years, children and grandchildren of Armenian orphans who were brought up as Muslims and of the small number of Armenians who remained in Turkey have begun to publish their own accounts and memoirs, filling in a key part of the historical record.[17]

These disparate sources agree in several areas, leaving little doubt about the nature and consequences of the Ottoman government's policy toward Armenians in 1915. One point of agreement is that Armenian families were given little or no warning before their expulsion. In almost all cases they had to leave their homes with hardly anything, and whatever they tried to carry was stolen from them en route. They either walked or were transported in cargo trains. Ahmet Refik, who was stationed in Eskişehir in 1915, described "women with crying children in their arms, unshaven fathers trying to carry their possessions in sacks on their shoulders, thousands of exhausted, sick, poor, and desperate families from all kinds of backgrounds trying to get off the train." He wrote that in a few days, as many as 20,000 Armenian families were camped by the train station.[18] After several days all these families, along with the mostly wealthy Armenians of Eskişehir, were marched out of town. In some cases Armenians were permitted to sell their property, but they had to do so in such a short time that even those who managed to sell could not get a fair value for their homes, land, or belongings. In most cases, even if they found buyers, they were forced to turn over their money to government officials.[19]

The new documentation leaves little room for doubt that the government's plan for evacuation was conceived and executed in a way meant to be as comprehensive as possible. Even though the Armenians in Istanbul, İzmir, and Aleppo were supposed to be exempted from orders of deportation, many Armenian intellectuals and political leaders were arrested in Istanbul and sent to eastern Anatolia in 1915. According to Morgenthau, "practically all other places where a single Armenian family lived now became scenes of unspeakable tragedies. Scarcely a single Armenian, whatever his education or wealth or whatever the social class to which he belonged, was exempt from the order."[20] Ahmet Refik wrote, "The right thing to do for a just and self-assured government under these circumstances would be to punish only those who had participated in armed rebellion against the state. But the CUP [Committee of Union and Progress] government decided to wipe out the entire Armenian population and solve the problem of six [Armenian] provinces in this way."[21] Halil Bey, who was president of the Ottoman parliament at the time, wrote in his memoirs about visiting the minister of the interior, Talat Bey, who is generally known as the architect of the plan to deport the Armenians. Halil Bey said that he found Talat deeply disturbed. He told Halil that he had heard very sad things concerning Armenians from the governor of Erzurum. "But," he said, "if I had not done this to them (meaning the Armenians) they would have done the same to my people—they had even started doing it. This is a struggle for national survival."[22] Some of the peasants who nowadays live in formerly Armenian villages in Turkey are aware of the history of their localities and are willing talk about what they know. A sixty-six-year-old woman living close to Elazığ, formerly a major center of Armenian life in the Ottoman Empire, spoke to a reporter in 2000, telling him that "they took the Armenians up there and killed them . . . they dug a hole for the bodies." She said that her grandmother had witnessed these events.[23]

All these sources, especially the survivors' stories, point out the prominent role played by Kurdish, Circassian, Bedouin, and other tribal irregular fighting units in the harassment, rape, and murder of countless civilians. As I discussed earlier, the purpose of constituting these auxiliary units was to draw the tribes to the government's side and entice them to settle down. Ahmet Refik described "murderers and thieves" who were released from prison and sent to Anatolia for this purpose.[24] He wrote about his conversation with a Circassian chief, Ahmet, who boasted of having cleared the entire province of Van. He said, "Today, you cannot find even a single Armenian there."[25] Far from being innocent bystanders, the regular military and the gendarmerie encouraged these groups, sometimes arming and protecting them and using them as auxiliary fighting forces.

Although the role played by Kurds and Circassians is well known, some of the literature, especially retrospective analyses of these events, tends to speak of these groups and the Turks as if they were homogeneous, acting in unison everywhere, all the time. But divisions within each of the groups ran deep. They had to do with language, religion, class, and region, as well as with political persuasion and preferences. Even during the most difficult years of the late nineteenth century, these divisions had made it possible for different political projects to develop among the Armenians, and important lines of communication and collaboration had developed between some Armenians and the CUP.[26] Similarly, it is unrealistic to imagine Kurds, Turks, and Armenians as uniformly constituted communities acting in opposition to one another. The missionary Henry Riggs wrote that some of the Kurdish tribes near Harput helped and protected

Armenians in 1915, mostly because of their own disagreements with the Ottoman government.[27] In western Anatolia, villagers have described how some Armenian youths stood guard outside the homes of Muslim villagers to protect them from occupying Greek troops in 1919.[28]

One source of debate among historians is whether an actual order for deportation was ever given, and if so, whether the government followed any legal procedure in designing this policy, to attempt to protect civilians.[29] This debate will never be settled to everyone's satisfaction, but it is known that it was only in May 1915, when the deportations were already being carried out, that the Ottoman government issued a decree providing legal cover for its actions. With this decree, the military was given the power to deport anyone whose loyalty was deemed suspect or whose activities suggested that he or she might be a spy or otherwise involved in treasonous activities.[30] Not only Armenians but also some Greeks, Jews, Chaldeans, and Nestorians were expelled from parts of the empire under this ruling, although in much smaller numbers.[31] Starting in 1916, the Ottoman government also relocated more than 5,000 Arab families from Syria to faraway places such as Edirne, Bursa, and İzmir as punishment for their Arabist policies.[32] Meanwhile, the flow of refugees into the shrinking empire, which had started in the late eighteenth century, continued. More than 400,000 Muslim refugees arrived from the Balkans and were settled in parts of Anatolia between 1912 and 1920.[33] Another 200,000 mostly Kurdish refugees fled the Bolshevik revolution in Russia and the war in Iran and took refuge in the eastern provinces of Diyarbakır, Mosul, and Urfa in 1917.[34]

Wartime purges and deportations continued to swell the numbers of people concentrating along the constantly shifting borders in the Balkans. At the end of World War I, Greece, Bulgaria, and the Ottoman Empire agreed to the voluntary exchange of populations in border areas in order to ease the pressure there. The Ottoman government was particularly interested in attracting certain Muslim communities from Bulgaria and Greece in order to boost security along the borders and to prevent their assimilation into Christian societies.[35] The idea of this planned and voluntary resettlement of people was quickly abandoned once war broke out between Greece and Turkey in 1919. During the war, which lasted until 1922, 300,000 Greeks and Armenians who had been expelled by the Ottoman government in 1914 returned to areas administered by occupying

Greek and French armies in western and southern Anatolia. The Greek administration resettled additional Greeks and Armenians in western Anatolia in order to alter the ethnic composition of people there.[36] This meant that Muslim inhabitants, some of whom had come as war refugees from the Balkans, lost their homes and became refugees all over again. They would return to western Anatolia only after the defeat and expulsion of the Greek army in September 1922 and the declaration of the Republic of Turkey the following year.

Almost the entire Greek and Armenian population of western Anatolia retreated from the interior along with the Greek army in 1922. Once these refugees arrived in İzmir, they were pushed onto the quay, where they were squeezed between the city, which was on fire and being taken over by Turkish nationalist forces, and the sea, where ships of the Allied Powers were anchored but refused to take the refugees on board. Large numbers of Greeks, Armenians, and Jews had also escaped to Istanbul and stayed in hospitals, schools, and churches. In the meantime, the Greek population of northern Anatolia was pushed into the coastal area between Trabzon and Samsun, where the people awaited ships that would take them to Greece. They had to find any means of transportation they could in order to get to the coast. Most of them ended up loading their possessions on animal carts and walking hundreds of miles, because trains were still rudimentary and charged high prices. Conditions on the roads and in the coastal areas deteriorated quickly. The accounts of survivors of these marches are full of rapes, robberies, disease, and death.[37] The new Turkish state, whose institutions were not yet fully formed, was in no position to contain the crisis. Indeed, for their own political and ideological goals, some agencies in the Turkish state actually helped pushed the process forward, making things worse for the people caught up in it.

In the fall of 1922, as a first step toward gaining control, the Turkish government began arresting young Christian men in the coastal areas and sending them to the interior and to the east to work on reconstruction projects. They also issued an ultimatum to Greece and other foreign governments to evacuate their remaining nationals in coastal towns.[38] Finally, Turkey and Greece reached an agreement for the mandatory exchange of populations in January 1924. It covered the remaining Greek residents of Anatolia—determined solely by their religion—and the Muslim residents of western Thrace. More than 1 million Greeks left Anatolia, and about

500,000 Muslim "Turks" made the opposite journey, moving into Turkey from northern Greece before, during, and after World War I and the Greco-Turkish War.[39]

The exchange of populations was supposed to be carried out in an orderly fashion. Special commissions were formed to record the identities and property of people leaving either country, so that they could be compensated adequately. The Turkish government established a new Ministry of Construction and Settlement shortly after the exchange treaty was signed, reflecting the importance and scope of the task at hand. In practice, however, the process unfolded chaotically. To begin with, the very definition of who would be exchanged was by no means clear. The broad definition of Greeks on the basis of religion included, for example, Orthodox Christian Arabs who belonged to the patriarchate in Antakya and had no relationship to Greece whatsoever. Although these people were eventually excluded from the treaty, the Turkish government continued to harass and try to expel them in subsequent years.[40] The Turkish-speaking Anatolian Greeks, known as Karamanlis, presented a different problem. Originally they assumed they would not be included in the treaty. They spoke no Greek, and their lives were thoroughly integrated into Anatolia and intertwined with those of other communities there. Even the Turkish delegation to the conference that produced the Treaty of Lausanne, whereby the Turkish republic gained international recognition, appeared to appreciate the special status of the Karamanlis, referring to them as "our Orthodox Turkish citizens." The Karamanlis waited as long as they could, hoping to win an exclusion, but in the end they were included in the treaty and deported in 1924.[41]

Although the new Ministry of Construction and Settlement was supposed to bring some clarity and coordination to the population exchange, in practice it went little farther than adding a new layer of bureaucracy to an issue so complicated that it demanded the attention of the entire Turkish government. People who had been sent into internal exile were detained in the interior and were not permitted to return to their homes to take care of their business and dispose of their property before leaving for Greece. They were required to make their way to one of the designated ports, where they were kept under difficult circumstances before embarking on ships that eventually came to transfer them.[42] Typically, women and children were deported separately from the men, and families were to be reunited in Greece.[43] The deportees had no hope of accessing their savings or collecting their debts.[44] They had to pay for their own and their animals' transportation, both overland and aboard ships. There was no way for the overburdened bureaucracy of the new state to keep track of the identities and property of roughly a million people. Having lost any resources they might have had, many of the deportees ended up walking barefoot long distances, which made them even more vulnerable to disease and attacks. The League of Nations, which monitored the exchange, estimated that of the more than 1 million refugees who arrived in Greece during and after the Greco-Turkish War, at most 300,000 came with sufficient resources to provide for themselves.[45] Ernest Hemingway, who was a reporter for the *Toronto Star* at the time, watched some of the Greek refugees as they crossed the Maritza River into Greece: "It is a silent procession. Nobody even grunts. It is all they can do to keep moving. Their brilliant peasant costumes are soaked and draggled. Chickens dangle by their feet from the carts. . . . A husband spreads a blanket over a woman in labor in one of the carts to keep off the driving rain. She is the only person making a sound. Her little daughter looks at her in horror and begins to cry. And the procession keeps moving."[46]

Once in Greece, the Anatolian refugees found that the best land vacated by the expelled Muslims, which was supposed to be used for their settlement, had already been confiscated by local people. Greeks greeted them with suspicion, resentment, and outright hostility. In several instances, local villagers even used force to prevent refugees from settling.[47] Although they had been expelled from Anatolia on the grounds that they were "Greeks," these people had more in common with other Anatolians than they did with the Greeks of Greece. Some did not even speak Greek. This led to further animosity and discrimination by locals. The immigrants were called names such as "sons of Turks," "baptized in yoghurt," and simply "Turks."[48] As a result, they gravitated toward their own communities and sought security among other refugees, keeping alive not only their memories of home but also their distinct culture and their ties, real and imagined, to Turkey. Decades after the events of the 1920s, one could still find in Greek cities refugee quarters such as Nea Philadelphia and Nea Smyrni, named after towns in Anatolia.[49]

Although their numbers were fewer, the experience of the Muslims leaving Greece was no easier. Conditions of travel to Greek ports from the hinterland and then transport to Turkey were extremely difficult. Like the Anatolian Greeks, Muslim deportees had to pay for the transport of their families and possessions. The owners of Turkish ships that were sent to carry them to Turkey insisted that payment be made in Turkish currency, which created opportunities for profiteers who camped in the ports. The two governments were eager to complete the process as quickly as possible, which made it necessary to carry out most of the exchange in the coldest months of winter, on vessels that were unsuitable for human travel.[50] So compressed was the process that a Muslim immigrant who was settled in Bursa described how, before leaving Greece, his family had to share its home with a family that had been expelled from Turkey. The two families lived together for six months, sharing their meager resources, before the Muslim family could leave for Turkey.[51]

An incoming refugee population that constituted one-quarter of the entire population of Greece made the population transfer a particularly difficult problem for Greece. But even though the number of Muslims was considerably smaller and Turkey's land mass larger, the Turkish government was constrained by the restrictions imposed on it by the victorious allies at the end of World War I.[52] Furthermore, unlike Greece, which received a loan from the League of Nations and was aided by an international commission, the Turkish government was on its own.

The new ministry in Turkey divided the country into ten major areas of settlement, corresponding to the areas where the deported Greeks and Armenians had lived. The Turkish government also divided the arriving Muslims into professions so that the land and property left behind by the Greeks and Armenians could be distributed to them according to their qualifications. But most of this property had been quickly claimed by local people, particularly officials—including some members of the settlement commissions—for their private use or for sale.[53] The first minister of construction and settlement, Mustafa Necati Bey, reported that of more than 100,000 houses abandoned by Greeks, no more than 25 percent were in the hands of the government.[54] Also, what was recorded did not always correspond to reality, which meant that people found themselves in places and with resources they did not know how to use.[55] This led to a secondary wave of migration in which people left their designated places of settlement. In response, the government passed a law in 1928 requiring that the immigrants stay on the land they were given for at least five years.[56] As a result of all this, Ottoman-Turkish agriculture suffered a serious setback during this transition period. Especially in the west, vineyards were left unattended, harvests were neglected, and one of the most prosperous and commercialized parts of Anatolia regressed considerably from the level of economic development it had reached in the nineteenth century.

There was, however, one aspect of this sad history in which the specialized offices of the Tanzimat and its aftermath worked the way they were supposed to. The information that the Ottoman government had collected proved indispensable for identifying and deporting almost the entire Greek and Armenian population of Anatolia between 1915 and 1923. The Greek population in the parts of the Ottoman Empire that subsequently became the Republic of Turkey was 1,540,359 in 1906–7. By 1927, when the new state conducted its first census, the count had dropped to 119,822. The numbers for Armenians in 1906–7 and 1927 were 1,031,708 and 64,745, respectively.[57]

There is no doubt that the mandatory uprooting of so many people from Anatolia in a relatively short time further wounded and crippled a society that had already suffered ten years of constant warfare, occupation, and destruction. For one thing, a significant part of the Greeks and Armenians who were eliminated from Anatolia in the early twentieth century came from an urbanized, artisan, and mercantile background. The loss of such a vital component of late Ottoman society could only have deeply a negative effect on Turkey's economy. It would take more than two decades for the rate of economic growth in Turkey to reach the growth rate that the Ottoman economy had attained before World War I.[58]

NATIONALISM AS CAUSE AND EFFECT

Both the exchange of population with Greece and the punitive measures taken against the Armenians targeted these ethnic groups without making distinctions on the basis of age, gender, income, legal status, or crimes people might have committed. The president of the Ottoman parliament stated clearly that the Greeks and Bulgarians were being expelled from the border regions en masse as retaliation for the perceived disloyalty of some of them during the Balkan Wars.[59] Both at the time and today, all explanations and justifications of the empire's policy toward the Armenians refer to the revolt of Armenian nationalist groups or the willingness of some of them to fight on the side of the Russians. Similar arguments were made for pushing the Greek population out of Anatolia, as if all Armenians had been in nationalist movements and all Greeks helped the occupying Greek army. This increasingly rigid and totalizing approach toward ethnic groups reflected a significant change in the way the Ottoman government approached its subject peoples in the late nineteenth and early twentieth centuries. And for this reason, I want to emphasize the substantive differences between the population movements instigated by the Ottoman government in previous centuries and those that affected the empire's Christian communities in the early twentieth century. So novel was this new way of identifying people and designing policy that even Ahmet Rıza, an important nationalist member of the CUP who was not known for his liberal views, criticized his party's pro-Turkish turn in 1916.[60]

It is difficult to ignore the decisive role played by nascent Turkish nationalism in the formulation and execution of the policies that targeted Greeks and Armenians in Anatolia in the first two decades of the twentieth century. Yet rather than being a fully formed ideological framework that led to staunchly nationalist policies, Turkish nationalism was still taking shape in these years. Indeed, it was the speed and efficiency with which Anatolia was remade that helped strengthen this ideology and renewed the self-confidence of the officials and laypeople who believed in it. Regardless of whether or not it had any bearing on reality, a degree of national homogeneity came to be seen by some ideologues and politicians as necessary for the preservation of Ottoman and then Turkish independence.

But the road from the Ottoman imperial kaleidoscope to the rigidly defined world of the successor nation-states was full of false starts, reversals, and uncharted alternatives. Initially, the idea of Turkish nationalism was used alongside policies that still reflected the imperial structures and priorities of the Ottoman government. Islam was considered a plausible tool to be used in reaction to the nationalisms of the Balkan peoples.[61] For example, toward the end of the nineteenth century the Ottoman government all but stopped accepting non-Muslim refugees while banning the emigration of Muslims.[62] But over time, especially when faced with Albanian nationalism and the Arab revolt, the Ottoman government became increasingly focused on an ethnically defined Turkish nationalism.[63] A law passed in 1916 made the use of Turkish mandatory for all companies in their correspondence and documents.[64] In the same year, the names of some villages and towns were changed from Kurdish and Armenian to Turkish.[65] In the end, the broad canvas that had been created with the institutional reforms and sedentarization policies of the previous centuries was broken down and given new content and substance with the emergence and strengthening of increasingly precise ideas and ideologies of national identity and the social movements these inspired.

The determining factor that prepared the ground for the transition to a more limited definition of identity was the international conjuncture. The territorial settlements reached at the end of World War I fractured the space in which alternative histories had been taking shape and made it possible for nationalist ideologies to gain strength. A similar shift is clearly observable in the other states that succeeded the Ottoman Empire, particularly in Greece.[66] The government there used the Anatolian immigrants to solidify its position and to increase the Greek proportion of the population in northern Greece and Macedonia. In both places the transition involved an increasingly essentialist definition of identity.

Kurds, who did not fit the idea of national homogeneity but who remained inside Turkey, became a major problem for the late Ottoman and the new Turkish state. Kurdish tribes were repeatedly relocated, and they and their leaders were constantly persecuted, despite the fact that some Kurdish tribes had fought on the side of the nationalist forces during the Greco-Turkish War.[67] The decision to set up a General Directorate of Tribes and Refugees in 1916 had mentioned "civilizing tribes" and preventing their movement as among the key mandates of the new agency.[68] In moving the Kurdish tribes, the late Ottoman and early Turkish governments were much more conscious of the ethnic and religious consequences of their decision than they had been in earlier decisions. Tribal leaders were separated from their followers, and officers were cautioned to disperse the Kurdish element so that there would be no heavy concentrations in their places of settlement.[69] In a continuation of the policy of encouraging individuation, which had started earlier in the nineteenth century, the government's orders of settlement during World War I emphasized the need to "undermine the migratory habits of the tribes" and "eradicate their distinct habits and languages."[70] The relocation of Kurds would remain a constant feature of the new state's eastern policy beginning in the 1920s and continuing into the twenty-first century.

But it was in the deportation and murder of Armenians and the mandatory exchange of Anatolian Greeks for the Muslims of western Thrace that the ethnic and racial definition of Turkishness became irreversibly important. It was the Turkish side that insisted on making the population exchange mandatory and designed it to be as comprehensive as possible.

The Turkish government insisted that Turkish vessels carry the immigrants from Greece, even though some foreign companies had won contracts to do so, because it was unacceptable to trust foreigners with the important task of bringing Turkish refugees home.[71] No one on either side was given grounds for claiming exemption from the deportation law. The Turkish government even refused to recognize the conversions of Greeks to Islam or the marriages of Greek women to Turkish men and hence their naturalization. The Greek government was equally skeptical about such changes, and finally the two parties agreed that neither government would accept any conversions taking place after the signing of the convention.[72] It would be two years before some severely disabled and sick people were allowed to remain.[73] After initially allowing Armenians to convert and stay, the Turkish government applied the ban to them as well. After passing this law, the state continued to keep a record of Armenians who had converted and monitored their movements and activities and those of the remaining non-Muslim and Turkish groups in Turkey. Reluctantly, the Turkish government agreed to leave the Istanbul Greeks out of the exchange, but it continued to pressure them to leave throughout the 1940s, 1950s, and 1960s. There is no doubt that the exchange of populations would never have become policy nor have been implemented without the hardening of nationalism in Turkey and Greece. One must also acknowledge the key part played by international organizations, especially the League of Nations, in making it possible for the measure to be carried out despite the wishes and preferences of an overwhelming majority of the people who were affected by it.[74]

Whereas the diversity of the Ottoman Empire was premised on the circulation of people of many different backgrounds, the new national entities strove above all else to put an end to this flux. The Ottoman government imposed a new rule in 1915 requiring its citizens to obtain permission even to travel within the empire.[75] By the end of the 1920s a degree of stasis had been achieved both in Turkey and in the new states created in the Balkans. But even a cursory examination of the new rules and conditions reveals that this stasis existed only on the surface. It was more a temporary respite from the ten years of conflict and movement that preceded it. Forces that pushed and pulled people in different directions continued to be strong, operating beneath the surface of this apparently calm containment. Pastoral nomadism continued to be widespread across the country. A survey conducted by the Ministry of the Interior in the 1940s found that as much as 63 percent of the land in Turkey was used at least in part for raising animals.[76] The survey also showed that many tribes continued to circulate, albeit over shorter distances, but frequently crossing Turkey's borders, especially those with Syria, Iraq, and Iran. During the major shuffle of the early twentieth century, families were separated from their close and extended kin, who were left in lands now designated as foreign. These organic ties provided another conduit for future migration. Similarly, the newly created diaspora communities extended the migratory networks centered in the former territories of the Ottoman Empire into the Americas, Africa, southern Asia, and the Pacific Ocean.

With enormous numbers of people caught up in the massive population shuffle of the late nineteenth and early twentieth centuries, migration emerged as the most common experience of an overwhelming majority of households in Turkey and the other states that succeeded the Ottoman Empire. The experience of moving was etched into the very fiber of all the national communities created in the Balkans and the Middle East. The factors that made migrant workers such a prominent feature in the Balkans and the Middle East in the twentieth century were linked, to a large extent, to these patterns, rooted in the region's history.

Notes

1. EMPIRE, STATE, AND PEOPLE

1   The other four areas of nomadic pastoralism are Africa south of the Sahara, the desert zones of Arabia, the Eurasian steppes, and the Tibetan plateau. The five zones are distinguished by the types of animals raised and the types of economic and political relations the nomadic communities maintained with sedentary populations and the outside world. Thomas Barfield, *The Nomadic Alternative* (Englewoods Cliffs, N.J.: Prentice Hall, 1993), 7–8.

2   For a masterly description of these early migrations and their integration into Anatolia, see Claude Cahen, *Pre-Ottoman Turkey* (New York: Taplinger, 1968).

3   As late as in 1950, before the big injection of machinery into Turkish agriculture, there were about 315,000 permanent agricultural workers in Turkey and more than 550,000 migrant workers. Eva Hirsch, *Poverty and Plenty on the Turkish Farm* (New York: Middle East Institute of Columbia University, 1970), 246. As Claude Cahen showed, these patterns have been remarkably consistent over a very long period. Cahen, *Pre-Ottoman Turkey,* 175–87. See also Çağlar Keyder, "Cycle of Sharecropping and the Consolidation of Small Peasant Ownership in Turkey," *Journal of Peasant Studies* 10, no. 2–3 (1983): 131–45.

4   Paul Wittek, *The Rise of the Ottoman Empire* (London: Royal Asiatic Society, 1938); Fuad Köprülü, *Osmanlı İmparatorluğu'nun Kuruluşu* (Istanbul: Ötüken,

1981). More recent additions to this discussion are Rudi Lindner, *Nomads in Medieval Ottoman Anatolia* (Bloomington: Indiana University Press, 1983); Colin Imber, "The Ottoman Dynastic Myth," *Turcica* 19 (1987): 7–27; Cemal Kafadar, *Between Two Worlds: The Construction of the Ottoman State* (Berkeley: University of California Press, 1995); and Heath Lowry, *The Nature of the Early Ottoman State* (Albany: State University of New York Press, 2003).

5   For example, Faruk Sümer treated Oğuz and Türkmen as synonomous and declared that the mental makeup of modern Anatolian Turks was identical to that of their Oğuz ancestors. He claimed that in the thousand-year history connecting Turkey to the Oğuz tribe, non-Turkish elements made no contribution whatsoever. Faruk Sümer, *Oğuzlar (Türkmenler) Tarihleri- Boy Teşkilatı-Destanları* (Istanbul: Türk Dünyası Araştırmaları Vakfı, 1980), xiv, xviii. For a summary of this literature and the way the debates in Europe influenced it, see Colin Heywood, "Boundless Dreams of the Levant: Paul Wittek, the Geroge-Kreis, and the Writing of Ottoman History," *Journal of the Royal Asiatic Society* 1 (1988): 7–25; and Halil Berktay, *Cumhuriyet İdeolojisi ve Fuat Köprülü* (Istanbul: Kaynak, 1983).

6   Ömer Lütfi Barkan, "Osmanlı İmparatorluğu'nda Bir İskân ve Kolonizasyon Metodu Olarak Vakıflar ve Temlikler: I. İstila devirlerinin Kolonizator Türk Dervişleri ve Zaviyeler," *Vakîflar Dergisi* 2 (1942): 279–386.

7   Rudi Lindner wrote that by the end of the fourteenth century, tribal form had ceased to be relevant for the Ottomans. Rudi Lindner, "What Was the Nomadic Tribe?" *Comparative Studies in Society and History* 25 (1982): 709. See also his *Nomads in Medieval Ottoman Anatolia*.

8   On this point, see Hakan Özoğlu, *Kurdish Notables and the Ottoman State: Evolving Identities, Competing Loyalties, and Shifting Boundaries* (Albany: State University of New York Press, 2004). Also see Baki Öz, *Osmanlı' da Alevi Ayaklanmaları* (Istanbul: Ant, 1992), and Fariba Zarinebaf-Shahr, "Qızılbash 'Heresy' and Rebellion in Ottoman Anatolia during the Sixteenth Century," *Anatolia Moderna* 7 (1997): 1–15.

9   Ibn Khaldun, *The Muqaddimah* (Princeton, N.J.: Princeton University Press, 1958). The best-known modern scholar who has used Ibn Khaldun extensively in his study of Muslim societies in North Africa is Ernest Gellner, in his *Muslim Society* (Cambridge: Cambridge University Press, 1981).

10   Cornell Fleischer, "Royal Authority, Dynastic Cyclism and 'Ibn Khaldûnism'" in Sixteenth-Century Letters," in *Ibn Khaldun and Islamic Ideology*, ed. Bruce Lawrence (Leiden: E. J. Brill, 1984), 46–68.

11   Simon Schama, *The Embarrassment of Riches* (New York: Knopf, 1987), 581–82.

12   Isabel Fonseca, *Bury Me Standing: The Gypsies and Their Journey* (New York: Knopf, 1995), 229.

13   For example, Denis Diderot, *Supplément au voyage de Bougainville* (Paris, 1796), cited in Dorinda Outram, *The Enlightenment* (Cambridge: Cambridge University Press, 1991), 67.

14 Karl Marx, "The Future Results of the British Rule in India," in Karl Marx, *Surveys from Exile* (London: Penguin, 1973), 320.

15 Emile Durkheim, *Selected Writings* (Cambridge: Cambridge University Press, 1972), 140–46.

16 Gellner, *Muslim Society;* Çağlar Keyder, "A Brief History of Modern Istanbul," in *Cambridge History of Modern Turkey,* vol. 4, ed. Reşat Kasaba (Cambridge: Cambridge University Press, 2008), 504–23.

17 James C. Scott, "La montagne et la liberté, ou Pourquoi les civilisations ne savant pas grimper," *Critique Internationale* 3 (2001): 85–104. Also see his *Seeing Like a State* (New Haven, Conn.: Yale University Press, 1998).

18 Ziya Gökalp, *Kürt Aşiretleri Hakkında Sosyolojik Tetkikler* (Istanbul: Sosyal, 1992 [1924]).

19 Daniel Bates, "The Role of the State in Peasant-Nomad Mutualism," *Anthropological Quarterly* 44, no. 3 (1971): 109–32; Richard Tapper, *Frontier Nomads of Iran: A Political and Social History of Shahsevan* (Cambridge: Cambridge University Press, 1997). See also the essays in *Tribes and State Formation in the Middle East,* ed. Philip Khoury and Joseph Kostiner (Berkeley: University of California Press, 1990).

20 Demirtaş Ceyhun, in *Ah Şu Biz Kara Bıyıklı Türkler* (Istanbul: E Yayınları, 1992), provides a humorous look at the restlessness that is germane to Turkish society.

21 Reşat Kasaba, "Do States Always Favor Stasis? The Changing Status of Tribes in the Ottoman Empire," in *Boundaries and Belonging: States and Societies in the Struggle to Shape Identities and Local Practices,* ed. Joel Migdal (Cambridge: Cambridge University Press, 2004), 27–48.

2. A MOVABLE EMPIRE

1 Wittek, *Rise of the Ottoman Empire;* Köprülü, *Osmanlı İmparatorluğu'nun Kuruluşu;* Lindner, *Nomads in Medieval Ottoman Anatolia;* Kafadar, *Between Two Worlds;* Lowry, *Nature of the Early Ottoman State.*

2 It is no coincidence that the training of scholars who tackled such questions early included not only history but also languages and literature. Among them, Fuad Köprülü is probably the best example.

3 Colin Imber, "Heath Lowry, *The Nature of the Early Ottoman State,*" book review, *Turkish Studies Association Journal* 27, nos. 1–2 (2003): 112.

4 See note 1, chapter 1.

5 Imber, "Ottoman Dynastic Myth."

6 Quoted in Ross Dunn, *The Adventures of Ibn Battuta, a Muslim Traveler of the Fourteenth Century* (Berkeley: University of California Press, 1985), 152.

7 Johannes Schlitberger, *Türkler ve Tatarlar Arasında* (Istanbul: İletişim, 1995), 52.

8 Halil İnalcık with Donald Quataert, eds., *An Economic and Social History of the Ottoman Empire, 1300–1914* (Cambridge: Cambridge University Press, 1994), 35.

9 Rhoads Murphey, "Some Features of Nomadism in the Ottoman Empire," *Journal of Turkish Studies* 8 (1984): 192. For obvious reasons, it is difficult to reliably estimate the number of nomads in the Ottoman Empire. In addition to the technical difficulties and the unreliability of most of the counts, there is also the problem of particular tribes and confederations disappearing from one registration to the next, because these groups rarely stayed in one place long enough to be recorded in successive registrations. Mübahat Kütükoğlu, *XV. ve XVI. Asırlarda İzmir Kazasının Sosyal ve İktisadi Yapısı* (İzmir: Büyükşehir Belediyesi, 2000), 104.

10 Halil İnalcık, "The Yürüks," in *Oriental Carpet and Textile Studies,* ed. R. Pinner and H. İnalcık (London: Oguz Press, 1986), 56.

11 Ömer Lütfi Barkan, "Osmanlı İmparatorluğunda Bir İskân ve Kolonizasyon Metodu Olarak Sürgünler," *İstanbul Üniversitesi İktisat Fakültesi Mecmuası,* part 1, vol. 11 (1949–50): 254–569; part 2, vol. 13 (1952): 56–79; and part 3, vol. 14 (1953–54): 209–36; İnalcık, "The Yürüks," 41.

12 Barkan, "Sürgünler," part 1, 547.

13 Halil İnalcık, "Osmanlı İmparatorluğu'nun Kuruluş ve İnkişafı Devrinde Türkiye'nin İktisadi Vaziyeti Üzerine Bir Tetkik Münasebetiyle," in Halil İnalcık, *Osmanlı İmparatorluğu: Toplum ve Ekonomi* (Istanbul: Eren, 1993), 157.

14 Barkan, "Sürgünler," part 3, 227.

15 See Lindner, *Nomads in Medieval Ottoman Anatolia.*

16 Lowry, *Nature of the Early Ottoman State.*

17 See Sanjay Subrahmanyam, "A Tale of Three Empires: Mughals, Ottomans, and Habsburgs in a Comparative Context," *Common Knowledge* 12, no. 1 (2006): 66–92.

18 Fuad Köprülü, *Bizans Müesseselerinin Osmanlı Müesseselerine Etkisi* (Istanbul: Ötüken, 1981). Speros Vryonis, in his *Decline of Medieval Hellenism in Asia Minor* (Berkeley: University of California Press, 1971), 194, mistakenly portrayed the Türkmen tribes who arrived in Anatolia as purely nomadic-pastoral-warrior forces that had a fateful effect on the "stability of the highly developed sedentary society of the Byzantine Christians."

19 Machiavelli, quoted in Perry Anderson, *Lineages of the Absolutist State* (London: Verso, 1974), 397–98.

20 M. A. Cook, ed., *A History of the Ottoman Empire to 1730* (Cambridge: Cambridge University Press, 1976), 59; Huri İslamoğlu-Inan, *State and Peasant in the Ottoman Empire* (Leiden: E. J. Brill, 1984), 25.

21 Cengiz Orhonlu, *Osmanlı İmparatorluğu'nda Aşiretlerin İskânı* (Istanbul: Eren, 1987), 12; Xavier de Planhol, "Geography, Politics and Nomadism in Anatolia," *International Social Science Journal* 11, no. 4 (1959): 527.

22 Murphey, "Some Features of Nomadism," 192; Planhol, "Geography, Politics," 527; Cengiz Orhonlu, *Osmanlı İmparatorluğu'nda Aşiretlerin İskânı*, 21 n. 54; Lütfü Güçer, *XVI. ve XVII. Asırlarda Osmanlı İmparatorluğunda Hububat Meselesi ve Hububattan Alınan Vergiler* (Istanbul: Semet, 1964), 13, 15.

23 Salahaddin Çetintürk, "Osmanlı İmparatorluğu'nda Yürük Sınıfı ve Hukuki Statüleri," *Ankara Üniversitesi Dil ve Tarih Coğrafya Fakültesi Dergisi* 2 (1943): 107-16; İnalcık, "The Yürüks."

24 Faruk Sümer, "Anadolu, Suriye, ve Irak'ta yaşayan Türk Aşiretlerine Umumi Bir Bakış," *Istanbul Üniversitesi İktisat Fakültesi Mecmuası* 11 (1949-50): 511.

25 Halil İnalcık, "Introduction," in İnalcık with Quataert, *Economic and Social History*, 32-37; Martin van Bruinessen, *Evliya Çelebi in Diyarbekir* (Leiden: E. J. Brill, 1988), 27.

26 Çetintürk, "Osmanlı İmparatorluğu'nda," 111; İnalcık, "The Yürüks," 42-43; Sümer, "Anadolu, Suriye ve Irak'ta," 515-16; Feridun Emecen, *XVI. Asırda Manisa Kazası* (Ankara: Türk Tarih Kurumu, 1989), 128.

27 İnalcık, "The Yürüks," 47.

28 Hüseyin Özdeğer, "Haleb Bölgesi Türkmenleri," *Türk İktisat Tarihi Yıllığı: Istanbul Üniversitesi İktisat Fakültesi Türk İktisat ve İçtimaiyat Tarihi Araştırmalar Merkezi* 1 (1987): 178.

29 Kütükoğlu, *XV. ve XVI. Asırlarda İzmir*, 97.

30 Fikret Adanır, "The Ottoman Peasantries, c. 1360-1860," in *The Peasantries of Europe from the Fourteenth to Eighteenth Centuries*, ed. Tom Scott (London: Longman, 1998), 275.

31 Çetintürk, "Osmanlı İmparatorluğu'nda," 114; Orhonlu, *Osmanlı İmparatorluğu'nda*, 20.

32 Tufan Gündüz, *Anadolu'da Türkmen Aşiretleri* (Ankara: Bilge Yayınları, 1997), 105; Planhol, "Geography, Politics," 527.

33 Van Bruinessen, *Evliya Çelebi*, 28; Suraiya Faroqhi, "Crisis and Change," in İnalcık with Quataert, *Economic and Social History*, 444.

34 Faruk Söylemez, *Osmanlı Devletinde Aşiret Yönetimi* (Istanbul: Kültür ve Turizm Bakanlığı, 2007).

35 Sümer, "Anadolu, Suriye, ve Irak'ta," 511; Orhonlu, *Osmanlı İmparatorluğu'nda*, 19; Çetintürk, "Osmanlı İmparatorluğu'nda," 111.

36 Elena Marushiakova and Vesselin Popov, *Gypsies in the Ottoman Empire: A Contribution to the History of the Balkans* (Hatfield, U.K.: University of Hertfordshire Press, 2001), 34.

37 Orhonlu, *Osmanlı İmparatorluğu'nda*, 15.

38 Robert Dankoff, *Evliya Çelebi in Bitlis* (Leiden: E. J. Brill, 1990), 14.

39 Dror Ze'evi, *An Ottoman Century: The District of Jerusalem in the 1600s* (Albany: State University of New York Press, 1996), 113.

40 Martin van Bruinessen, *Agha, Sheikh and State: The Social and Political Structures of Kurdistan* (London: Zed, 1992), 144-45.

41 Lowry, *Nature of the Early Ottoman State*, 91.

42 Dankoff, *Evliya*, 15.

43 Ibid., 12–18, 273–90. See also Tom Sinclair, "The Ottoman Arrangements for the Tribal Principalities of the Lake Van Region of the Sixteenth Century," *International Journal of Turkish Studies* 9, nos. 2–3 (2003): 119–43.

44 Rhoads Murphey, ed., *Kanuname-i Sultâani Li Aziz Efendi* (Cambridge, Mass.: Harvard University Press, 1985), 14.

45 Ibid., 16.

46 Ibid., 15.

47 Ibid., 7.

48 Ze'evi, *Ottoman Century*, 96.

49 Barfield, *Nomadic Alternative*, 17.

50 For examples, see the governmental orders reprinted in Ahmet Refik, *Anadolu'da Türk Aşiretleri* (Istanbul: Devlet Matbaası, 1930).

51 Originally the term *levend* referred only to sailors, including those who jumped ship, but over time it became a general term used for all roaming vagabonds. Mehmet Zeki Pakalın, *Osmanlı Tarih Deyimleri ve Terimleri Sözlüğü*, vol. 2 (Istanbul: M. E. B. Devlet Basımevi, 1971), 358.

52 Halil İnalcık, "Osmanlılarda Raiyyet Rüsumu," in Halil İnalcık, *Osmanlı İmparatorluğu: Toplum ve Ekonomi* (Istanbul: Eren, 1993), 41–42; Pakalın, *Osmanlı Tarih*, vol. 1, 297.

53 Sümer, "Anadolu, Suriye, ve Irak'ta," 518; Orhonlu, *Osmanlı İmparatorluğu'nda Aşiretlerin*, 23–25; Çetintürk, "Osmanlı İmparatorluğu'nda," 110–11; İnalcık, "Osmanlilarda Raiyyet."

54 Ahmet Refik, *Anadolu'da*, 36, 37 (documents 67, 70 [1579]).

55 Murphey, "Some Features of Nomadism," 191.

56 Ömer Lutfi Barkan, "Research on the Ottoman Fiscal Surveys," in *Studies in the Economic History of the Middle East,* ed. M. A. Cook (London: Oxford University Press, 1970), 165.

57 See Ahmet Yaşar Ocak, *Osmanlı Toplumunda Zındıklar ve Mülhidler* (Istanbul: Tarih Vakfı, 1998).

58 On Gypsies, see Marushiakova and Popov, *Gypsies in the Ottoman Empire;* on Kurds, see van Bruinessen, *Agha, Sheikh, and State.*

59 Fernand Braudel, *The Mediterranean and the Mediterranean World in the Age of Philip II,* vol. 1 (London: Fontana, 1972), 94.

60 İnalcık, "Introduction," 37.

61 Güçer, *XVI. ve XVII. Asırlarda,* 13–15; Murphey, "Some Features of Nomadism," 195. For a description of similar policies during the republican period, see Bates, "Role of the State."

62 For an example encompassing all these elements, see Feridun Emecen, "The History of an Early Sixteenth-Century Migration: Sirem Exiles in Gallipoli," in *Hungarian-Ottoman Military and Diplomatic Relations in the Age of Süleyman the Magnificent,* eds. Geza David and Pal Fodor (Budapest: Acta Orientalia Academiae Scientiarum Hungaricae, 1994), 77–91.

63 Suraiya Faroqhi, *Coping with the State: Political Conflict and Crime in the Ottoman Empire, 1520–1750* (Istanbul: İsis, 1995), 32.

64 Ahmet Refik, *Osmanlı Devrinde Türkiye Madenleri* (Istanbul: Enderun Kitabevi, 1989), 19.

65 Emecen, *XVI. Asırda Manisa*, 134–35.

66 Tayyip Gökbilgin, *Rumeli'de Yürükler, Tatarlar ve Evlad-ı Fatihan* (Istanbul: Osman Yalçın Matbaası, 1957), 49–51.

67 Faroqhi, *Coping with the State*.

68 Ahmet Refik, *Anadolu'da*, 7.

69 Marushiakova and Popov, *Gypsies in the Ottoman Empire*, 38.

70 Emecen, *XVI. Asırda Manisa*, 135.

71 United Kingdom, Public Records Office, Foreign Office, Consular Correspondence (hereafter FO) 78/868: 94–103 (1850); FO 78/1450: 72 (1858).

72 Braudel, *The Mediterranean*, 87.

73 Ya'akov Firestone, "Land Equalization and Factor Scarcities: Holding Size and the Burden of Impositions in Imperial Russia and the Late Ottoman Levant," *Journal of Economic History* 41 (December 1981): 813–33.

74 İnalcık, "The Yürüks," 40; Sümer "Anadolu, Suriye, ve Irak'ta," 516.

75 Ze'evi, *Ottoman Century*, 106.

76 İnalcık, "The Yürüks," 46; Sümer "Anadolu, Suriye, ve Irak'ta," 516.

77 Ze'evi, *Ottoman Century*, 102; Amy Singer, *Palestinian Peasants and Ottoman Officials: Rural Administration around Sixteenth-Century Jerusalem* (Cambridge: Cambridge University Press, 1994), 113.

78 Halil İnalcık, "'Arab' Camel Drivers in Western Anatolia in the Fifteenth Century," *Revue d'Histoire Maghrebine* 10, nos. 31–32 (1983): 260.

79 Ahmet Refik, *Hicri Onikinci Asırda İstanbul Hayatı* (Istanbul: Devlet Matbaası, 1930), 78–79; Güçer, *XVI. ve XVII. Asırlarda*, 15–16; Orhonlu, *Osmanlı İmparatorluğu'nda*, 21–22, 27 n. 84.

80 For examples, see Ahmet Refik, *Anadolu'da;* İnalcık, "'Arab' Camel Drivers"; Çetintürk, "Osmanlı İmparatorluğu'nda."

81 İnalcık, "Introduction," 15.

82 Gökbilgin, *Rumeli'de Yürükler*.

83 In Cemal Kafadar's words: "The Ottoman success was due to the fact that they harnessed that mobility to their own ends while shaping and taming it to conform to their stability-seeking centralizing vision." Kafadar, *Between Two Worlds*, 141.

84 Barkan, "Sürgünler," 61, 72; Adanır, "Ottoman Peasantries," 277.

85 Charles Thornton Forster and F. H. Blackburne Daniell, eds., *The Life and Letters of Ogier Ghiselin de Busbecq* (London, 1881), 219; Rhoads Murphey, *Ottoman Warfare, 1500–1700* (New Brunswick, N.J.: Rutgers University Press, 1999), 70–71.

86 Ze'evi, *Ottoman Century*, 98–99.

87 Murphey, "Some Features of Nomadism," 192.

88   Ibid., 193.

89   Güçer, *XVI. ve XVII. Asırlarda,* 29–30, 32.

90   Lowry, *Nature of the Early Ottoman State,* 138.

91   Ira Lapidus, "Sufism and Ottoman Islamic Society," in *The Dervish Lodge,* ed. Raymond Lifchez (Berkeley: University of California Press, 1992), 25.

92   V. J. Parry, "The Reigns of Bayezid II and Selim I, 1481–1520," in Cook, *History of the Ottoman Empire,* 64.

93   Zarinebaf-Shahr, "Qızılbash 'Heresey'"; Colin Imber, "The Persecution of Ottoman Shi'ites according to the Muhimme Defterleri," *Der Islam* 56 (1979): 245–73.

94   Irène Mélikoff, "Bektaşilik/Kızılbaşlık Tarihsel Bölünme ve Sonuçları," in *Alevi Kimliği,* ed. T. Olsson, E. Özdalga, and C. Raudvere (Istanbul: Tarih Vakfı, 1999), 3–11.

95   John Robert Barnes, "The Dervish Orders in the Ottoman Empire," in Lifchez, *Dervish Lodge,* 36.

96   Barkan, "Temlikler," 356.

97   Braudel, *The Mediterranean,* 102.

98   Barkan, "Sürgünler," 70; Ibrahim Gökçen, *Saruhan'da Yürük ve Türkmenler* (Istanbul: Marifet Basımevi, 1946).

99   Planhol, "Geography, Politics," 531. See also İnalcık, "The Yürüks," 46.

100 Barkan, "Research on the Ottoman Fiscal Surveys," 169.

101 Emecen, *XVI. Asırda Manisa,* 142.

102 Şevket Pamuk makes a similar argument concerning the monetary policies of the Ottoman Empire. Şevket Pamuk, *A Monetary History of the Ottoman Empire* (Cambridge: Cambridge University Press, 2000).

103 Jeremy Black, *Maps in History* (New Haven, Conn.: Yale University Press, 1997), 25.

104 Braudel, *The Mediterranean,* 23.

105 Cemal Kafadar, "A Death in Venice: Anatolian Muslim Merchants Trading in the Serenissima," *Journal of Turkish Studies* 10 (1986): 191–218; Bronwen Wilson, "Foggie diverse di vestire de'Turchi: Turkish Costume Illustration and Cultural Transition," *Journal of Medieval and Early Modern Studies* 37, no. 1 (2007): 105; Palmira Brummett, "Visions of the Mediterranean: A Classification," *Journal of Medieval and Early Modern Studies* 37, no. 1 (2007): 9–55. See also Faruk Tabak, *The Waning of the Mediterranean, 1550–1870* (Baltimore, Md.: Johns Hopkins University Press, 2008).

106 Pamuk, *Monetary History.*

107 Colin Heywood, "The Frontier in Ottoman History: Old Ideas and New Myths," in *Writing Ottoman History* (London: Variorum, 2002), 228–50.

108 Lucette Valensi, *The Birth of the Despot* (Ithaca, N.Y.: Cornell University Press, 1993), 53.

109 I am indebted to Selim Kuru for this observation.

110 Ahmet Karamustafa, "Introduction to Ottoman Cartography," in *The His-*

tory of Cartography, vol. 2, book 1, *Cartography in the Traditional Islamic and South Asian Societies,* ed. J. B. Harley and David Woodward (Chicago: University of Chicago Press, 1992), 206–8.

111 J. M. Rogers, "Itineraries and Town Views in Ottoman Histories," in Harley and Woodward, *Cartography,* 237; Ahmet Karamustafa, "Military, Administrative, and Scholarly Maps and Plans," in Harley and Woodward, *Cartography,* 212–13. Among the sources that come close to providing a comprehensive description of the Ottoman possessions, two stand out for their brilliance. These are Matrakçı's *Menzilname* and Piri Reis's *Kitabı Bahriye.* They are both products of the sixteenth century, when the empire reached its most extensive borders. Matrakçı accompanied Sultan Süleyman I (Süleyman the Magnificent) and the Ottoman army during the expedition against the Safavids in Persia in 1533. Matrakçı's drawings of Baghdad, Alanya, and especially Istanbul are admired as exquisite gems for their detail and the wealth of information they provide. But texts such as *Menzilname* also include many inconsistent and superficial pictures and hence can be considered only partial renderings of the imperial possessions.

112 Rogers, "Itineraries and Town Views," 231–35. See also Thomas Goodrich, *The Ottoman Turks and the New World: A Study of Tarih-i Hind-i Garbi and Sixteenth-Century Americana* (Wiesbaden: O. Harrassowitz, 1990).

113 J. H. Elliott, *The Old World and the New* (Cambridge: Cambridge University Press, 1970), 88.

114 Rogers, "Itineraries," 237.

115 James Krokar, *The Ottoman Presence in Southeastern Europe, 16th–19th Centuries: A View in Maps,* collection of slides with explanatory text (Chicago, 1997). See also Brummett, "Visions of the Mediterranean," 3–25.

116 Cited in Caroline Finkel, *Osman's Dream* (New York: Basic Books, 2005), 323.

117 Viorel Panatie, *The Ottoman Law of War and Peace: The Ottoman Empire and Tribute Payers* (Boulder, Colo.: East European Monographs, 2000), 238.

118 Ze'evi, *Ottoman Century,* 94.

119 Dina Rizk Khoury, *State and Provincial Society in the Ottoman Empire: Mosul, 1540–1834* (Cambridge: Cambridge University Press, 1997), 40; Ze'evi, *Ottoman Century,* 99–101.

120 Singer, *Palestinian Peasants,* 114.

121 Reşat Ekrem Koçu, *Osmanlı Muahedeleri ve Kapitülasyonlar, 1300–1920 — ve Lozan Muahedesi, 24 Temmuz 1923* (Istanbul: Muallim Ahmet Halim Kütüphanesi, 1934), 45.

122 Gabor Agoston, "A Flexible Empire: Authority and Its Limits on the Ottoman Frontiers," *International Journal of Turkish Studies* 9, nos. 1–2 (2003): 15–31.

123 Panatie, *Ottoman Law,* 148–70.

124 Halil İnalcık, *Fatih Devri Üzerine Tetkikler ve Vesikalar* (Ankara: Türk Tarih Kurumu, 1954), 182.

125 Lowry, *Nature of the Early Ottoman State,* 58.

126 Steven Runciman, *The Fall of Constantinople* (Cambridge: Cambridge University Press, 1965), 84.

127 This gun had a bronze barrel more than twenty-six feet long and eight inches thick, and it fired cannonballs weighing 800 pounds. Lisa Jardine, *Worldly Goods: A New History of the Renaissance* (New York: Doubleday, 1996), 42.

128 Lowry, *Nature of the Early Ottoman State*, 116.

129 Runciman, *Fall of Constantinople*, 84.

130 Cemal Kafadar, "A Rome of One's Own: Reflections on Cultural Geography and Identity in the Lands of Rum," *Muqarnas* 24 (2007): 7–25. See also Karen Barkey, *Empire of Difference: The Ottomans in Comparative Perspective* (Cambridge: Cambridge University Press, 2008).

131 Kafadar, *Between Two Worlds*, 71, 169–70.

132 F. Babinger, *Mehmed the Conqueror and His Time* (Princeton, N.J.: Princeton University Press, 1978), 66.

133 İlber Ortaylı, *Osmanlı İmparatorluğunda Aile* (Istanbul: Pan, 2000), 37.

134 Ehud Toledano, *The Ottoman Slave Trade and Its Suppression, 1840–1890* (Princeton, N.J.: Princeton University Press, 1982).

135 The only official source in which Mehmet II's mother is identified is a deed of a pious foundation in which she is mentioned as "Hatun bint-Abdulah," the standard way converts to Islam from other religions are mentioned in Ottoman legal documents. This establishes her non-Muslim origin. Babinger, *Mehmed the Conqueror*, 11–12.

136 Leslie Peirce, *The Imperial Harem: Women and Sovereignty in the Ottoman Empire* (New York: Oxford University Press, 1993), 221.

137 Ibid., 222.

138 Metin Kunt, *The Sultan's Servants: The Transformation of Ottoman Provincial Government, 1550–1650* (New York: Columbia University Press, 1983), 33.

139 Faroqhi, *Coping with the State*, 97.

140 Cornell Fleischer, *Bureaucrat and Intellectual in the Ottoman Empire: The Historian Mustafa Ali, 1541–1600* (Princeton, N.J.: Princeton University Press, 1983), 159.

141 Halil İnalcık, "The Rise of the Ottoman Empire," in Cook, *History of the Ottoman Empire*, 42.

142 Daniel Goffman, *İzmir and the Levantine World* (Seattle: University of Washington Press, 1990); Edhem Eldem, Daniel Goffman, and Bruce Masters, *Ottoman City between East and West* (Cambridge: Cambridge University Press, 1999).

143 Halil İnalcık, "Istanbul," in *The Encyclopaedia of Islam, New Edition*, vol. 4 (Leiden: E. J. Brill, 1978), 239.

144 Kütükoğlu, *XV. ve XVI. Asırlarda*, 32–33.

145 Münir Aktepe, "XIV. ve XV. Asırlarda Rumeli'nin Türkler Tarafından İskânına Dair," *Türkiyat Mecmuası* 10 (1951–53): 299–312.

146 Orhonlu, *Osmanlı İmparatorluğu'nda*, 103.

147 Koçu, *Osmanlı Muahedeleri*, 11; John Freely, *Istanbul, the Imperial City* (London: Penguin, 1998), 167.

148 Barkan, "Sürgünler," part 2, 69; Orhonlu, *Osmanlı İmparatorluğu'nda*, 103–4. On Tatarpazari, see Barkan, "Sürgünler," part 3, 210.

149 Emecen, "History of an Early Sixteenth-Century Migration."

150 Aleksandar Fotic, "Yürük ve sipahi," H-TURK, H-Net: Humanities and Social Sciences Online (www.h-net.msu.edu), January 16, 1999.

151 İnalcık, "Istanbul," 240.

152 Ahmet Refik, *Hicri Onikinci Asırda*, 140.

153 Kenneth Setton, "Lutheranism and the Turkish Peril," *Balkan Studies* 3 (1962): 142.

154 Ibid., 139.

155 George Forell, "Luther and the War against the Turks," *Church History* 14, no. 4 (1945): 260.

156 Setton, "Lutheranism," 151.

157 See Forell, "Luther"; and Harvey Buchanan, "Luther and the Turks," *Archiv für Reformationgeschichte* 47, no. 2 (1956): 145–60.

158 Ira Lapidus, *A History of Islamic Societies* (Cambridge: Cambridge University Press, 1988), 26–27.

159 Barkan, "Temlikler," 295–96.

160 Barnes, "Dervish Orders," 33.

161 Ahmet Karamustafa, *God's Unruly Friends* (Salt Lake City: University of Utah Press, 1994), 2.

162 I am indebted to Nadide Karkıne for this information. For a detailed description of an Alevi community in Anatolia, see Yavuz Ziya Yörükan, *Anadolu'da Aleviler ve Tahtacılar* (Ankara: Kültür Bakanlığı, 1998). See also Fulya Doğruel, *"İnsaniyetleri Benzer: Hatay'da Çoketnili Ortak Yaşam Kültürü"* (Istanbul: İletişim, 2005).

163 Barnes, "Dervish Orders," 34–35.

164 See, for example, Edwin Seroussi, "The Peşrev as a Vocal Genre in Ottoman Hebrew Sources," *Turkish Music Quarterly*, Summer 1991: 1–2. I thank Maureen Jackson for this source.

165 See Barkan, "Temlikler," 282–83; Mélikoff, "Bektaşilik/Kızılbaşlık Tarihsel Bölünme ve Sonuçları," 7.

166 Raymond Lifchez, "Introduction," in Lifchez, *Dervish Lodge*, 5.

167 İnalcık, "Istanbul," 226.

168 Lapidus, "Sufism," 32n. 31; Köprülü, *Osmanlı İmparatorluğunun Kuruluşu*, 162–63.

169 Koçu, *Osmanlı Muahedeleri*, 57.

1   Ahmet Refik, *Anadolu'da*, 103–6 (document 157 [1691]). For example, a tribe named Civanşir was described as "Civanşir community, which is governed by Musa kethüda, İvaz kethüda, and Cücük Yusuf kethüda [*Musa kethüda, ve İvaz kethüda, ve Cücük Yusuf kethüdaya tâbi Civanşir cemaati*]."

2   Virginia Aksan, "Ottoman Sources of Information on Europe in the Eighteenth Century," *Archivum Ottomanicum* 11 (1986): 8.

3   Quoted in Eleazar Birnbaum, "The Questing Mind: Kâtib Chelebi, 1609–1657. A Chapter in Ottoman Intellectual History," in *Corolla Torontonensis: Studies in Honour of Ronald Morton Smith*, ed. Emmet Robbins and Stella Sandahl (Toronto: TSAR, 1994), 141.

4   Rifa'at A. Abou-El-Haj, "Ottoman Diplomacy at Karlowitz," *Journal of the American Oriental Society* 87, no. 4 (1967): 498–512.

5   Dusan Djordjevich, H-TURK, H-Net: Humanities and Social Sciences Online (www.h-net.msu.edu), November 2, 2001.

6   On Westphalia, see Jeremy Black, "Warfare, Crisis, and Absolutism," in *Early Modern Europe*, ed. Euan Cameron (Oxford: Oxford University Press, 1999), 215–16.

7   Finkel, *Osman's Dream*, 321–22.

8   Abou-El-Haj, "Ottoman Diplomacy."

9   İsmail Hakkı Uzunçarşılı, *Osmanlı Tarihi*, vol. 4, part 1 (Ankara: Türk Tarih Kurumu, 1947), 4.

10 J. C. Hurewitz, *Diplomacy in the Middle East: A Documentary Record* (Princeton, N.J.: Princeton University Press, 1956), 43.

11 Virginia Aksan, "War and Peace," in *The Cambridge History of Turkey*, vol. 3, *The Later Ottoman Empire*, ed. Suraiya Faroqhi (Cambridge: Cambridge University Press, 2006), 86.

12 Uzunçarşılı, *Osmanlı Tarihi*, 4.

13 Bruce McGowan, "Population and Migration," in İnalcık with Quataert, *Economic and Social History*, 647.

14 Yusuf Hallaçoğlu, *XVIII. Yüzyılda Osmanlı İmparatorluğu'nun İskân Siyaseti ve Aşiretlerin Yerleştirilmesi* (Ankara: Türk Tarih Kurumu, 1988), 79.

15 Mary Lucille Shay, *The Ottoman Empire from 1720 to 1734 as Revealed in Dispatches of the Venetian Baili* (Westport, Conn.: Greenwood Press, 1978), 25.

16 Mehmet Genç, "Osmanlı Maliyesinde Malikâne Sistemi," in *Türkiye İktisat Tarihi Semineri*, ed. Osman Okyar and Ünal Nalbantoğlu (Ankara: Hacettepe Universitesi Yayınları, 1975), 231–96.

17 Halil İnalcık, "Military and Fiscal Transformation in the Ottoman Empire, 1600–1700," *Archivum Ottomanicum* 6 (1980): 283–337.

18 Mustafa Cezar, *Osmanlı Tarihinde Levendler* (Istanbul: Çelikcilt, 1965), 227; İnalcık, "Military and Fiscal Transformation," 304–11.

19 Kütükoğlu, *XV ve XVI. Asırlarda İzmir*, 201.

20 Ibid.

21 Ahmet Refik, *Hicri Onikinci Asırda Istanbul Hayatı.*

22 İnalcık, "Istanbul."

23 Cezar, *Osmanlı Tarihinde Levendler,* 229; see also Cengiz Orhonlu, *Osmanlı İmparatorluğu'nda Derbend Teşkilatı* (Istanbul: Eren, 1990), 11.

24 Ahmet Ağa, *Viyana Kuşatması Günlüğü,* trans. Esat Nermi (Istanbul: Milliyet Yayınları, 1970,) 114.

25 Ibid., 129.

26 Walter L. Wright, ed., *Ottoman Statecraft: The Book of Counsel for Vezirs and Governors of Sarı Mehmed Pasha, the Defterdar* (Princeton, N.J.: Princeton University Press, 1935), 126.

27 Cited by Dusan J. Djordjevich, H-TURK, H-Net: Humanities and Social Sciences Online (www.h-net.msu.edu), November 2, 2001.

28 A. N. Kurat and J. S. Bromley, "The Retreat of the Turks, 1683–1730," in Cook, *History of the Ottoman Empire,* 192.

29 Aksan, "War and Peace," 100.

30 Shay, *Ottoman Empire from 1720 to 1734,* 28.

31 Wright, *Ottoman Statecraft,* 126 n. 20.

32 Finkel, *Osman's Dream,* 312.

33 Stanford Shaw and Ezel Kuran Shaw, *History of the Ottoman Empire and Modern Turkey,* vol. 1 (Cambridge: Cambridge University Press, 1976), 219.

34 Ibid., 206–7; Madeline Zilfi, "The Kadızadelis: Discordant Revivalism in Seventeenth Century Istanbul," *Journal of Near Eastern Studies* 45 (1986), 251–74; Marc Baer, *Bound by the Glory of Islam* (New York: Oxford University Press, 2008), 65–80.

35 Ariel Salzmann, "The Age of Tulips: Confluence and Conflict in Early Modern Consumer Culture," in *Consumption Studies and the History of the Ottoman Empire,* ed. D. Quataert (Albany: State University of New York Press, 2000), 83–106; Ahmet Evin, "Tulip Age and Definitions of Westernization," in *Social and Economic History of Turkey,* ed. Osman Okyar and Halil İnalcık (Ankara: Meteksan, 1980), 131–45.

36 Faik Reşit Unat, *Osmanlı Sefirleri ve Sefaretnameleri* (Ankara: Türk Tarih Kurumu, 1968), 19–20.

37 Virginia Aksan, "Ottoman Political Writing, 1768–1808," *International Journal of Middle East Studies* 25 (1993): 56.

38 Birnbaum, "Questing Mind," 145.

39 Aksan, "Ottoman Political Writing"; Riffa'at Ali Abou-El-Haj, "The Ottoman Nasihatname as a Discourse over Morality," *Mélanges Robert Mantran, Revue Histoire Maghrebine* 47–48 (1987) 17–30; Fleischer, *Bureaucrat and Intellectual.*

40 Fleischer, "Royal Authority."

41 Ibid., 50.

42 Wright, *Ottoman Statecraft,* 127.

43 Two crucial sources for the early policies of sedentarization are Ahmet Refik's

Anadolu'da Türk Aşiretleri and Cengiz Orhonlu's *Osmanlı İmparatorluğu'nda Aşiretlerin İskânı.* Ahmet Refik's book is a compilation of the orders issued by the central government to administer and settle the nomadic tribes. Even though it is not (and could not have been) a comprehensive list, it is a valuable source that brings together 244 orders covering the period between 1558 and 1785.

44   Tayyib Gökbilgin, *Rumeli'de Yürükler, Tatarlar ve Evlad-ı Fatihan* (Istanbul: Osman Yalçın Matbaası, 1957).

45   Finkel, *Osman's Dream,* 308–10.

46   Ahmet Refik, *Anadolu'da,* 107 (document 159, 1692).

47   Ibid., 96 (document 147, 1690).

48   Ibid., 128 (document 180, 1700).

49   Ibid., 93–94 (document 144, 1690).

50   Ibid., 96 (document 147, 1690).

51   Ibid., 95 (document 146, 1690).

52   Ibid. See also 97 (document 148, 1690), 105 (document 157, 1691); Orhonlu, *Osmanlı İmparatorluğu'nda Aşiretlerin İskânı,* 49.

53   Orhonlu, *Osmanlı İmparatorluğu'nda Aşiretlerin İskânı,* 57–65, 107–9.

54   Ibid., 59–60.

55   Hallaçoğlu, *XVIII. Yüzyılda Osmanlı,* 51.

56   Orhonlu, *Osmanlı İmparatorluğu'nda Aşiretlerin İskânı,* 71.

57   Ahmet Refik, *Anadolu'da,* 117 (document 169, 1698).

58   Ibid.

59   Fuat Dündar, *İttihat ve Terakki'nin Müslümanları İskân Politikası* (Istanbul: İletişim, 2001), 50.

60   Ahmet Refik, *Anadolu'da,* 15–16 (no. 29, July 8, 1572).

61   Orhonlu, *Osmanlı İmparatorluğu'nda Aşiretlerin İskânı,* 108–9.

62   Rifa'at Abou-El-Haj, *Formation of the Modern State: The Ottoman Empire, Sixteenth to Eighteenth Centuries* (Albany: State University of New York Press, 1991).

63   Orhonlu, *Osmanlı İmparatorluğu'nda Aşiretlerin İskânı,* 52–53.

64   Hallaçoğlu, *XVIII. Yüzyılda Osmanlı,* 109.

65   Orhonlu, *Osmanlı İmparatorluğu'nda Aşiretlerin İskânı,* 77, 110–11; Hallaçoğlu, *XVIII. Yüzyılda Osmanlı,* 96.

66   Orhonlu, *Osmanlı İmparatorluğu'nda Aşiretlerin İskânı,* 101.

67   Orhonlu, *Osmanlı İmparatorluğu'nda Derbend Teşkilatı,* 13.

68   Orhonlu, *Osmanlı İmparatorluğu'nda Aşiretlerin İskânı,* 47–48, 52 n. 79.

69   Orhonlu, *Osmanlı İmparatorluğu'nda Derbend Teşkilatı,* 85–99.

70   Suraiya Faroqhi, "Rural Life," in Faroqhi, *Later Ottoman Empire,* 379.

71   Ahmet Refik, *Anadolu'da,* 80–81 (document 136).

72   Ibid., 110–11 (document 162, 1695).

73   Ibid., 81–91 (documents 137–139, 1689).

74 Gökbilgin, *Rumeli'de Yürükler,* 38.

75 Ibid., 20, 31–34.

76 Ibid., 255–56; Uzunçarşılı, *Osmanlı Tarihi,* 31. Ahmet Refik published the sultan's order concerning the registration of Yürüks and the formation of the Evlad-ı Fatihan in *Anadolu'da,* 114–17 (documents 167–68, 1697–98). Much of the information in this paragraph is from that source.

77 Ahmet Refik, *Anadolu'da,* 95 (document 146, 1690), 97 (document 148, 1690), 105 (document 157, 1691). Typically, "avarız-ı divaniyye ve sayir rusumu raiyyet üzerlerinden muaf ve müsellem olup."

78 Orhonlu, *Osmanlı İmparatorluğu'nda Aşiretlerin İskânı,* 55–56.

79 Ahmet Refik, *Anadolu'da,* 95 (document 146, 1690), 116 (document 168, 1698).

80 Orhonlu, *Osmanlı İmparatorluğu'nda Aşiretlerin İskânı,* 117.

81 Ibid., 33, 49.

82 Ahmet Refik, *Anadolu'da,* 165 (document 206, 1719).

83 Ibid., 100–102.

84 Ibid., 101 (document 154, 1690).

85 Hallaçoğlu, *XVIII. Yüzyılda Osmanlı,* 31 n. 216.

86 Ahmet Refik, *Anadolu'da,* 80 (document 136, 1689).

87 Ibid., 135 (document 186, 1706).

88 On this point and on the way this relationship was part of a state-building strategy in the Ottoman Empire, see Karen Barkey, *Bandits and Bureaucrats: The Ottoman Route to State Centralization* (Ithaca, N.Y.: Cornell University Press, 1994).

89 Ahmet Refik, *Anadolu'da,* 105 (document 157, 1691).

90 Ibid., 102 (document 156, 1691).

91 Ibid., 121 (document 172, 1699).

92 Orhonlu, *Osmanlı İmparatorluğu'nda Aşiretlerin İskânı,* 53 n. 94.

93 Ahmet Refik, *Anadolu'da,* 79 (document 134).

94 Cezar, *Osmanlı Tarihinde Levendler,* 221.

95 Shay, *Ottoman Empire from 1720 to 1734,* 27.

96 Cezar, *Osmanlı Tarihinde Levendler,* 227.

97 M. A. Cook, *Population Pressure in Rural Anatolia, 1450–1600* (Oxford: Oxford University Press, 1972), 40.

98 Ahmet Refik, *Anadolu'da,* 120 (document 171, 1699).

99 For example, ibid., 201 (document 231, 1735).

100 For example, Kemal Güngör concluded that "despite the differences in their skull shapes and skin colors, just like the Türkmens, yürüks belong to the Grand Turkish Unity [sic]." Kemal Güngör, *Cenubi Anadolu Yürüklerinin Etno-Antroplojik Tetkiki* (Ankara: İdeal, 1941), 2. Also see Sadi Irmak, *Yürüklerin Kan Gurupları* (Istanbul: Devlet, 1937).

101 Ahmet Refik, *Anadolu'da,* documents 67 (1579), 70 (1579), 35 (1573), 37 (1573).

102 Orhonlu, *Osmanlı İmparatorluğu'nda Aşiretlerin İskânı,* 89–90.

103 Ahmet Refik, *Anadolu'da*, 190–91 (document 265, 1732).

104 Yücel Özkaya, *Osmanlı İmparatorluğu'nda Dağlı İsyanları* (Ankara: Dil ve Tarih Coğrafya Fakültesi Basımevi, 1983).

105 Cezar, *Osmanlı Tarihinde Levendler*, 248–49.

106 Dina Rizk Khoury, "The Ottoman Centre versus Provincial Power Holders: An Analysis of the Historiography," in Faroqhi, *Later Ottoman Empire*, 143; Bruce Masters, "Semi-Autonomous Forces in the Arab Provinces," in Faroqhi, *Later Ottoman Empire*, 196.

107 Ahmet Refik, *Anadolu'da*, 104 (document 157, 1691).

108 Orhonlu, *Osmanlı İmparatorluğu'nda Aşiretlerin İskânı*, 76.

109 Suraiya Faroqhi, "Introduction," in Faroqhi, *Later Ottoman Empire*, 12; Aksan, "War and Peace," 102.

110 Orhonlu, *Osmanlı İmparatorluğu'nda Aşiretlerin İskânı*, 59, 65, 70, and appendix map.

111 Cezar, *Osmanlı Tarihinde Levendler*, 248–49.

112 Orhonlu, *Osmanlı İmparatorluğu'nda Aşiretlerin İskânı*, 108.

113 Cevdet Türkay, *Osmanlı İmparatorluğu'nda Oymak, Aşiret, ve Cemaatler* (Istanbul: İşaret, 2001).

114 Mehmet Genç, "Ottoman Industry in the 18th Century: General Framework, Characteristics and Main Trends," in *Manufacturing in the Ottoman Empire and Turkey, 1500–1950*, ed. Donald Quataert (Albany: State University of New York Press, 1994), 59–86; Mehmet Genç, "Osmanlı Ekonomisi ve Savaş," *Yapıt* 49, no. 4 (1984): 52–56, and 50, no. 5 (1984): 86–93; Elena Frangakis-Syrett, *The Commerce of Smyrna in the Eighteenth Century* (Athens: Centre for Asia Minor Studies, 1992); Bruce Masters, *The Origins of Western Economic Dominance in the Middle East: Mercantilism and Islamic Economy in Aleppo, 1600–1750* (New York: New York University Press, 1988).

115 Yücel Özkaya, *Osmanlı İmparatorluğu'nda Dağlı İsyanları* (Ankara, 1983).

116 İnalcık with Quataert, *Social and Economic History*, 637–758.

4. BUILDING STASIS

1 Mark Sykes, "The Kurdish Tribes of the Ottoman Empire," *Journal of the Royal Anthropological Institute of Great Britain and Ireland* 38 (1908): 456.

2 Andrew Gordon Gould, "Pashas and Brigands: Ottoman Provincial Reform and Its Impact on the Nomadic Tribes of Sothern Anatolia" (Ph.D. diss., University of California, Los Angeles, 1973), 17.

3 See note 105, this chapter.

4 Yaşar Kemal popularized some stories of tribal resistance in a series of novels, the best known of which is *Memed My Hawk*.

5 Gould, "Pashas and Brigands," 27–28.

6   Menemencioğlu Ahmet Bey, *Menemencioğlu Tarihi*, ed. Yilmaz Kurt (Ankara: Akçağ, 1997), xxi.

7   William Francis Ainsworth, *A Personal Narrative of the Euphrates Expedition*, vol. 1 (London, 1888), 106; Cevdet Paşa, *Tezâkir, 21–39* (Ankara: Türk Tarih Kurumu, 1986), 126, 145; Norman Lewis, *Nomads and Settlers in Syria and Jordan* (Cambridge: Cambridge University Press, 1987), 7.

8   Colin Heywood, "The Ottoman Menzilhane and Ulak System in Rumeli in the Eighteenth Century," in *Türkiye'nin Sosyal ve Ekonomik Tarihi, 1071–1920*, ed. Osman Okyar and Halil İnalcık (Ankara: Meteksan, 1980), 179–86; Yücel Özkaya, "XVIII. Yüzyılda Menzilhane Sorunu," *Ankara Üniversitesi Dil ve Tarih Coğrafya Dergisi* 28, nos. 3–4 (1970): 339–68.

9   FO 78/615, Kayseri, March 8, 1845; James Baillie Fraser, *Constantinople to Tehran*, vol. 1 (London, 1838), 82, 136–37; Charles Fellows, *Travels and Researches in Asia Minor, More Particularly in Lycia* (London, 1852), 28.

10 Fikret Adanır, "Semi-Autonomous Provincial Forces in the Balkans and Anatolia," in Faroqhi, *Later Ottoman Empire*, 176.

11 Fellows, *Travels and Researches*, 325–27.

12 Cevdet Paşa, *Tezâkir*, 163.

13 Fellows, *Travels and Researches*, 388–89.

14 Ainsworth, *Personal Narrative*, vol. 1, 41.

15 Enver Beşe, "Anadolu'da Göçebe Türkler," *Türk Folklor Araştırmaları* 31 (1952).

16 Virginia Aksan, *Ottoman Wars, 1700–1870* (Harlow, U.K.: Pearson, 2007), 343ff.

17 Shaw and Shaw, *History of the Ottoman Empire*, vol. 2, 31; Aksan, *Ottoman Wars*, 346.

18 Alexander Sergeevich Pushkin, *A Journey to Arzrum* (Ann Arbor, Mich.: Ardis, 1974), 58.

19 Ibid., 61, 68.

20 *Seattle Times*, December 28, 2005.

21 Fraser, *Constantinople to Tehran*, 25; Robert Curzon, *Armenia: A Year at Erzurum and the Frontier of Russia, Turkey, and Persia* (New York, 1854), 188.

22 Fraser, *Constantinople to Tehran*, 254.

23 Ibid., 255.

24 Curzon, *Armenia*, 188.

25 Fraser, *Constantinople to Tehran*, 314–15.

26 Ibid., 313–14, 318.

27 Shaw and Shaw, *History of the Ottoman Empire*, vol. 2, 32.

28 Fraser, *Constantinople to Tehran*, 300–301, 318, 404.

29 H. Von Möltke, *Türkiye Mektupları* (Istanbul: Varlık, 1982), 101–7.

30 Sinan Marufoğlu, *Osmanlı Döneminde Kuzey Irak* (Istanbul: Eren, 1998), 150.

31 FO 78/615, March 8, 1845.

32   FO 78/491, January 1842.

33   Ufuk Gülsoy, *Osmanlı Rus Savaşında Rumeli'den Rusya'ya Göçürülen Reaya, 1828–1829* (Istanbul: Türk Kültürün Araştırma Enstitüsü, 1993).

34   Eren, *Türkiye'de Göç ve Göçmen Meseleleri*, 36.

35   Khaled Fahmy describes the underlying difficulties, corruption, and cheating that made the Egyptian army less spectacular than the façade it put forth. Khaled Fahmy, *All the Pasha's Men: Mehmed Ali, His Army and the Making of Modern Egypt* (Cambridge: Cambridge University Press, 1997), esp. ch. 4.

36   Ainsworth, *Personal Narrative*, vol. 1, 130.

37   Lewis, *Nomads and Settlers*, 40–41.

38   Gould, "Pashas and Brigands," 14; Cevdet Paşa, *Tezâkir*, 110; Menemencioğlu Ahmet Bey, *Menemencioğlu Tarihi*.

39   A number of fine studies have been published in recent years explaining the rise of local notables in different parts of the empire. See Khoury, *State and Provincial Society*; Beshara Doumani, *Rediscovering Palestine: Merchants and Peasants in Jabal Nablus, 1700–1900* (Berkeley: University of California Press, 1995); and Thomas Philipp, *Acre: The Rise and Fall of a Palestinian City* (New York: Columbia University Press, 2001). Michael Meeker, *A Nation of Empire: The Ottoman Legacy of Turkish Modernity* (Berkeley: University of California Press, 2002).

40   Ainsworth, *Personal Narrative*, vol. 1, 39. See also "A Turkish Watering Place," *Blackwood's Edinburgh Magazine* 380 (June 1847): 745.

41   Ainsworth, *Personal Narrative*, vol. 1, 99–101.

42   Ainsworth, *Personal Narrative*, vol. 2, 71–75; Yitzhak Nakash, *The Shi'is of Iraq* (Princeton, N.J.: Princeton University Press, 1994), 26, 27.

43   Anthony Bryer, "The Last Laz Risings and the Downfall of the Pontic Derebeys, 1812–1840," in *People and Settlement in Anatolia and the Caucasus* (London: Variorum, 1988), 201–5.

44   Ibid., 206.

45   FO 78/533, January 26, 1843.

46   Bryer, "Last Laz Risings," 194.

47   FO 78/443, September 1841.

48   Curzon, *Armenia*, 84.

49   Cevdet Paşa, *Tezâkir*, 127.

50   Ibid., 109, 130.

51   Ibid., 108.

52   FO 78/896, December 18, 1849.

53   FO 78/796, June 27, 1849.

54   Wolfram Eberhard, "Nomads and Farmers in Southeastern Turkey: Problems of Settlement," *Oriens* 6 (1953): 45.

55   Cevdet Paşa, *Tezâkir*, 117.

56   Ibid., 114.

57   Ibid.

58 Ibid., 143.

59 Ibid., 110.

60 Ibid. See also Menemencioğlu Ahmet Bey, *Menemencioğlu Tarihi*.

61 Cevdet Paşa, *Tezâkir*, 131–32.

62 Gould, "Pashas and Brigands," 129. At the time there were 1,300 households in Zeytun, all but 20 to 30 of which were Armenian. Ibid., 60–62.

63 Ibid., 106.

64 Cevdet Paşa, *Tezâkir*, 182.

65 Enver Ziya Karal, *Osmanlı İmparatorluğu'nda İlk Nüfus Sayımı, 1831* (Ankara: İstatistik Umum Müdürlüğü, 1943); Nakash, *Shi'is of Iraq*, 32; Marufoğlu, *Osmanlı Döneminde*, 20.

66 Marufoğlu, *Osmanlı Döneminde*, 50.

67 Fellows, *Travels and Researches*, 260.

68 FO 78/835, September 27, 1849

69 Marufoğlu, *Osmanlı Döneminde*, 66.

70 Möltke, *Türkiye Mektupları*, 107.

71 Gould, "Pashas and Brigands," 41; FO 78/614, June 13, 1845; FO 78/796, June 27, 1849.

72 Aksan, *Ottoman Wars*, 470.

73 Ibid., 358.

74 Çağatay Uluçay, *18. ve 19. Yüzyıllarda Saruhan'da Eşkiyalık ve Halk Hareketleri* (Istanbul: Berksoy, 1955), 31, 70–73, 80–81; Sabri Yetkin, *Ege'de Eşkiyalar* (Istanbul: Tarih Vakfı, 1996); John Koliopoluos, *Brigands with a Cause* (Oxford: Clarendon Press, 1987).

75 Lewis, *Nomads and Settlers*, 30; Gould, "Pashas and Brigands," 130–32; Möltke, *Türkiye Mektupları*, 111.

76 Gould, "Pashas and Brigands," 41.

77 FO 78/835, September 27, 1849.

78 Cevdet Paşa, *Tezâkir*, 134–36.

79 Cevdet Paşa's rivals in the government put him in charge of the army, partly to keep him away from Istanbul. Gould, "Pashas and Brigands," 81.

80 Cevdet Paşa wrote, "15 tabur piyade artı 2 alay suvari artı 5–600 Gürcü, Çerkes, Kürt atlılar." Conversions are per Nuri Yavuz's message to H-TURK, September 6, 2004: a *tabur* equals 400–600 soldiers, and an *alay* equals 5,000 soldiers. Some estimates vary. See Gould, "Pashas and Brigands," 82. Note that these are the maximum possible numbers. In reality, quotas were never filled because of difficulties in recruitment.

81 Gould, "Pashas and Brigands," 85–86.

82 Cevdet Paşa, *Tezâkir*, 148, 151.

83 Ibid., 141–42.

84 Ibid., 126–27, 140; Reşat Kasaba, "Diversity in Antakya: A Historical Perspective," in *The Mediterranean World: The Idea, The Past and Present*, ed. Eyüp Özveren et al. (Istanbul: İletişim, 2006), 216.

85 Cevdet Paşa, *Tezâkir,* 154, 161.

86 Ibid., 144.

87 Ibid., 142, 146, 151, 162.

88 Gould, "Pashas and Brigands," 131.

89 Cevdet Paşa, *Tezâkir,* 142–43, 45.

90 While repairing the Niğolu castle, the Ottomans discovered a stone on which they read that the castle had already been repaired once before, by the forces of Alexander the Great. This suggests that many similar expeditions had been carried out in the region throughout history. Ahmet Cevdet noted that his men placed the stone back in the foundation of the Niğolu citadel for safe-keeping. Cevdet Paşa, *Tezâkir,* 150.

91 Gould, "Pashas and Brigands," 201.

92 Cevdet Paşa, *Tezâkir,* 21–39, 172, 178–79, 183–87; Gould, "Pashas and Brigands," 229–33.

93 *Kavanin ve Nizamat Mecmuası,* cited in Marufoğlu, *Osmanlı Döneminde,* 177.

94 Marufoğlu, *Osmanlı Döneminde,* 178.

95 Ömer Lütfi Barkan, "Türk Toprak Hukuku Tarihinde Tanzimat ve 1274 (1858) Tarihli Arazi Kanunnamesi," in *Türkiye'de Toprak Meselesi* (Istanbul: Gözlem, 1980), 281–375.

96 Eugene Rogan, *Frontiers of the State in the Late Ottoman Empire* (Cambridge: Cambridge University Press, 1999), 85–86; Nakash, *Shi'is of Iraq,* 34; Lewis, *Nomads and Settlers,* 50.

97 Wolf-Dieter Hütteroth, "The Influence of Social Structure on Land Division and Settlement in Inner Anatolia," in *Turkey: Geographic and Social Perspectives,* ed. P. Benedict, E. Tümertekin, and F. Mansur (Leiden: E. J. Brill, 1974), 23; Lewis, *Nomads and Settlers,* 50. One unexpected result of the 1858 code was that it turned the Ottoman sultan into one of the biggest landlords in the empire. Lewis, *Nomads and Settlers,* 43.

98 Lewis, *Nomads and Settlers,* 30; Gould, "Pashas and Brigands," 121.

99 A survey from 1848 describes the settlement of Avşars among the Pehlivanlı and Pörtük tribes. Başbakanlık Arşivi, Maliye Nezaret Ceride Odası (hereaf-ter ML-CRD), 1377. For the original settlement of Avşars, see FO 78/796, June 27, 1849, and FO 78/835, September 27, 1849; Cevdet Paşa, *Tezâkir,* 157; and Earl Percy, *Highlands of Asiatic Turkey* (London, 1901), 89–90.

100 Lewis, *Nomads and Settlers,* 42–43.

101 Gould, "Pashas and Brigands," 138, 146.

102 Nakash, *Shi'is of Iraq,* 32–33.

103 Marufoğlu, *Osmanlı Döneminde,* 181.

104 Fellows, *Travels and Researches,* 136–37.

105 This collection is held at the Başbakanlık Arşivi in Istanbul. The collection is catalogued under Maliye Ceride ML-CRD (Maliye Nezareti Ceride Odası). Most folios are four to five pages, but some elaborate on issues that had to do

with military service or tax arrears, in which case they can run to eighty pages or more.

106 ML-CRD 270 (1838).

107 ML-CRD 269 (1834); ML-CRD 388 (1833, 1839); ML-CRD 677 (1841).

108 ML-CRD 1496 (1850); ML-CRD 609 (1840); ML-CRD 1881 (1863); ML-CRD 2024 (no date).

109 ML-CRD 896 (1845).

110 ML-CRD 1494 (1845).

111 ML-CRD 179 (1255); ML-CRD 1146 (1846).

112 For example, nine adult Armenians and sixteen sons from two to twenty-two years old were counted in the Koçgiri tribe in 1838 (ML-CRD 217 [1838]).

113 It is largely because of the collection of such information that modern scholars such as Ahmet Refik, Cengiz Orhonlu, Peter Andrews, and Cevdet Türkay have been able to trace the histories and political status of thousands of tribes in Anatolia and the Arab provinces over a long period of time. Ahmet Refik, *Anadolu'da;* Orhonlu, *Osmanlı İmparatorluğu'nda Aşiretlerin İskanı;* Peter Andrews, *Ethnic Groups in the Republic of Turkey* (Wiesbaden: Reichert, 1989); Türkay, *Osmanlı İmparatorluğu'nda Oymak.*

114 See Justin McCarthy and Dennis Hyde, "Ottoman Imperial and Provincial Salnames," *Middle East Studies Association Bulletin* 13, no. 1 (1978): 46–48.

115 Halil İnalcık, "Tanzimat'ın Uygulanması ve Sosyal Tepkileri," *Belleten* 28 (1964): 623–90.

116 Fellows, *Travels and Researches,* 409.

117 FO 78/614, June 13, 1845.

118 Aksan, *Ottoman Wars,* 386.

119 Sykes, "Kurdish Tribes," 456.

120 Gould, "Pashas and Brigands," 45. On Kara Fatma, see Ayşe Hür, "Sizin Kahramanınız Hangi Kara Fatma?" *Taraf,* March 8, 2009.

121 Kemal Karpat, "Muslim Migration: Response to Aldeeb Abu-Sahlieh," in Kemal Karpat, *Studies on Ottoman Social and Political History* (Leiden: E. J. Brill, 2002 [1996]), 321.

122 Alan Fisher, "Emigration of Muslims from the Russian Empire in the Years after the Crimean War," in *A Precarious Balance: Conflict, Trade and Diplomacy on the Russian-Ottoman Frontier* (Istanbul: İsis, 1999), 181.

123 Eren, *Türkiye'de Göç ve Göçmen Meseleleri,* 49–50.

124 Dündar, *İttihat ve Terakki'nin Müslümanları İskân Politikası,* 49; Hütteroth, "Influence of Social Structure," 36.

125 Hütteroth, "Influence of Social Structure," 23.

126 Lewis, *Nomads and Settlers,* 44.

127 Eren, *Türkiye'de Göç ve Göçmen Meseleleri,* 70–74.

128 Ahmet Akgündüz, "Migration to and from Turkey, 1783–1960: Types, Numbers and Ethno-Religious Dimensions," *Journal of Ethnic and Migration Studies* 24, no. 1 (1998): 101.

129 Eren, *Türkiye'de Göç ve Göçmen Meseleleri,* 55–58.

130 Dündar, *İttihat ve Terakki'nin Müslümanları İskân Politikası,* 58.

131 Faruk Kocacık, "XIX. Yüzyılda Göçmen Köylerine İlişkin Bazı Yapı Planları," *Istanbul Üniversitesi Edebiyat Fakültesi Tarih Dergisi* 32 (March 1979): 422.

132 Rogan, *Frontiers of the State,* 73; Lewis, *Nomads and Settlers,* 99. See also Kemal Karpat, "The Status of the Muslim under European Rule: The Eviction and Settlement of the Çerkes," in Karpat, *Studies on Ottoman Social and Political History,* 647–75.

133 Roderic Davison, *Reform in the Ottoman Empire* (Princeton, N.J.: Princeton University Press, 1963), 263; Carter Findley, *Bureaucratic Reform in the Ottoman Empire, 1789–1922* (Princeton, N.J.: Princeton University Press, 1980), 188; Kemal Karpat, "Millets and Nationality: The Roots of the Incongruity of Nation and State in the Post-Ottoman Era," in Karpat, *Studies on Ottoman Social and Political History,* 639.

134 Nakash, *Shi'is of Iraq,* 34–35.

135 Cihan Osmanağaoğlu, *Tanzimat Dönemi İtibarıyla Osmanlı Tabiiyetinin (Vatandaşlığının) Gelişimi* (Istanbul: Legal, 2004), 198–249; Marufoğlu, *Osmanlı Döneminde,* 58.

136 Selim Deringil, *The Well Protected Domains* (London: I. B. Tauris, 1998). See also Aksan, *Ottoman Wars.*

137 Hasan Kayalı, *Arabs and the Young Turks* (Berkeley: University of California Press, 1997), 49.

138 Deringil, *Well Protected Domains,* 19, 41; Selim Deringil, "They Live in a State of Nomadism and Savagery: The Late Ottoman Empire and the Post-Colonial Debate," *Comparative Studies in Society and History* 45 (2003): 311–42.

139 Marufoğlu, *Osmanlı Döneminde,* 181.

140 Lewis, *Nomads and Settlers,* 24.

141 Earl Percy, *Highlands of Asiatic Turkey,* 132.

142 See Ussama Makdisi, "Ottoman Orientalism," *American Historical Review* 102, no. 3 (1997): 786–96; Deringil, "They Live in a State"; Thomas Kühn, "An Imperial Borderland as Colony: Knowledge Production and the Elaboration of Difference in Ottoman Yemen, 1872–1918," *MIT Electronic Journal of Middle East Studies* 3 (2003): 5–17; and Isa Blumi, "Beyond the Margins of Empire: Issues concerning Ottoman Boundaries in Yemen and Albania," *MIT Electronic Journal of Middle East Studies* 3 (2003): 18–26. For an early discussion of this topic, see Şerif Mardin, "Center-Periphery Relations: A Key to Turkish Politics," *Daedalus* 102, no. 1 (1973): 169–90.

143 Gould, "Pashas and Brigands," 156.

144 Kocacık, "XIX. Yüzyılda Göçmen Köylerine İlişkin Bazı Yapı Planları," 419.

145 Ibid., 423.

146 Eren, *Türkiye'de Göç ve Göçmen Meseleleri,* 89–90; Bela Howarth, *Anadolu 1913* (Istanbul: Tarih Vakfı, 1996 [1929]).

147 Başbakanlık Arşivi, Dahiliye Nezareti, Muhaberat-ı Umumiye İdare Kalemi (hereafter DH MUI) 67/9 (1910).

148 DH MUI 13-3/2 (1907).

149 Marufoğlu, *Osmanlı Döneminde*, 170-71; Başbakanlık Arşivi, Meclis-i Vükela Mazbataları (hereafter MV) 20/6 (1886).

150 MV 22/50 (1886), 24/48 (1887).

151 MV 22/75 (1886).

152 MV 27/53 (1887).

153 DH MUI 29/37 (1887); Marufoğlu, *Osmanlı Döneminde*, 170-71.

154 MV 35/51 (1887).

155 MV 14/24 (1886).

156 MV 15/56 (1886).

157 MV 22/49 (1886).

158 Gould, "Pashas and Brigands," 208-9.

159 Ibid., 248-50; Yonca Köksal, "Coercion and Mediation: Centralization and Sedentarization of Tribes in the Ottoman Empire," *Middle Eastern Studies* 42, no. 3 (2006): 469-91; Lewis, *Nomads and Settlers*, 36-37, 56-57.

160 Gould, "Pashas and Brigands," 181.

161 Ibid., xv.

162 Nakash, *Shi'is of Iraq*, 35.

163 Orhonlu, *Osmanlı İmparatorluğunda Aşiretlerin İskânı*, 117.

164 Hütteroth, "Influence of Social Structure," 20-39; Lewis, *Nomads and Settlers*, 41; Firestone, "Land Equalization."

165 Gould, "Pashas and Brigands," 146-67.

166 Kocacık, "XIX. Yüzyılda Göçmen Köylerine İlişkin Bazı Yapı Planları," 419.

167 Halit Ziya Uşaklıgil, *Kırk Yıl* (Istanbul: Varlık, 1987), 80.

168 Lewis, *Nomads and Settlers*, 99; Rogan, *Frontiers of the State*, 73.

169 Rogan, *Frontiers of the State*, 75-76.

170 Kocacık, "XIX. Yüzyılda Göçmen Köylerine İlişkin Bazı Yapı Planları," 420; Percy, *Highlands of Asiatic Turkey*, 86.

171 Gould, "Pashas and Brigands," 155.

172 Lewis, *Nomads and Settlers*, 45.

173 Orhonlu, *Osmanlı İmparatorluğunda Aşiretlerin İskânı*, 50 n. 87.

174 Nakash, *Shi'is of Iraq*, 35-45.

175 Van Bruinessen, *Agha, Sheikh and State*, 186. On the Hamidiye regiments, see Bayram Kodaman, "Hamidiye Hafif Süvari Alayları (II. Abdülhamid ve Doğu Anadolu Aşiretleri)," *Tarih Dergisi* 32 (March 1975): 427-80; and Janet Klein, "Power in the Periphery: The Hamidiye Light Cavalry and the Struggle over Ottoman Kurdistan, 1890-1914" (Ph.D. diss., Princeton University, 2002).

176 Van Bruinessen, *Agha, Sheikh and State*, 188.

177 Marufoğlu, *Osmanlı Döneminde*, 172.

178 Ibid., 61.

179 Ibid., 70.

180 Norman Lewis, "The Syrian Steppe during the Last Century of Ottoman Rule: Hawran and the Palmyrena," in *The Transformation of Nomadic Society in the Arab East,* ed. Matha Mundy and Basim Musallam (Cambridge: Cambridge University Press, 2000), 37.

181 Marufoğlu, *Osmanlı Döneminde,* 181–82.

182 Gould, "Pashas and Brigands," 201.

183 Karen Barkey, in *Bandits and Bureaucrats,* makes this argument for an earlier period in discussing the Ottoman government's relations with local notables.

184 For a description of the schism that split the Christian communities and the differences among them, see Bruce Masters, *Christians and Jews in the Ottoman Arab World* (Cambridge: Cambridge University Press, 2001), 45–47.

185 Earl Percy, *Highlands of Asiatic Turkey,* 192.

186 Marufoğlu, *Osmanlı Döneminde,* 149.

187 Sykes, "Kurdish Tribes," 465.

188 MV 17/26 (1886).

5. THE IMMOVABLE STATE

1 Hasan Kayalı, "Elections and the Electoral Process in the Ottoman Empire," *International Journal of Middle East Studies* 27, no. 3 (1995): 265–86.

2 Fevzi Demir, "İkinci Meşrutiyet Dönemi Meclis-i Mebusanında Etnik Grubların Temsiline İlişkin Bazı Gözlem ve Veriler," in *Tarih ve Milliyetçilik* (Mersin: Mersin Üniversitesi, 1999), 348–68.

3 The number of refugees in Europe at the end of World War I is estimated to have been about 9.5 million. According to some sources, Europe had not witnessed mass movement on this scale since the barbarian invasions. See Michael Marrus, *The Unwanted: European Refugees in the Twentieth Century* (New York: Oxford University Press, 1985), 51–121; also Norman Naimark, *Fires of Hatred: Ethnic Cleansing in Twentieth-Century Europe* (Cambridge, Mass.: Harvard University Press, 2001), 17–56.

4 The term "unmixing of people," originally used by Lord Curzon, was expanded upon by Rogers Brubaker in *Nationalism Reframed* (Cambridge: Cambridge University Press, 1996), 148–78. So complex was the social makeup of the Balkans in the late nineteenth century that 100 years later the process of disentangling communities was still incomplete, leading to yet another Balkan war in the 1990s.

5 See the essays in Joel Migdal, ed., *Boundaries and Belonging: States and Societies in the Struggle to Shape Identities and Local Politics* (Cambridge: Cambridge University Press, 2004).

6 Reşat Kasaba, "Migrant Labor in Western Anatolia," in *Landholding and Commercial Agriculture in the Middle East,* ed. Çağlar Keyder and Faruk Tabak (Albany: State University of New York Press, 1991), 113–21; Reşat Kasaba, "A

Time and a Place for the Nonstate: Social Change in the Ottoman Empire during the 'Long Nineteenth Century,'" in *State Power and Social Forces,* ed. Joel Migdal, Atul Kohli, and Vivienne Shue (Cambridge: Cambridge University Press, 1994); Kasaba, "Do States Always Favor Stasis?" 27–48; Gersaimos Augustinos, *The Greeks of Asia Minor* (Kent, Ohio: Kent State University Press, 1992), 26–32.

7   Augustinos, *Greeks of Asia Minor,* 22.

8   Anastasia Karakasidou, *Fields of Wheat, Hills of Blood* (Chicago: University of Chicago Press, 1997); Mark Mazower, *The Balkans: A Short History* (New York: Modern Library, 2000), 113–44. See also L. S. Stavrianos, *The Balkans since 1453* (New York: Rinehart, 1958); and Barbara Jelavich and Charles Jelavich, *The Establishment of Balkan National States* (Seattle: University of Washington Press, 1977).

9   Carnegie Endowment, *The Other Balkan Wars: A Carnegie Endowment Inquiry* (Washington, D.C., 1993), 148–207.

10   See Taner Akçam, *Türk Ulusal Kimliği ve Ermeni Sorunu* (Istanbul: Su Yayınları, 2001); Taner Akçam, *A Shameful Act: The Armenian Genocide and the Question of Turkish Responsibility* (New York: Metropolitan Books, 2006); Fikret Adanır, "Armenian Deportations and Massacres in 1915," in *Ethnopolitical Conflict,* ed. Daniel Chirot and Martin Seligman (Washington, D.C.: American Psychological Association, 2001), 71–82; and Ronald Suny, "Religion, Ethnicity and Nationalism: Armenians, Turks and the End of the Ottoman Empire," in *In God's Name: Genocide and Religion in the Twentieth Century,* ed. Omer Bartov and Phyllis Mack (New York: Berghahn Books, 2001), 23–61.

11   Deringil, *Well Protected Domains,* 84–91.

12   Arman Kirakossian, ed., *The Armenian Massacres, 1894–1896* (Detroit: Wayne State University Press, 2004); Stina Katchadourian, ed., *Great Need over the Water: The Letters of Theresa Huntington Ziegler, Missionary to Turkey, 1898–1905* (Ann Arbor, Mich.: Gomidas Institute, 1999).

13   James Barton, ed., *Turkish Atrocities: Statements of American Missionaries on the Destruction of Christian Communities in Ottoman Turkey: 1915–1917* (Ann Arbor, Mich.: Gomidas Institute, 1998); Henry Riggs, *Days of Tragedy in Armenia: Personal Experiences in Harpoot, 1915–1917* (Ann Arbor, Mich.: Gomidas Institute, 1997).

14   Henry Morgenthau, *Ambassador Morgenthau's Story* (New York: Doubleday, 1918); Leslie Davis, *The Slaughterhouse Province: An American Diplomat's Report on the Armenian Genocide, 1915–1917,* ed. Susan Blair (New Rochelle, N.Y.: Aristide Caratazas, 1989); Samantha Powers, *A Problem from Hell* (New York: Perennial, 2003).

15   Ahmet Refik, *İki Komite, İki Kıtal* (Ankara: Kebikeç, 1994); Halil Menteşe, *Osmanlı Mebusan Meclisi Reisi Halil Menteşe'nin Anıları* (Istanbul: Hürriyet Vakfı Yayınları, 1986).

16 Donald Miller and Lorna Touryan Miller, eds., *Survivors: An Oral History of the Armenian Genocide* (Berkeley: University of California Press, 1993); Peter Balakian, *Black Dog of Fate* (New York: Basic Books, 1997).

17 For example, Fethiye Çınar, *Anneannem* (Istanbul: Metis, 2005).

18 Refik, *İki Komite*, 30.

19 Ibid., 45.

20 Morgenthau, *Ambassador Morgenthau's Story*, 309.

21 Refik, *İki Komite*, 45.

22 Menteşe, *Osmanlı Mebusan Meclisi*, 216.

23 "Turkish Region Recalls Massacre of Armenians," *New York Times*, May 10, 2000.

24 Refik, *İki Komite*, 27.

25 Ibid., 42.

26 Adanır, "Armenian Deportations and Massacres," 74.

27 Riggs, *Days of Tragedy*, 111.

28 Raif Kaplanoğlu, *Bursa'da Mübadele* (Bursa: Avrasya Etnografya Yayınları 1999), 41. Many thanks to Ali İğmen for bringing this book to my attention.

29 The literature about the Armenian genocide is vast. Three recent additions that also provide comprehensive reviews are Akçam, *A Shameful Act*; Guenter Lewy, *The Armenian Massacres in Ottoman Turkey: A Disputed Genocide* (Salt Lake City: University of Utah Press, 2005); and Donald Bloxham, *The Great Game of Genocide: Imperialism, Nationalism, and the Destruction of the Ottoman Armenians* (Oxford: Oxford University Press, 2005). See also Murat Bardakçı, *Talât Paşa'nın Evrak-ı Metrukesi* (Istanbul: Everest, 2008).

30 Dündar, *İttihat ve Terakki'nin*, 63.

31 Ibid., 65.

32 Ibid., 104; Kayalı, *Arabs and Young Turks*, 194.

33 Stephen Ladas, *The Exchange of Minorities: Bulgaria, Greece, and Turkey* (New York: Macmillan, 1932); A. A. Pallis, "Racial Migrations in the Balkans during the Years 1912–1924," *Geographical Journal* 66 (October 1925): 315–33; Engin Berber, *Sancılı Yıllar: İzmir, 1918–1922* (Anakara: Ayraç, 1997).

34 Dündar, *İttihat ve Terakki'nin*, 151; Kemal Arı, *Büyük Mübadele* (Istanbul: Tarih Vakfı, 1995), 9.

35 Dündar, *İttihat ve Terakki'nin*, 71.

36 Ibid., 91; Onur Yıldırım, *Diplomasi ve Göç: Türk-Yunan Mübadelesinin Öteki Yüzü* (Istanbul: Bilgi Üniversitesi, 2007), 150–51.

37 Theo Halo, *Not Even My Name* (New York: Picador, 2000); Küçük Asya Araştırmalar Merkezi, *Göç: Rumlar'ın Anadolu'dan Mecburi Ayrılışı* (Istanbul: İletişim, 2001).

38 See Reşat Kasaba, "İzmir 1922: A Port City Unravels," in *Modernity and Culture,* ed. Leila Tarazi Fawaz and C. A. Bayly (New York: Columbia University Press, 2002), 204–29; Arı, *Büyük Mübadele*, 7.

39   Dündar, *İttihat ve Terakki'nin,* 57; Yıldırım, *Diplomasi ve Göç; Arı, Büyük Mübadele,* 7; Ladas, *Exchange of Minorities,* 420–42.

40   Yıldırım, *Diplomasi ve Göç,* 190; Kasaba, "Diversity in Antakya."

41   Richard Clogg, "Anadolu Hritiyan Karındaşlarımız: The Turkish-Speaking Greeks of Asia Minor," in *Neohellenism,* ed. John Burke and Stahis Gauntlett (Canberra: Australian National University, 1992), 65–91; Argiris Petronotis, *Hacıustalar: Akdağmadeni'nden Aridea'ya Bir Mübadele Öyküsü* (Istanbul: Kitap Yayınları, 2004).

42   Yıldırım, *Diplomasi ve Göç,* 210–14.

43   Petronotis, *Hacıustalar,* 46.

44   Yıldırım, *Diplomasi ve Göç,* 203–5.

45   League of Nations, *The Settlement of Greek Refugees* (Geneva, 1924), 3.

46   Ernest Hemingway, *The Wild Years* (New York: Dell, 1962), 200.

47   Karakasidou, *Fields of Wheat,* 164–69; Elisabeth Kontogiorgi, *Population Exchange in Greek Macedonia* (Oxford: Oxford University Press, 2006), 140–62, 175–85.

48   Kontogiorgi, *Population Exchange,* 168.

49   Renée Hirschon, *Heirs of the Greek Catastrophe* (New York: Berghahn, 1998). See also Kemal Yalçın, *Emanet Çeyiz* (Istanbul: Doğan Kitap, 1998); and Peter Loizos, "Ottoman Half-Lives: Long-Term Perspectives on Particular Forced Migrations," *Journal of Refugee Studies* 12, no. 3 (1999): 237–63.

50   Arı, *Büyük Mübadele,* 83–84.

51   Kaplanoğlu, *Bursa'da Mübadele,* 47.

52   Yıldırım, *Diplomasi ve Göç,* 154–56.

53   Arı, *Büyük Mübadele,* 52–53; Yıldırım, *Diplomasi ve Göç,* 159–60.

54   Arı, *Büyük Mübadele,* 12.

55   Yıldırım, *Diplomasi ve Göç,* 244.

56   Arı, *Büyük Mübadele,* 155.

57   Kemal Karpat, *Ottoman Population* (Madison: University of Wisconsin Press, 1985), 168; Cem Behar, *Osmanlı İmparatorluğu'nun ve Türkiye'nin Nüfusu, 1500–1927* (Ankara: Devlet İstatistik Enstitüsü, 1996), 56; Umumi Nüfus Tahriri, *28 Teşrinievvel 1927* (Ankara: Hüsnütabiat Matbaası, 1929), 31; Bardakçı, *Talât Paşa'nın.*

58   Roger Owen and Şevket Pamuk, *A History of Middle East Economies in the Twentieth Century* (Cambridge, Mass.: Harvard University Press, 1998).

59   Menteşe, *Osmanlı Mebusan Meclisi,* 166.

60   Dündar, *İttihat ve Terakki'nin,* 72.

61   See Deringil, *Well Protected Domains.*

62   Dündar, *İttihat ve Terakki'nin,* 53. Kemal Karpat, in a series of articles reprinted in his book *Studies on Ottoman Social and Political History* (Leiden: E. J. Brill, 2002), explained the various aspects of changing migration policy in the Ottoman Empire in the nineteenth century. See his chapters "Muslim

Migration," 311–23; "Ottoman Migration, Ethnopolitics, and the Formation of Nation States in South-East Europe and Israel," 752–82; "Ottoman Immigration Policies and Settlement in Palestine," 783–99; "The Ottoman Emigration to America, 1862–1914," 90–131; and "Jewish Population Movements in the Ottoman Empire, 1862–1914," 146–68.

63 Dündar, İttihat ve Terakki'nin, 108–23.

64 Kayalı, Arabs and Young Turks, 194.

65 Dündar, İlttihat ve Terakki'nin, 83.

66 For the effects of ethnic unmixing on Salonica, see Mark Mazower, Salonica: City of Ghosts (New York: Knopf, 2005). On the (re)formation of Greek nationalism, see Michael Herzfeld, Ours Once More (New York: Pella, 1986), and Michael Llewellyn Smith, Ionian Vision: Greece in Asia Minor, 1919–1922 (Ann Arbor: University of Michigan Press, 1998 [1973]). For a more focused study of these processes in Macedonia, see Karakasidou, Fields of Wheat.

67 Dündar, İttihat ve Terakki'nin, 139–40; Yıldırım, Diplomasi ve Göç, 158.

68 Dündar, İttihat ve Terakki'nin, 60.

69 Ibid., 137–55, 167.

70 Ibid., 142.

71 Yıldırım, Diplomasi ve Göç, 217.

72 Ladas, Exchange of Minorities, 390.

73 Yıldırım, Diplomasi ve Göç, 177–78.

74 Mazower, The Balkans, 119–20.

75 Dündar, İttihat ve Terakki'nin, 65.

76 Marcel Clerget, La Turquie passé et présent (Paris: A. Colin, 1947), 89.

Bibliography

ARCHIVAL SOURCES

Turkey
Başbakanlık Arşivi
    Dahiliye Nezareti, Muhaberat-ı Umumiye Idare Kalemi (DH MUI)
    Maliye Nezaret Ceride Odası (ML-CRD)
    Meclis-i Vükela Mazbataları (MV)

United Kingdom
Public Records Office, Foreign Office, FO/78 Consular Correspondence.

PUBLISHED SOURCES

Abou-El-Haj, Rifa'at Ali. *Formation of the Modern State: The Ottoman Empire, Sixteenth to Eighteenth Centuries.* Albany: State University of New York Press, 1991.
———. "Ottoman Diplomacy at Karlowitz." *Journal of the American Oriental Society* 87, no. 4 (1967): 498–512.
———. "The Ottoman Nasihatname as a Discourse over Morality." *Mélanges Robert Mantran, Revue Histoire Maghrebine* 47–48 (1987): 17–30.
Adanır, Fikret. "Armenian Deportations and Massacres in 1915." In *Ethnopolitical Conflict,* ed. Daniel Chirot and Martin Seligman, 71–82. Washington, D.C.: American Psychological Association, 2001.

————. "The Ottoman Peasantries, c. 1360–1860." In *The Peasantries of Europe from the Fourteenth to Eighteenth Centuries*, ed. Tom Scott, 269–310. London: Longman, 1998.

————. "Semi-Autonomous Provincial Forces in the Balkans and Anatolia." In *The Cambridge History of Turkey*, vol. 3, *The Later Ottoman Empire*, ed. Suraiya Faroqhi, 157–85. Cambridge: Cambridge University Press, 2006.

Agoston, Gabor. "A Flexible Empire: Authority and Its Limits on the Ottoman Frontiers." *International Journal of Turkish Studies* 9, no. 1–2 (2003): 15–31.

Ahmet Ağa. *Viyana Kuşatması Günlüğü*. Trans. Esat Nermi. Istanbul: Milliyet Yayınları, 1970.

————. *Hicri Onikinci Asirda Istanbul Hayatı*. Istanbul: Devlet Matbaası, 1930.

————. *İki Komite, İki Kıtal*. Ankara: Kebikeç, 1994.

————. *Osmanlı Devrinde Türkiye Madenleri*. Istanbul: Enderun Kitabevi, 1989.

Ahmet Refik. Anadolu'da Türk Aşiretleri. Istanbul: Devlet Matbaası, 1930.

Ainsworth, William Francis. *A Personal Narrative of the Euphrates Expedition*. 2 vols. London, 1888.

Akçam, Taner. *A Shameful Act: The Armenian Genocide and the Question of Turkish Responsibility*. New York: Metropolitan Books, 2006.

————. *Türk Ulusal Kimliği ve Ermeni Sorunu*. Istanbul: Su Yayınları, 2001.

Akgündüz, Ahmet. "Migration to and from Turkey, 1783–1960: Types, Numbers and Ethno-Religious Dimensions." *Journal of Ethnic and Migration Studies* 24, no. 1 (1998): 97–120.

Aksan, Virginia. "Ottoman Political Writing, 1768–1808." *International Journal of Middle East Studies* 25 (1993): 53–69.

————. "Ottoman Sources of Information on Europe in the Eighteenth Century." *Archivum Ottomanicum* 11 (1986): 5–16.

————. *Ottoman Wars, 1700–1870*. Harlow, U.K.: Pearson, 2007.

————. "War and Peace." In *The Cambridge History of Turkey*, vol. 3, *The Later Ottoman Empire*, ed. Suraiya Faroqhi, 81–117. Cambridge: Cambridge University Press, 2006.

Aktepe, Münir. "XIV. ve XV. Asırlarda Rumeli'nin Türkler Tarafından İskânına Dair." *Türkiyat Mecmuası* 10 (1951–53): 299–312.

Anderson, Perry. *Lineages of the Absolutist State*. London: Verso, 1974.

Andrews, Peter. *Ethnic Groups in the Republic of Turkey*. Wiesbaden: Reichert, 1989.

Arı, Kemal. *Büyük Mübadele*. Istanbul: Tarih Vakfı, 1995.

Augustinos, Gersaimos. *The Greeks of Asia Minor*. Kent, Ohio: Kent State University Press, 1992.

Babinger, F. *Mehmed the Conqueror and His Time*. Princeton, N.J.: Princeton University Press, 1978.

Baer, Marc. *Bound by the Glory of Islam*. New York: Oxford University Press, 2008.

Balakian, Peter. *Black Dog of Fate*. New York: Basic Books, 1997.

Bardakçı, Murat. Talât Paşa'nın Evrak-ı Metrukesı: Sadrazam Talat Pasa'nın özel arşivinde bulunan Ermeni tehciri konusndaki belgeler ve hususi yaısmalar. Istanbul: Everest, 2008.

Barfield, Thomas. *The Nomadic Alternative*. Englewood Cliffs, N.J.: Prentice Hall, 1993.

Barkan, Ömer Lütfi. "Osmanlı İmparatorluğunda Bir İskân ve Kolonizasyon Metodu Olarak Sürgünler." *İstanbul Üniversitesi İktisat Fakültesi Mecmuası*, part 1, vol. 11 (1949–50): 254–569; part 2, vol. 13 (1952): 56–79; part 3, vol. 14 (1953–54): 209–36.

———. "Osmanlı İmparatorluğu'nda Bir İskân ve Kolonizasyon Metodu Olarak Vakıflar ve Temlikler: I. İstila devirlerinin Kolonizator Türk Dervişleri ve

———. "Research on the Ottoman Fiscal Surveys." In *Studies in the Economic History of the Middle East*, ed. M. A. Cook. London: Oxford University Press, 1970.

———. "Türk Toprak Hukuku Tarihinde Tanzimat ve 1274 (1858) Tarihli Arazi Kanunnamesi." In *Türkiye'de Toprak Meselesi*, 281–375. Istanbul: Gözlem, 1980.

Barkey, Karen. *Bandits and Bureaucrats: The Ottoman Route to State Centralization*. Ithaca, N.Y.: Cornell University Press, 1994.

———. *Empire of Difference: The Ottomans in Comparative Perspective*. Cambridge: Cambridge University Press, 2008.

Barnes, John Robert. "The Dervish Orders in the Ottoman Empire." In *The Dervish Lodge*, ed. Raymond Lifchez, 33–48. Berkeley: University of California Press, 1992.

Barton, James, ed. *Turkish Atrocities: Statements of American Missionaries on the Destruction of Christian Communities in Ottoman Turkey: 1915–1917*. Ann Arbor, Mich.: Gomidas Institute, 1998.

Bates, Daniel. "The Role of the State in Peasant-Nomad Mutualism." *Anthropological Quarterly* 44, no. 3 (1971): 109–32.

Behar, Cem. *Osmanlı İmparatorluğu'nun ve Türkiye'nin Nüfusu, 1500–1927*. Ankara: Devlet İstatistik Enstitüsü, 1996.

Berber, Engin. *Sancılı Yıllar: İzmir, 1918–1922*. Ankara: Ayraç, 1997.

Berktay, Halil. *Cumhuriyet İdeolojisi ve Fuat Köprülü*. Istanbul: Kaynak, 1983.

Beşe, Enver. "Anadolu'da Göçebe Türkler." *Türk Folklor Araştırmaları* 31 (1952).

Birnbaum, Eleazar. "The Questing Mind: Kâtib Chelebi, 1609–1657. A Chapter in Ottoman Intellectual History." In *Corolla Torontonensis: Studies in Honour of Ronald Morton Smith*, ed. Emmet Robbins and Stella Sandahl, 133–59. Toronto: TSAR, 1994.

Black, Jeremy. *Maps in History*. New Haven, Conn.: Yale University Press, 1997.

———. "Warfare, Crisis, and Absolutism." In *Early Modern Europe*, ed. Euan Cameron, 206–30. Oxford: Oxford University Press, 1999.

Bloxham, Donald. *The Great Game of Genocide: Imperialism, Nationalism, and the Destruction of the Ottoman Armenians*. Oxford: Oxford University Press, 2005.

Blumi, Isa. "Beyond the Margins of Empire: Issues concerning Ottoman Boundaries in Yemen and Albania." *MIT Electronic Journal of Middle East Studies* 3 (2003): 18–26.

Braudel, Fernand. *The Mediterranean and the Mediterranean World in the Age of Philip II*, vol. 1. London: Fontana, 1972.

Brubaker, Rogers. *Nationalism Reframed*. Cambridge: Cambridge University Press, 1996.

Brummett, Palmira. "Visions of the Mediterranean: A Classification." *Journal of Medieval and Early Modern Studies* 37, no. 1 (2007): 9–55.

Bryer, Anthony. "The Last Laz Risings and the Downfall of the Pontic Derebeys, 1812–1840." In *People and Settlement in Anatolia and the Caucasus*, 191–200. London: Variorum, 1988.

Buchanan, Harvey. "Luther and the Turks." *Archiv für Reformationgeschichte* 47, no. 2 (1956): 145–60.

Cahen, Claude. *Pre-Ottoman Turkey*. New York: Taplinger, 1968.

Carnegie Endowment. *The Other Balkan Wars: A Carnegie Endowment Inquiry*. Washington, D.C., 1993.

Çetintürk, Salahaddin. "Osmanlı İmparatorluğu'nda Yürük Sınıfı ve Hukuki Statüleri." *Ankara Üniversitesi Dil ve Tarih Coğrafya Fakültesi Dergisi* 2 (1943): 107–16.

Cevdet Paşa. *Tezâkir, 21–39*. Ankara: Türk Tarih Kurumu, 1986.

Ceyhun, Demirtaş. *Ah Şu Biz Kara Bıyıklı Türkler*. Istanbul: E Yayınları, 1992.

Cezar, Mustafa. *Osmanlı Tarihinde Levendler*. Istanbul: Çelikcilt, 1965.

Çınar, Fethiye. *Anneannem*. Istanbul: Metis, 2005.

Clerget, Marcel. *La Turquie passé et présent*. Paris: A. Colin, 1947.

Clogg, Richard. "Anadolu Hristiyan Karındaşlarımız: The Turkish-Speaking Greeks of Asia Minor." In *Neohellenism*, ed. John Burke and Stahis Gauntlett, 65–91. Canberra: Australian National University, 1992.

Cook, M. A. *Population Pressure in Rural Anatolia, 1450–1600*. Oxford: Oxford University Press, 1972.

———, ed. *A History of the Ottoman Empire to 1730*. Cambridge: Cambridge University Press, 1976.

Curzon, Robert. *Armenia: A Year at Erzurum and the Frontier of Russia, Turkey and Persia*. New York, 1854.

Dankoff, Robert. *Evliya Çelebi in Bitlis*. Leiden: E. J. Brill, 1990.

Davis, Leslie. *The Slaughterhouse Province: An American Diplomat's Report on the Armenian Genocide, 1915–1917*. Ed. Susan Blair. New Rochelle, N.Y.: Aristide Caratazas, 1989.

Davison, Roderic. *Reform in the Ottoman Empire*. Princeton, N.J.: Princeton University Press, 1963.

Demir, Fevzi. "Ikinci Meşrutiyet Dönemi Meclis-i Mebusanında Etnik Grubların

Temsiline İlişkin Bazı Gözlem ve Veriler." In *Tarih ve Milliyetçilik,* 348–68. Mersin: Mersin Üniversitesi, 1999.

Deringil, Selim. "They Live in a State of Nomadism and Savagery: The Late Ottoman Empire and the Post-Colonial Debate." *Comparative Studies in Society and History* 45 (2003): 311–42.

————. *The Well Protected Domains.* London: I. B. Tauris, 1998.

Doğruel, Fulya. *Hatay'da Çoketnili Ortak Yaşam Kültürü İnsaniyetleri Benzer.* Istanbul: İletişim, 2005.

Doumani, Beshara. *Rediscovering Palestine: Merchants and Peasants in Jabal Nablus, 1700–1900.* Berkeley: University of California Press, 1995.

Dündar, Fuat. *İttihat ve Terakki'nin Müslümanları İskân Politikası.* Istanbul: İletişim, 2001.

Dunn, Ross. *The Adventures of Ibn Battuta, a Muslim Traveler of the Fourteenth Century.* Berkeley: University of California Press, 1985.

Durkheim, Emile. *Selected Writings.* Ed. Anthony Giddens. Cambridge: Cambridge University Press, 1972.

Eberhard, Wolfram. "Nomads and Farmers in Southeastern Turkey: Problems of Settlement." *Oriens* 6 (1953): 2–49.

Eldem, Edhem, Daniel Goffman, and Bruce Masters. *Ottoman City between East and West.* Cambridge: Cambridge University Press, 1999.

Elliott, J. H. *The Old World and the New.* Cambridge: Cambridge University Press, 1970.

Emecen, Feridun. *XVI. Asırda Manisa Kazası.* Ankara: Türk Tarih Kurumu, 1989.

————. "The History of an Early Sixteenth-Century Migration: Sirem Exiles in Gallipoli." In *Hungarian-Ottoman Military and Diplomatic Relations in the Age of Süleyman the Magnificent,* ed. Geza David and Pal Fodor, 77–91. Budapest: Acta Orientalia Academiae Scientiarum Hungaricae, 1994.

Eren, Ahmet Cevat. *Türkiye'de Göç ve Göçmen Meseleleri.* Istanbul: Nurgök, 1966.

Evin, Ahmet. "Tulip Age and Definitions of Westernization." In *Social and Economic History of Turkey,* ed. Osman Okyar and Halil İnalcık, 131–45. Ankara: Meteksan, 1980.

Fahmy, Khaled. *All the Pasha's Men: Mehmed Ali, His Army and the Making of Modern Egypt.* Cambridge: Cambridge University Press, 1997.

Faroqhi, Suraiya. *Coping with the State: Political Conflict and Crime in the Ottoman Empire, 1520–1750.* Istanbul: Isis, 1995.

————. "Crisis and Change." In *An Economic and Social History of the Ottoman Empire, 1300–1914,* ed. Halil İnalcık with Donald Quataert, 411–636. Cambridge: Cambridge University Press, 1994.

————. "Introduction." In *The Cambridge History of Turkey,* vol. 3, *The Later Ottoman Empire, 1603–1839,* ed. Suraiya Faroqhi, 3–17. Cambridge: Cambridge University Press, 2006.

————. "Rural Life." In *The Cambridge History of Turkey,* vol. 3, *The Later Otto-*

man Empire, 1603–1839, ed. Suraiya Faroqhi, 376–90. Cambridge: Cambridge University Press, 2006.

Fellows, Charles. *Travels and Researches in Asia Minor, More Particularly in Lycia.* London, 1852.

Findley, Carter. *Bureaucratic Reform in the Ottoman Empire, 1789–1922.* Princeton, N.J.: Princeton University Press, 1980.

Finkel, Caroline. *Osman's Dream.* New York: Basic Books, 2005.

Firestone, Ya'akov. "Land Equalization and Factor Scarcities: Holding Size and the Burden of Impositions in Imperial Russia and the Late Ottoman Levant." *Journal of Economic History* 41 (December 1981): 813–33.

Fisher, Alan. "Emigration of Muslims from the Russian Empire in the Years after the Crimean War." In Alan Fisher, *A Precarious Balance: Conflict, Trade and Diplomacy on the Russian-Ottoman Frontier,* 171–91. Istanbul: Isis, 1999.

Fleischer, Cornell. *Bureaucrat and Intellectual in the Ottoman Empire: The Historian Mustafa Ali, 1541–1600.* Princeton, N.J.: Princeton University Press, 1983.

———. "Royal Authority, Dynastic Cyclism and 'Ibn Khaldunism' in Sixteenth-Century Ottoman Letters." In *Ibn Khaldun and Islamic Ideology,* ed. Bruce Lawrence, 46–68. Leiden: E. J. Brill, 1984.

Fonseca, Isabel. *Bury Me Standing: The Gypsies and Their Journey.* New York: Knopf, 1995.

Forell, George. "Luther and the War against the Turks." *Church History* 14, no. 4 (1945): 256–71.

Forster, Charles Thornton, and F. H. Blackburne Daniell, eds. *The Life and Letters of Ogier Ghiselin de Busbecq.* London, 1881.

Frangakis-Syrett, Elena. *The Commerce of Smyrna in the Eighteenth Century.* Athens: Centre for Asia Minor Studies, 1992.

Fraser, James Baillie. *Constantinople to Tehran,* vol. 1. London, 1838.

Freely, John. *Istanbul, the Imperial City.* London: Penguin, 1998.

Gellner, Ernest. *Muslim Society.* Cambridge: Cambridge University Press, 1981.

Genç, Mehmet. "Osmanlı Ekonomisi ve Savaş." *Yapıt* 49, no. 4 (1984): 52–56, and 50, no. 5 (1984): 86–93.

———. "Osmanlı Maliyesinde Malikâne Sistemi." In *Türkiye İktisat Tarihi Semineri,* ed. Osman Okyar and Ünal Nalbantoğlu, 231–96. Ankara: Hacettepe Universitesi Yayınları, 1975.

———. "Ottoman Industry in the 18th Century: General Framework, Characteristics and Main Trends." In *Manufacturing in the Ottoman Empire and Turkey, 1500–1950,* ed. Donald Quataert, 59–86. Albany: State University of New York Press, 1994.

Goffman, Daniel. *İzmir and the Levantine World.* Seattle: University of Washington Press, 1990.

Gökalp, Ziya. *Kürt Aşiretleri Hakkında Sosyolojik Tetkikler.* Istanbul: Sosyal, 1992 [1924].

Gökbilgin, Tayyib. *Rumeli'de Yürükler, Tatarlar ve Evlad-ı Fatihan*. Istanbul: Osman Yalçın Matbaasi, 1957.

Gökçen, Ibrahim. *Saruhan'da Yürük ve Türkmenler*. Istanbul: Marifet Basımevi, 1946.

Goodrich, Thomas. *The Ottoman Turks and the New World: A Study of Tarih-i Hind-i Garbi and Sixteenth-Century Americana*. Wiesbaden: O. Harrassowitz, 1990.

Gould, Andrew Gordon. "Pashas and Brigands: Ottoman Provincial Reform and Its Impact on the Nomadic Tribes of Sothern Anatolia." Ph.D. diss., University of California at Los Angeles, 1973.

Güçer, Lütfü. *XVI. ve XVII. Asırlarda Osmanlı İmparatorluğunda Hububat Meselesi ve Hububattan Alınan Vergiler*. Istanbul: Semet, 1964.

Gülsoy, Ufuk. *Osmanlı Rus Savaşında Rumeli'den Rusya'ya Göçürülen Reaya, 1828–1829*. Istanbul: Türk Kültürün Araştırma Enstitüsü, 1993.

Gündüz, Tufan. *Anadolu'da Türkmen Aşiretleri*. Ankara: Bilge Yayınları, 1997.

Güngör, Kemal. *Cenubi Anadolu Yürüklerinin Etno-Antroplojik Tetkiki*. Ankara: İdeal, 1941.

Hallaçoğlu, Yusuf. *XVIII. Yüzyılda Osmanlı İmparatorluğu'nun İskân Siyaseti ve Aşiretlerin Yerleştirilmesi*. Ankara: Türk Tarih Kurumu, 1988.

Halo, Theo. *Not Even My Name*. New York: Picador, 2000.

Hemingway, Ernest. *The Wild Years*. New York: Dell, 1962.

Herzfeld, Michael. *Ours Once More*. New York: Pella, 1986.

Heywood, Colin. "Boundless Dreams of the Levant: Paul Wittek, the Geroge-Kreis, and the Writing of Ottoman History." *Journal of the Royal Asiatic Society* 1 (1988): 7–25.

———. "The Frontier in Ottoman History: Old Ideas and New Myths." In *Writing Ottoman History*, 228–50. London: Variorum, 2002.

———. "The Ottoman Menzilhane and Ulak System in Rumeli in the Eighteenth Century." In *Türkiye'nin Sosyal ve Ekonomik Tarihi, 1071–1920*, ed. Osman Okyar and Halil İnalcık, 179–86. Ankara: Meteksan, 1980.

Hirsch, Eva. *Poverty and Plenty on the Turkish Farm*. New York: Middle East Institute of Columbia University, 1970.

Hirschon, Renée. *Heirs of the Greek Catastrophe*. New York: Berghahn Books, 1998.

Howarth, Bela. *Anadolu 1913*. Istanbul: Tarih Vakfı, 1996 (1929).

Hür, Ayşe. "Sizin Kahramanınız Hangi Kara Fatma?" *Taraf*, March 8, 209; http://www.taraf.com.tr/makale/4405.htm.

Hurewitz, J. C. *Diplomacy in the Middle East: A Documentary Record*. Princeton, N.J.: Princeton University Press, 1956.

Hütteroth, Wolf-Dieter. "The Influence of Social Structure on Land Division and Settlement in Inner Anatolia." In *Turkey: Geographic and Social Perspectives*, ed. P. Benedict, E. Tümertekin, and F. Mansur, 19–47. Leiden: E. J. Brill, 1974.

Ibn Khaldun. *The Muqaddimah*. Princeton, N.J.: Princeton University Press, 1958.

Imber, Colin. "Heath Lowry, *The Nature of the Early Ottoman State*," book review. *Turkish Studies Association Journal* 27, nos. 1–2 (2003): 108–16.

———. "The Ottoman Dynastic Myth." *Turcica* 19 (1987): 7–27.

———. "The Persecution of Ottoman Shi'ites according to the Muhimme Defterleri." *Der Islam* 56 (1979): 245–73.

İnalcık, Halil. "'Arab' Camel Drivers in Western Anatolia in the Fifteenth Century." *Revue d'Histoire Maghrebine* 10, nos. 31–32 (1983): 247–70.

———. *Fatih Devri Üzerine Tetkikler ve Vesikalar*. Ankara: Türk Tarih Kurumu, 1954.

———. "Introduction: Empire and Population." In *An Economic and Social History of the Ottoman Empire, 1300–1914*, ed. Halil İnalcık with Donald Quataert, 11–43. Cambridge: Cambridge University Press, 1994.

———. "Istanbul." In *The Encyclopaedia of Islam, New Edition*, vol. 4, 224–48. Leiden: E. J. Brill, 1978.

———. "Military and Fiscal Transformation in the Ottoman Empire." *Archivum Ottomanicum* 6 (1980): 283–337.

———. "Osmanlı İmparatorluğu'nun Kuruluş ve İnkişafı Devrinde Türkiye'nin İktisadi Vaziyeti Üzerine Bir Tetkik Münasebetiyle." In *Osmanlı İmparatorluğu: Toplum ve Ekonomi*, 139–86. Istanbul: Eren, 1993.

———. "Osmanlılarda Raiyyet Rüsumu." In *Osmanlı İmparatorluğu: Toplum ve Ekonomi*, 31–66. Istanbul: Eren, 1993.

———. "The Rise of the Ottoman Empire." In *A History of the Ottoman Empire to 1730*, ed. M. A. Cook, 10–53. Cambridge: Cambridge University Press, 1976.

———. "Tanzimat'ın Uygulanması ve Sosyal Tepkileri." *Belleten* 28 (1964): 623–90.

———. "The Yürüks." In *Oriental Carpet and Textile Studies*, ed. R. Pinner and H. İnalcık, 39–65. London: HALI, 1986.

İnalcık, Halil, with Donald Quataert, eds. *An Economic and Social History of the Ottoman Empire, 1300–1914*. Cambridge: Cambridge University Press, 1994.

Irmak, Sadi. *Yürüklerin Kan Grupları*. Istanbul: Devlet, 1937.

İslamoğlu-Inan, Huri. *State and Peasant in the Ottoman Empire*. Leiden: E. J. Brill, 1984.

Jardine, Lisa. *Worldly Goods: A New History of the Renaissance*. New York: Doubleday, 1996.

Jelavich, Barbara, and Charles Jelavich. *The Establishment of Balkan National States*. Seattle: University of Washington Press, 1977.

Kafadar, Cemal. *Between Two Worlds: The Construction of the Ottoman State*. Berkeley: University of California Press, 1995.

———. "A Death in Venice: Anatolian Muslim Merchants Trading in the Serenissima." *Journal of Turkish Studies* 10 (1986): 191–218.

———. "A Rome of One's Own: Reflections on Cultural Geography and Identity in the Lands of Rum." *Muqarnas* 24 (2007): 7–25.

Kaplanoğlu, Raif. *Bursa'da Mübadele*. Bursa: Avrasya Etnografi Yayınları, 1999.

Karakasidou, Anastasia. *Fields of Wheat, Hills of Blood.* Chicago: University of Chicago Press, 1997.

Karal, Enver Ziya. *Osmanlı İmparatorluğu'nda İlk Nüfus Sayımı, 1831.* Ankara: İstatistik Umum Müdürlüğü, 1943.

Karamustafa, Ahmet. *God's Unruly Friends.* Salt Lake City: University of Utah Press, 1994.

———. "Introduction to Ottoman Cartography." In *The History of Cartography,* vol. 2, book 1, *Cartography in the Traditional Islamic and South Asian Societies,* ed. J. B. Harley and David Woodward, 206-8. Chicago: University of Chicago Press, 1992.

———. "Military, Administrative and Scholarly Maps and Plans." In *The History of Cartography,* vol. 2, book 1, *Cartography in the Traditional Islamic and South Asian Societies,* ed. J. B. Harley and David Woodward, 209-27. Chicago: University of Chicago Press, 1992.

Karpat, Kemal. "Jewish Population Movements in the Ottoman Empire, 1862-1914." In Karpat, *Studies on Ottoman Social and Political History,* 146-68.

———. "Millets and Nationality: The Roots of the Incongruity of Nation and State in the Post-Ottoman Era." In Karpat, *Studies on Ottoman Social and Political History,* 611-46.

———. "Muslim Migration: Response to Aldeeb Abu-Sahlieh." In Karpat, *Studies on Ottoman Social and Political History,* 311-23.

———. "The Ottoman Emigration to America, 1862-1914." In Karpat, *Studies on Ottoman Social and Political History,* 90-131.

———."Ottoman Immigration Policies and Settlement in Palestine." In Karpat, *Studies on Ottoman Social and Political History,* 783-99.

———. "Ottoman Migration, Ethnopolitics, and the Formation of Nation States in South-East Europe and Israel." In Karpat, *Studies on Ottoman Social and Political History,* 752-82.

———. *Ottoman Population.* Madison: University of Wisconsin Press, 1985.

———. "The Status of the Muslim under European Rule: The Eviction and Settlement of the Çerkes." In Karpat, *Studies on Ottoman Social and Political History,* 646-75.

———. *Studies on Ottoman Social and Political History.* Leiden: E. J. Brill, 2002.

Kasaba, Reşat. "Diversity in Antakya: A Historical Perspective." In *The Mediterranean World: The Idea, The Past and Present,* ed. Eyüp Özveren et al., 207-22. Istanbul: İletişim, 2006.

———. "Do States Always Favor Stasis? The Changing Status of Tribes in the Ottoman Empire." In *Boundaries and Belonging: States and Societies in the Struggle to Shape Identities and Local Practices,* ed. Joel Migdal, 27-48. Cambridge: Cambridge University Press, 2004.

———. "İzmir 1922: A Port City Unravels." In *Modernity and Culture,* ed. Leila Tarazi Fawaz and C. A. Bayly, 204-29. New York: Columbia University Press, 2002.

———. "Migrant Labor in Western Anatolia." In *Landholding and Commercial Agriculture in the Middle East,* ed. Çağlar Keyder and Faruk Tabak, 113–21. Albany: State University of New York Press, 1991.

———. "A Time and a Place for the Nonstate: Social Change in the Ottoman Empire during the 'Long Nineteenth Century.'" In *State Power and Social Forces,* ed. Joel Migdal, Atul Kohli, and Vivienne Shue, 207–30. Cambridge: Cambridge University Press, 1994.

Katchadourian, Stina, ed. *Great Need over the Water: The Letters of Theresa Huntington Ziegler, Missionary to Turkey, 1898–1905.* Ann Arbor, Mich.: Gomidas Institute, 1999.

Kayalı, Hasan. *Arabs and the Young Turks.* Berkeley: University of California Press, 1997.

———. "Elections and the Electoral Process in the Ottoman Empire." *International Journal of Middle East Studies* 27, no. 3 (1995): 265–86.

Keyder, Çağlar. "A Brief History of Modern Istanbul." In *Cambridge History of Modern Turkey,* vol. 4, ed. Reşat Kasaba, 504–23. Cambridge: Cambridge University Press, 2008.

———. "Cycle of Sharecropping and the Consolidation of Small Peasant Ownership in Turkey." *Journal of Peasant Studies* 10, no. 2–3 (1983): 131–45.

Khoury, Dina Rizk. "The Ottoman Centre versus Provincial Power Holders: An Analysis of the Historiography." In *The Cambridge History of Turkey,* vol. 3, *The Later Ottoman Empire,* ed. Suraiya Faroqhi, 135–56. Cambridge: Cambridge University Press.

———. *State and Provincial Society in the Ottoman Empire: Mosul, 1540–1834.* Cambridge: Cambridge University Press, 1997.

Khoury, Philip, and Joseph Kostiner, eds. *Tribes and State Formation in the Middle East.* Berkeley: University of California Press, 1990.

Kirakossian, Arman, ed. *The Armenian Massacres, 1894–1896.* Detroit, Mich.: Wayne State University Press, 2004.

Klein, Janet. "Power in the Periphery: The Hamidiye Light Cavalry and the Struggle over Ottoman Kurdistan, 1890–1914." Ph.D. diss., Princeton University, 2002.

Kocacık, Faruk. "XIX. Yüzyılda Göçmen Köylerine İlişkin Bazı Yapı Planları." *Istanbul Üniversitesi Edebiyat Fakültesi Tarih Dergisi* 32 (March 1979): 415–26.

Koçu, Reşat Ekrem. *Osmanlı Muahedeleri ve Kapitülasyonlar, 1300–1920—ve Lozan Muahedesi, 24 Temmuz 1923.* Istanbul: Muallim Ahmet Halim Kütüphanesi, 1934.

Kodaman, Bayram. "Hamidiye Hafif Süvari Alayları (II. Abdülhamid ve Doğu Anadolu Aşiretleri)." *Tarih Dergisi* 32 (March 1975): 427–80.

Köksal, Yonca. "Coercion and Mediation: Centralization and Sedentarization of Tribes in the Ottoman Empire." *Middle Eastern Studies* 42, no. 3 (2006): 469–91.

Koliopoulos, John. *Brigands with a Cause.* Oxford: Clarendon Press, 1987.

Kontogiorgi, Elisabeth. *Population Exchange in Greek Macedonia*. Oxford: Oxford University Press, 2006.

Köprülü, Fuad. *Bizans Müesseselerinin Osmanlı Müesseselerine Etkisi*. Istanbul: Ötüken, 1981.

———. *Osmanlı İmparatorluğu'nun Kuruluşu*. Istanbul: Ötüken, 1981.

Krokar, James P. *The Ottoman Presence in Southeastern Europe, 16th-19th Centuries: A View in Maps*. Collection of slides with explanatory text. Chicago, 1997.

Küçük Asya Araştırmalar Merkezi. *Göç: Rumlar'ın Anadolu'dan Mecburi Ayrılışı*. Istanbul: İletişim, 2001.

Kühn, Thomas. "An Imperial Borderland as Colony: Knowledge Production and the Elaboration of Difference in Ottoman Yemen, 1872-1918." *MIT Electronic Journal of Middle East Studies* 3 (2003): 5-17.

Kunt, Metin. *The Sultan's Servants: The Transformation of Ottoman Provincial Government, 1550–1650*. New York: Columbia University Press, 1983.

Kurat, A. N., and J. S. Bromley. "The Retreat of the Turks, 1683-1730." In *A History of the Ottoman Empire to 1730*, ed. M. A. Cook. Cambridge: Cambridge University Press, 1976.

Kütükoğlu, Mübahat. *XV. ve XVI. Asırlarda İzmir Kazasının Sosyal ve Iktisadi Yapısı*. İzmir: Büyükşehir Belediyesi, 2000.

Ladas, Stephen. *The Exchange of Minorities: Bulgaria, Greece, and Turkey*. New York: Macmillan, 1932.

Lapidus, Ira. *A History of Islamic Societies*. Cambridge: Cambridge University Press, 1988.

———. "Sufism and Ottoman Islamic Society." In *The Dervish Lodge*, ed. Raymond Lifchez, 15-32. Berkeley: University of California Press, 1992.

League of Nations. *The Settlement of Greek Refugees*. Geneva, 1924.

Lewis, Norman. *Nomads and Settlers in Syria and Jordan*. Cambridge: Cambridge University Press, 1987.

———. "The Syrian Steppe during the Last Century of Ottoman Rule: Hawran and the Palmyrena." In *The Transformation of Nomadic Society in the Arab East*, ed. Matha Mundy and Basim Musallam, 33-43. Cambridge: Cambridge University Press, 2000.

Lewy, Guenter. *The Armenian Massacres in Ottoman Turkey: A Disputed Genocide*. Salt Lake City: University of Utah Press, 2005.

Lifchez, Raymond, ed. *The Dervish Lodge*. Berkeley: University of California Press, 1992.

Lindner, Rudi. *Nomads in Medieval Ottoman Anatolia*. Bloomington: Indiana University Press, 1983.

———. "What Was the Nomadic Tribe?" *Comparative Studies in Society and History* 24 (1982): 689-711.

Loizos, Peter. "Ottoman Half-Lives: Long-Term Perspectives on Particular Forced Migrations." *Journal of Refugee Studies* 12, no. 3 (1999): 237-63.

Lowry, Heath. *The Nature of the Early Ottoman State*. Albany: State University of New York Press, 2003.

Makdisi, Ussama. "Ottoman Orientalism." *American Historical Review* 102, no. 3 (1997): 786–96.

Mardin, Şerif. "Center-Periphery Relations: A Key to Turkish Politics." *Daedalus* 102, no. 1 (1973): 169–90.

Marrus, Michael. *The Unwanted: European Refugees in the Twentieth Century*. New York: Oxford University Press, 1985.

Marufoğlu, Sinan. *Osmanlı Döneminde Kuzey Irak*. Istanbul: Eren, 1998.

Marushiakova, Elena, and Vesselin Popov. *Gypsies in the Ottoman Empire: A Contribution to the History of the Balkans*. Hatfield, U.K.: University of Hertfordshire Press, 2001.

Marx, Karl. "The Future Results of the British Rule in India." In Karl Marx, *Surveys from Exile*, 319–24. London: Penguin, 1973.

Masters, Bruce. *Christians and Jews in the Ottoman Arab World*. Cambridge: Cambridge University Press, 2001.

———. *The Origins of Western Economic Dominance in the Middle East: Mercantilism and Islamic Economy in Aleppo, 1600–1750*. New York: New York University Press, 1988.

———. "Semi-Autonomous Forces in the the Arab Provinces." In *The Cambridge History of Turkey*, vol. 3, *The Later Ottoman Empire*, ed. Suraiya Faroqhi, 186–206. Cambridge: Cambridge University Press, 2006.

Mazower, Mark. *The Balkans: A Short History*. New York: Modern Library, 2000.

———. *Salonica: City of Ghosts*. New York: Knopf, 2005.

McCarthy, Justin, and Dennis Hyde. "Ottoman Imperial and Provincial Salnames." *Middle East Studies Association Bulletin* 13, no. 1 (1978): 46–48.

McGowan, Bruce. "Population and Migration." In *An Economic and Social History of the Ottoman Empire, 1300–1914*, ed. Halil İnalcık with Donald Quataert. Cambridge: Cambridge University Press, 1994.

Meeker, Michael. *A Nation of Empire: The Ottoman Legacy of Turkish Modernity*. Berkeley: University of California Press, 2002.

Mélikoff, Irène. "Bektaşilik/Kızılbaşlık Tarihsel Bölünme ve Sonuçları." In *Alevi Kimliği*, ed. T. Olsson, E. Özdalga, and C. Raudvere. Istanbul: Tarih Vakfı, 1999.

Menemencioğlu Ahmet Bey. *Menemencioğlu Tarihi*. Ed. Yilmaz Kurt. Ankara: Akçağ, 1997.

Menteşe, Halil. *Osmanlı Mebusan Meclisi Reisi Halil Menteşe'nin Anıları*. Istanbul: Hürriyet Vakfı Yayınları, 1986.

Migdal, Joel, ed. *Boundaries and Belonging: States and Societies in the Struggle to Shape Identities and Local Politics*. Cambridge: Cambridge University Press, 2004.

Miller, Donald, and Lorna Touryan Miller, eds. *Survivors: An Oral History of the*

Armenian Genocide. Berkeley: University of California Press, 1993.

Möltke, H. Von. *Türkiye Mektupları*. Istanbul: Varlık, 1982.

Morgenthau, Henry. *Ambassador Morgenthau's Story*. New York: Doubleday, 1918.

Murphey, Rhoads. *Ottoman Warfare, 1500–1700*. New Brunswick, N.J.: Rutgers University Press, 1999.

———. "Some Features of Nomadism in the Ottoman Empire: A Survey Based on Tribal Census and Judicial Appeal Documentation from Archives in Istanbul and Damascus." *Journal of Turkish Studies* 8 (1984).

———, ed. *Kanuname-i Sultâani Li Aziz Efendi*. Cambridge, Mass.: Harvard University Press, 1985.

Naimark, Norman. *Fires of Hatred: Ethnic Cleansing in Twentieth-Century Europe*. Cambridge, Mass.: Harvard University Press, 2001.

Nakash, Yitzhak. *The Shi'is of Iraq*. Princeton, N.J.: Princeton University Press, 1994.

Ocak, Ahmet Yaşar. *Osmanlı Toplumunda Zındıklar ve Mülhidler*. Istanbul: Tarih Vakfı, 1998.

Orhonlu, Cengiz. *Osmanlı İmparatorluğu'nda Aşiretlerin İskânı*. Istanbul: Eren, 1987.

———. *Osmanlı İmparatorluğu'nda Derbend Teşkilatı*. Istanbul: Eren, 1990.

Ortaylı, İlber. *Osmanlı İmparatorluğunda Aile*. Istanbul: Pan, 2000.

Osmanağaoğlu, Cihan. *Tanzimat Dönemi İtibarıyla Osmanlı Tabiiyetinin (Vatandaşlığının) Gelişimi*. Istanbul: Legal, 2004.

Outram, Dorinda. *The Enlightenment*. Cambridge: Cambridge University Press, 1991.

Owen, Roger, and Şevket Pamuk. *A History of Middle East Economies in the Twentieth Century*. Cambridge, Mass.: Harvard University Press, 1998.

Öz, Baki. *Osmanlı da Alevi Ayaklanmaları*. Istanbul: Ant, 1992.

Özdeğer, Hüseyin. "Haleb Bölgesi Türkmenleri." *Türk İktisat Tarihi Yıllığı: Istanbul Üniversitesi İktisat Fakültesi Türk İktisat ve İçtimaiyat Tarihi Araştırmalar Merkezi* 1 (1987): 177–224.

Özkaya, Yücel. *Osmanlı İmparatorluğu'nda Dağlı İsyanları*. Ankara: Dil ve Tarih Coğrafya Fakültesi Basımevi, 1983.

———. "XVIII. Yüzyılda Menzilhane Sorunu." *Ankara Üniversitesi Dil ve Tarih Coğrafya Dergisi* 28, nos. 3–4 (1970): 339–68.

Özoğlu, Hakan. *Kurdish Notables and the Ottoman State: Evolving Identities, Competing Loyalties, and Shifting Boundaries*. Albany: State University of New York Press, 2004.

Pakalın, Mehmet Zeki. *Osmanlı Tarih Deyimleri ve Terimleri Sözlüğü*. 2 vols. Istanbul: M. E. B. Devlet Basımevi, 1971.

Pallis, A. A. "Racial Migrations in the Balkans during the Years 1912–1924." *Geographical Journal* 66 (Oct. 1925): 315–33.

Pamuk, Şevket. *A Monetary History of the Ottoman Empire*. Cambridge: Cambridge University Press, 2000.

Panatie, Viorel. *The Ottoman Law of War and Peace: The Ottoman Empire and Tribute Payers.* Boulder, Colo.: East European Monographs, 2000.

Parry, V. J. "The Reigns of Bayezid II and Selim I, 1481–1520." In *A History of the Ottoman Empire to 1730,* ed. M. A. Cook, 54–78. Cambridge: Cambridge University Press, 1976.

Peirce, Leslie. *The Imperial Harem: Women and Sovereignty in the Ottoman Empire.* New York: Oxford University Press, 1993.

Percy, Earl Henry A. G. *Highlands of Asiatic Turkey.* London, 1901.

Petronotis, Argiris. *Hacıustalar: Akdağmadeni'nden Aridea'ya Bir Mübadele Öyküsü.* Istanbul: Kitap Yayınları, 2004.

Philipp, Thomas. *Acre: The Rise and Fall of a Palestinian City.* New York: Columbia University Press, 2001.

Planhol, Xavier de. "Geography, Politics and Nomadism in Anatolia." *International Social Science Journal* 11, no. 4 (1959): 525–31.

Powers, Samantha. *A Problem from Hell.* New York: Perennial, 2003.

Pushkin, Alexander Sergeevich. *A Journey to Arzrum.* Ann Arbor, Mich.: Ardis, 1974.

Riggs, Henry. *Days of Tragedy in Armenia: Personal Experiences in Harpoot, 1915–1917.* Ann Arbor, Mich.: Gomidas Institute, 1997.

Rogan, Eugene. *Frontiers of the State in the Late Ottoman Empire.* Cambridge: Cambridge University Press, 1999.

Rogers, J. M. "Itineraries and Town Views in Ottoman Histories." In *The History of Cartography,* vol. 2, book 1, *Cartography in the Traditional Islamic and South Asian Societies,* eds. J. B. Harley and David Woodward, 228–51. Chicago: University of Chicago Press, 1992.

Runciman, Steven. *The Fall of Constantinople.* Cambridge: Cambridge University Press, 1965.

Salzmann, Ariel. "The Age of Tulips: Confluence and Conflict in Early Modern Consumer Culture." In *Consumption Studies and the History of the Ottoman Empire, 1550–1922: An Introduction,* ed. D. Quataert, 83–106. Albany: State University of New York Press, 2000.

Schama, Simon. *The Embarrassment of Riches.* New York: Knopf, 1987.

Schlitberger, Johannes. *Türkler ve Tatarlar Arasında.* Istanbul: İletişim, 1995.

Scott, James C. "La montagne et la liberté, ou Pourquoi les civilisations ne savant pas grimper." *Critique Internationale* 3 (2001): 85–104.

———. *Seeing Like a State.* New Haven, Conn.: Yale University Press, 1998.

Seroussi, Edwin. "The Peşrev as a Vocal Genre in Ottoman Hebrew Sources." *Turkish Music Quarter,* Summer 1991: 1–9.

Setton, Kenneth. "Lutheranism and the Turkish Peril." *Balkan Studies* 3 (1962): 133–68.

Shaw, Stanford, and Ezel Kuran Shaw. *History of the Ottoman Empire and Modern Turkey.* 2 vols. Cambridge: Cambridge University Press, 1976.

Shay, Mary Lucille. *The Ottoman Empire from 1720 to 1734 as Revealed in Dispatches* of the Venetian Baili. Westport, Conn.: Greenwood Press, 1978.

Sinclair, Tom. "The Ottoman Arrangements for the Tribal Principalities of the Lake Van Region of the Sixteenth Century." *International Journal of Turkish Studies* 9, no. 2–3 (2003): 119–43.

Singer, Amy. *Palestinian Peasants and Ottoman Officials: Rural Administration around Sixteenth-Century Jerusalem*. Cambridge: Cambridge University Press, 1994.

Smith, Michael Llewellyn. *Ionian Vision: Greece in Asia Minor, 1919–1922*. Ann Arbor: University of Michigan Press, 1998 [1973].

Söylemez, Faruk. *Osmanlı Devletinde Aşiret Yönetimi*. Istanbul: Kültür ve Turizm Bakanlığı, 2007.

Stavrianos, L. S. *The Balkans since 1453*. New York: Rinehart, 1958.

Subrahmanyam, Sanjay. "A Tale of Three Empires: Mughals, Ottomans, and Habsburgs in a Comparative Context." *Common Knowledge* 12, no. 1 (2006): 66–92.

Sümer, Faruk. "Anadolu, Suriye, ve Irak'ta yaşayan Türk Aşiretlerine Umumi Bir Bakış." *Istanbul Üniversitesi İktisat Fakültesi Mecmuası* 11 (1949–50): 509–23.

———. *Oğuzlar (Türkmenler) Tarihleri- Boy Teşkilatı-Destanları*. Istanbul: Türk Dunyası Araştırmaları Vakfi, 1980.

Suny, Ronald. "Religion, Ethnicity and Nationalism: Armenians, Turks and the End of the Ottoman Empire." In *In God's Name: Genocide and Religion in the Twentieth Century*, ed. Omer Bartov and Phyllis Mack, 23–61. New York: Berghahn Books, 2001.

Sykes, Mark. "The Kurdish Tribes of the Ottoman Empire." *Journal of the Royal Anthropological Institute of Great Britain and Ireland* 38 (1908): 451–86.

Tabak, Faruk. *The Waning of the Mediterranean, 1550–1870*. Baltimore, Md.: Johns Hopkins University Press, 2008.

Tapper, Richard. *Frontier Nomads of Iran: A Political and Social History of Shahsevan*. Cambridge: Cambridge University Press, 1997.

Toledano, Ehud. *The Ottoman Slave Trade and Its Suppression, 1840–1890*. Princeton, N.J.: Princeton University Press, 1982.

Türkay, Cevdet. *Osmanlı İmparatorluğu'nda Oymak, Aşiret, ve Cemaatler*. Istanbul: İşaret, 2001.

Uluçay, Çağatay. *18. ve 19. Yüzyıllarda Saruhan'da Eşkiyalık ve Halk Hereketleri*. Istanbul: Berksoy, 1955.

Umumi Nüfus Tahriri. *28 Teşrinievvel 1927*. Ankara: Hüsnütabiat Matbaası, 1929.

Unat, Faik Reşit. *Osmanlı Sefirleri ve Sefaretnameleri*. Ankara: Türk Tarih Kurumu, 1968.

Uşaklıgil, Halit Ziya. *Kırk Yıl*. Istanbul: Varlik, 1987.

Uzunçarşılı, İsmail Hakkı. *Osmanlı Tarihi*, vol. 4, part 1. Ankara: Türk Tarih Kurumu, 1947.

Valensi, Lucette. *The Birth of the Despot*. Ithaca, N.Y.: Cornell University Press, 1993.

van Bruinessen, Martin. *Agha, Sheikh and State: The Social and Political Structures of Kurdistan*. London: Zed, 1992.

———, ed. *Evliya Çelebi in Diyarbekir*. Leiden: E. J. Brill, 1988.

Vryonis, Speros. *Decline of Medieval Hellenism in Asia Minor*. Berkeley: University of California Press, 1971.

Wilson, Bronwen. "Foggie diverse di vestire de'Turchi: Turkish Costume Illustration and Cultural Transition." *Journal of Medieval and Early Modern Studies* 37, no. 1 (2007): 97–139.

Wittek, Paul. *The Rise of the Ottoman Empire*. London: Royal Asiatic Society, 1938.

Wright, Walter L., ed. *Ottoman Statecraft: The Book of Counsel for Vezirs and Governors of Sarı Mehmed Pasha, the Defterdar*. Princeton, N.J.: Princeton University Press, 1935.

Yalçın, Kemal. *Emanet Çeyiz*. Istanbul: Doğan Kitap, 1998.

Yetkin, Sabri. *Ege'de Eşkiyalar*. Istanbul: Tarih Vakfı, 1996.

Yıldırım, Onur. *Diplomasi ve Göç: Türk-Yunan Mübadelesinin Öteki Yüzü*. Istanbul: Bilgi Üniversitesi, 2007.

Yörükan, Yavuz Ziya. *Anadolu'da Aleviler ve Tahtacılar*. Ankara: Kültür Bakanlığı, 1998.

Zarinebaf-Shahr, Fariba. "Qızılbash 'Heresey' and Rebellion in Ottoman Anatolia during the Sixteenth Century." *Anatolia Moderna* 7 (1997): 1–15.

Ze'evi, Dror. *An Ottoman Century: The District of Jerusalem in the 1600s*. Albany: State University of New York Press, 1996.

Zilfi, Madeline. "The Kadızadelis: Discordant Revivalism in Seventeenth-Century Istanbul." *Journal of Near Eastern Studies* 45 (1986): 251–74.

Index

Greek(s), 45, 46, 51, 92, 106, 124–27,
130–32, 135–37; nationalism of, 138;
Orthodox, 125; Pontic, 95; refugee,
133–35; workers, 125
Greek Revolution, 92, 130
Gypsies, 24, 28, 29, 31, 88, 106

Habsburg Empire, 10, 41, 55, 57, 63. *See
also* Austria
Haçin, 98
Hafsa Sultan, 44
hajj, 72
Hakkari, 121
Haleb, 66, 67, 69; Türkmeni, 23, 79. *See
also* Aleppo
Halil Bey, 128–29
Halvetis, 48, 51. *See also* Sufi: orders
Hamawand, 84–85, 86, 90, 115, 120, 122
Hamidiye regiments, 119
Harput, 129
Hassa, 102
Hazinedaroğlu, 95
Hejaz, 119
Hemingway, Ernest, 133
Hemvend. *See* Hamawand
Holy League, 57
Humbaracı Ahmed Paşa. *See* Bon-
neval, Comte de
Hungary, 52, 55, 57, 62–63, 73
Hürrem Sultan, 45
Hussein, Saddam, 84, 85

Iberian empires, 19
Ibn Batuta, 15
Ibn Khaldun, 5, 7, 65, 142*n9*
Ibrahim Müteferrika, 64
Ibrahim Paşa, 93, 119
il, 21
Ilgın, 62
İmam Ali, 36
İnalcık, Halil, 18, 43
India, 46
Iraq, 84, 90, 96, 99, 108, 116, 139

Iran, 7, 25, 29, 30, 35, 42, 58, 69, 92, 95,
105, 108, 130, 139. *See also* Persia
Iranian(s), 14, 29, 42, 46, 92, 112, 115
Ishak Paşa, 90
İşkodra, 115
iskân başı, 77
İskân Dairesi (Office of Settlements),
70
İskenderun, 98, 101
Islam, 4, 9, 41, 43, 44, 45, 48, 49–51,
64, 89, 136, 138, 150*n135*; abode of,
42; community of, 113; faith, 50, 65;
law of, 111, 112; and orthodoxy, 13, 35;
rulers of, 44; Sufi interpretation of,
64; Shi'i, 25, 29, 35, 36, 49–50, 95, 112;
Sunni, 25, 49, 119, 121; Turkish, 4. *See
also* Alevi; Muslim; Shi'i; Sufi
Islamic civilization, 41; empires, 20;
scholars of, 14
Ismail, Shah, 35–36
İsmail Paşa, 116
Istanbul, 27, 28, 31, 45, 48, 51, 53, 55, 61,
63, 64, 69, 77, 78, 92–95, 101–2, 106,
114, 117, 120, 128, 131, 138, 149*n111*. *See
also* Byzantium; Constantinople
istimalet, 25
İzmir, 23, 32, 46, 60–61, 69, 115, 130, 131
Izziye, 102

Jaff. *See* Caf
Janissaries, 52, 62
Janum Hodja, 77–78
Jerusalem, 32, 42
Jew(s), 28, 46, 48, 51, 106, 124, 130, 131;
expelled from Russia, 109; expelled
from Spain, 49

kabile, 21. *See also* tribes
kadı, 24, 31, 47, 60
Kadiris, 51, 88, 120. *See also* Sufi: orders
Kadirli, 67
Kadızadeliler, 63
Kafadar, Cemal, 147*n83*

112–16, 119, 120; confederations of, 10, 94, 101, 121; in frontier areas, 39; hierarchies of, 110; and livestock, 32–33, 34; and manufacturing, 32–33; nomadic, 3–5, 7–9, 14, 15, 18, 19, 21, 23, 24, 28–30, 34–37, 52, 54, 55, 66, 68, 73–75, 83, 84, 88, 89, 91, 92, 110, 116, 118, 124, 141*n*7; and the Ottoman state, 3, 7, 9, 10, 35–37; registration of, 55, 56, 73, 78, 79, 82, 144*n*9; and trade, 32–33, 87; resistance by, 79, 84, 85, 96, 124, 156*n*4; Turkic, 15, 50. *See also* Afşar; Al-Cerba; Al-Bu Hamned; Alevi; Arab; Arablı; Arıklı; Atçeken; Baban; Badıllı; Bedouin; Beğmişli; Boz Koyunlu; Caf; Çeng; Çepeni; Çerçili; Cerid; Cirid; Civanşir; Cubur; Dimlik; Döğerli; Hamawand; Kadirli; Kara Şeyhli; Kaşıkçı; Keçili; Kıcılu; Kırıntılı; Koçgiri; *Konar-göçer;* Koyuncu; Koyuneri; Kürkçü; Lek; Mamali; Mihmadlu; Milan; Öksüzler; Ravala; Rişvanlı; Safavid; Sakallı; Saraç; Simre; Şammar; Şehitler; Süryani; Tajiboğlu; Talabani; Tecirli; Türkmen; Tuzcuoğlu; Ulaşlı; Yağcı; Yarı Çoban; Yaycı; Yürük; Zilanlı

Tripoli, 77–78, 102

Tulip Age, 64

Turabalı, 68

Turkey, 8, 62, 125, 132; agriculture, 141*n*3; census of, 135; government of, 134, 137, 138; independence, 136; and Islam, 4; and nationalism, 11, 131, 135–39; and Turkish refugees, 138; Republic of, 131, 135

Türkmen, 15, 21, 35–36, 47, 67, 73, 75, 77, 79, 120, 94, 101, 120, 121, 142*n*5, 144*n*18, 155*n*100. *See also* Haleb Türkmeni; Şam Türkmeni; Üsküdar Türkmeni

Turks, 49, 126, 129, 132, 133, 142*n*5

Tuzcuoğlu, 95

Ukraine, 45, 55, 57

Ulaşlı, 95

ulus, 21, 24

Urfa, 130

Uşaklıgil, Halit Ziya, 117

Üsküdar Türkmeni, 23

Van, 108, 129

Venice, 45, 62

Vienna, 52, 57, 62

Viran Han, 68

Viranşehir, 68

Vlachs, 23, 34

voyvodas, 24

Wahhabi, 99

Walachia, 42, 92

Westphalia, Treaty of, 57, 58

World War I, 11, 54, 125, 130, 132, 134, 135, 137, 164*n*3

Yağcı, 26

Yahud (Yehud), 28. *See also* Jew(s)

Yarı Çoban, 26

Yarı-göçebe, 21

Yaycı, 26

Yeğen Osman, 77

Yemen, 115

Yezidi, 29, 42, 90

Yozgat, 95, 101

Yürük, 21, 23, 27, 30, 31, 33, 70, 73, 74, 79, 144*n*9, 155*n*100

Zeybek, 100, 101

Zeytun, 98, 159*n*62

Zilanlı, 90

zimmi, 28

Zubair, Sheikh, 94